DIVORCE
STRESS SYNDROME

Dr. David E. Pastrana
Divorce Attorney & Emeritus Professor of Legal Studies, CSULB
pastrana@cuslb.edu

ABRUZZI PRESS CORPORATION

ABRUZZI PRESS CORPORATION

850 E. Ocean Boulevard, Suite 1402
Long Beach, California 90802-5456

This book contains public information about celebrities, public figures, and public office holders. All said individuals are listed by their actual names. References to *friends, neighbors, married couples,* and *former clients* are all to fictionalized and fictitious individuals and are not intended or portrayed to represent any such individuals, persons, couples, or clients. Any and all possible resemblance to any actual persons, living or deceased, is entirely coincidental. The names of my two ex-wives have also been changed to protect their privacy.

DIVORCE STRESS SYNDROME Copyright © 2011

by

ABRUZZI PRESS CORPORATION, confirmation pending.

ISBN 978-0-578-09083-2

Published in the United States by ABRUZZI PRESS CORPORATION. Bulk sale discounts are available to civic, educational, non-profit, religious, or other groups; please contact the publisher at the above address. Speaking and lecture presentations can be scheduled by contacting the author at C/O of the publisher.

This book is also available in ebook formats and can be at most ebook vendors.

Printed in the United States of America © 2011

Contact website information:
www.mydisso.com and www.divorcestresssyndrome.com

Cover design, typography and site design – www.kirks-graphics.com

Mom and Dad, this book is for you.

Disclaimers and Disclosures

The content provided in this book is for a general and diverse reading audience. It is not intended as a substitute for medical, psychiatric or psychological attention, or competent legal advice. All content is for reading purposes only. Any and all decisions made with respect to individual or collective needs, problems, or conditions must be made in consultation with appropriate physicians, qualified psychologists, or other licensed professionals as necessary.

The material reflects an interdisciplinary and collaborative effort among lawyers, psychologists, sociologists, and other subject-related PhDs. The findings and conclusions are based on prevailing standards and majority opinions. They are not subject-specific; thus, the foregoing provides only general knowledge and are given as such. There are no claims, guarantees, or representations made, either expressed or implied, as to the accuracy, benefits or effectiveness provided in said materials herein. There are also no implied warranties of merchantability or implied warranties of fitness for a particular purpose, condition, or ailment. Central to the cure and treatment of any condition or person is the required professional attention, family history, and other necessary and required diagnosis particular to the individual. None of the foregoing is a part of this book. While the information provided herein is not applicable to any particular diagnosis, case, or individual, it is presented as general topics for broad discussion.

Samples of Prenuptial and Postnuptial Agreements in the Appendix are provided for information purposes only. These sample copies may not be applicable to your individual needs and may not be enforceable in your particular state. Be sure you seek appropriate professional assistance for your legal needs. The material presented is current through November 30, 2010; legal precedents can change daily and must always be checked daily.

Years of university teaching have provided your author opportunities to perfect civility toward all. Because the study of divorce comes with built-in pejorative and unfair conclusions about women, your author has endeavored to be sensitive in writing about women's issues, and yet retain accuracy and fairness in content. He has also tried not to be professorial or preachy in his presentations; however, 36-year-old work habits die hard.

Much of this volume is autobiographical, biographical, and cathartic. The book is also historical, holistic, and humorous and encompasses a novel approach to understanding divorce and self-help recovery.

Contents

Preface

THIS BOOK evolved over three decades of my divorce law practice and 72 semesters of teaching law at California State University Long Beach (CSULB). It started as a series of short, single-subject informational pamphlets; over the years, these individual pamphlets were consolidated, enhanced with relevant celebrity examples, and seasoned with selective humor. These expanded pamphlets improved my clients' understanding of their respective divorce issues and advanced acceptance of their dissolution outcomes. I later added post-divorce recovery suggestions and dating advice, along with remarriage and cohabitation warnings.

For many, the word *divorce* carries negative connotations like guilt, failure, and rejection. Mere mention of the "D" word can trigger visceral recollections of regretful deeds or ruthless responses that often followed unacceptable marital behavior. At first, I imagined that persons involved in troubled relationships or strained marriages might be hesitant to purchase a book with "divorce" in its title. Yet, this one book provides relevant advice to engaged couples evaluating their marital potential. These future partners can review relationship compatibilities, discover latent landmines found in all marriages, and work on necessary modifications to defuse future marital expositions. Estranged couples can address their trying issues and consider suggested settlement solutions to help find their lost marital bliss.

This book will serve as a beacon for divorcing individuals entering the cold, stormy, unknown waters of divorce. It will also provide multiple exit-channels for those still seeking an outlet from their *completed* divorces. Both individuals will gain from simplified divorce law explanations, sequential divorce-process guidance, and recovery recommendations for dealing with lasting divorce issues or residual hostile feelings.

Divorced/divorcing individuals must forgive their mistakes and the errors of others. Failure to do so can result in self-imposed emotional confinement, via a life of personal suffering, continuous stress, and an inability to enjoy later happiness found in reconciliation or remarriage.

Introduction

We Marry in Poetry and Divorce in Prose

Clinicians and physicians now recognize the combined emotional, mental, and physical trauma of divorce as Divorce Stress Syndrome. This syndrome affects millions. Recent U.S. Census Bureau figures state that 55 percent of first marriages end in divorce, 67 percent of second marriages end in divorce, and 74 percent of third marriages end in divorce. Given the foregoing, the late philosopher Henny Youngman may have said it best: "The secret to a happy marriage remains a secret."

This book will help divorcing and divorced women and men understand their pre-, present-, and post-divorce stresses. Each phase of **Divorce Stress Syndrome (DSS)** is carefully examined for its underlying causes and upsetting consequences. With this information in hand, you'll soon recognize which divorce circumstances can be changed or resolved and accept realities that cannot be altered. These distinctions, along with recommended proactive coping strategies, provide assistance for dealing with your own divorce demons.

As a tenured full professor in the Department of Legal Studies at CSULB, and active divorce lawyer, I engaged in extensive academic and legal research. I have published for the heavily footnoted scholastic community and societies of professional legal journals. Here I've written for the reader who wants an informative, educational read without the gates and fences of academic or professional publications. This integrated work includes collaborative contributions from colleagues, my experiences in having taught more than 300 law classes (over thirty-six years), as well as having advised and represented hundreds of individuals who divorced.

Seasoned teaching techniques are applied throughout this book. Because repetition reinforces recall, major theme topics introduced in previous chapters are selectively repeated in later chapters. This provides for subconscious reviews and cumulative content layering.

The book chapters are coordinated and presented in the usual unfolding sequence of divorce happenings. This approach allows for cumulative coverage of pre-divorce triggering events, brewing emotions, and the onset of loss of marital bliss. Understanding divorce and recovering from its consequences can be difficult, yet "understanding divorce and its destruction" and "realizing recovery recommendations" must be presented together. These different tasks require coordinated platforms to ensure that readers are not inundated with too much of one and not enough of the other.

Accordingly, the "understanding part of divorce" is offered in Chapters 1, 2 and 7 - 10. These chapters include essential explanations regarding the chief causes of divorce, how to exit a lifeless marriage, as well as details pertaining to increasing divorce rates across America. This "understanding" background material also provides an overview of the entire divorce process, and suggestions for dealing with your estranged spouse, lawyers, and creditors. Prenuptial and Postnuptial Agreement explanation details are also included. All this material is presented as if you were a student in one of my undergraduate classes. These serious topics are lightened with celebrity references and occasional humor to aid readers in dealing with what has become a common event.

The "recovery part of divorce" is set forth in Chapters 3 - 6, 11, and 12 and attends to personal and private topics. These topics include healing yourself, spending time alone, coping mechanisms, and divorce stress reduction remedies which will help readers comprehend their individual circumstances and aid them in dealing with their complex challenges. These concerns are addressed in a more intimate setting, as if only you and I were engaged in thoughtful conversation, and they are delivered with optimism, forgiveness, and self-improvement in mind. These subjects are accompanied by a review of reconciliation realities, post-divorce dating, and warnings about cohabitation and remarriage.

Early in my academic career, I discovered that effective teaching could be greatly enhanced with reference to divorced celebrities and public figures. These significant examples are helpful to us because we are often fascinated by accomplished individuals who have achieved stellar success in commerce, entertainment, and government.

Granted, the listed celebrities on the coming pages may not exemplify typical marriages, where average couples struggle to get by; nevertheless, not only do these talented and successful persons make the same marital mistakes as the rest of us, they also suffer many of the same consequences as we do, when dealing with difficult divorce issues. Celebrity divorces are also effective exemplars, for these spouses can certainly afford the best lawyers and effective therapists. Still, only a limited number of celebrity spouses and select average couples are able to overcome their marital obstacles and remain married; most are not successful and they eventually divorce.

To help illustrate significant problems, therefore, I've provided relevant public information details regarding the troubled marriages, reconciliation efforts, and divorce particulars of popular athletes, entertainers, and movie stars, as well as those of chief executive officers, public figures, and public officeholders. I have included several of their innovative reconciliation trials, divorce settlements, and remarriage outcomes which may be helpful to others.

The A through F and I grading system used in school can be applied to marriages: A – F for completed marriages, and I [incomplete] for those ending in divorce. Many interrupted divorce-ending marriages (and other ending long-term relationships) include extraordinary efforts to save their marriages on the part of one or both spouses, yet all too often even extraordinary efforts cannot save a troubled marriage. Such enduring efforts cannot and should not be characterized as failures. For all of these reasons and more, I long ago started referring to "incomplete" marriages as such, and not as failed marriages. Besides, we've had "no-fault" divorce laws for the past 45 years, and no one looks for fault. It's no longer legally relevant or required. Most countries throughout the word now have no-fault divorce laws. (Note: The Appendix contains brief comparisons of divorce law administration in various nations.)

Divorcing and returning to the single life are usually not as exciting, glamorous, or romantic as portrayed in movies, on television, and in stories from other singles. To some, the remaining groups of eligible men and women may be missing desired attributes. To others there are enlightened, quality, and loving individuals awaiting them.

The Capstone section at the end presents an assimilation of divorce recovery content and brings into logical focus what needs to be remembered and perhaps occasionally reviewed.

This book provides *GPS guidance* for engaged couples planning their premarital travels, and for married spouses searching for available avenues back to their lost happiness. DSS is no stranger to interrupted same-sex relationships and troubled marriages. These partners live through similar stresses and secondary sufferings. They experience the same symptoms and reprehensible reactions when ending a loving relationship. Most of the information provided in this book is applicable to their emotional disruptions, property divisions, and other divorce consequences.

Because of the plethora of excellent and exhaustive free materials provided by articulate academics and proficient professionals on the care, protection and welfare of children of divorce, I've respectfully omitted coverage about children in this work. One just has to Google "children of divorce" and some 37,360,070 sites instantly appear.

Being in the classroom helped me in the courtroom; being in the courtroom helped me in the classroom. Still most audiences (students, jurors and readers) have a limited capacity to retain complex information provided in concentrated dosages. It is as though we have a small cup in our brains and when the cup is filled, we can no longer take in additional information—we have reached, you might say, our "brain-cup" capacity. This causes our reading comprehension to wane; we start to lose interest and we sometimes tune out.

Long ago I devised the mental coffee break. This involves a relevant, brief and sometimes entertaining diversion from the lecture subject matter or heavy reading to enable all to catch their cerebral breath and make room for new information. Thus ample mental coffee breaks are provided throughout this book, allowing you to read on with greater interest, comprehension and enjoyment.

Psychologists tell us that journaling after divorce helps us heal. Journaling only requires pen, paper or your computer, and a private place. There are only a few rules that apply: date your daily entries, write freely about your deepest and darkest thoughts and feelings, as well as your reaction to your experiences and what you've learned along the way.

Appendix 2 provides helpful suggestions for starting your journal entries after you have finished reading the book.

Be you straight or gay, engaged or married, separated, divorcing or divorced, I wish you good reading as you begin your journey through the traumas and dramas of DSS. As you will discover, each of us has our own travel time for reaching fully divorced status; for most, it takes about two years to totally recover. With acceptance and forgiveness of your troubled past, your crisis, too, will pass. Who knows? The secret to a happy remarriage may be found within these pages. Greater happiness awaits you through self-help and the exhilaration of new beginnings.

Recall, that our marriages start with:

> "Dearly beloved, we are gathered here
> this day to join this man and this
> woman in marriage."

And incomplete marriages end with:

> "Are you the Petitioner in this matter?"
> "Yes."
>
> "Have irreconcilable differences arisen
> between you and the Respondent?"
>
> "Yes."
>
> "Will counseling or the further passage
> of time save your marriage?"
>
> "No."
>
> "I hereby grant your Dissolution
> Petition and dissolve your marriage as
> requested.
>
> "Next case!"

A PARTIAL LIST OF MENTIONED INDIVIDUALS

Actors: 26
Woody Allen
Jennifer Aniston
Ellen Barkin
Tom Cruise
Michael Douglas
Mia Farrow
Jane Fonda
Harrison Ford
Ava Gardner
Mel Gibson
Cary Grant
Katharine Hepburn
Angelina Jolie
Nicole Kidman
Lee Marvin
Marilyn Monroe
Bill Murray
Sean Penn
Brad Pitt
Denise Richards
Charlie Sheen
Brooke Shields
Elizabeth Taylor
Spencer Tracy**
Lana Turner
Robin Williams

Artist: 1
Pablo Picasso

Athletes: 12
Andre Agassi
Barry Bonds
Kobe Bryant**
Joe DiMaggio
Hulk Hogan
Michael Jordan

Billie Jean King
Martina Navratilova
Alex Rodriguez
O.J. Simpson
Michael Strahan
Tiger Woods

Celebrities: 6
Christie Brinkley
Johnny Carson
Rodney Dangerfield
Larry King
Rush Limbaugh
Anna Nicole Smith

CEOs: 15
Warren Buffett*
Jim Clark
George David
Carly Fiorina
Hugh Hefner
Howard Hughes
Lee Iacocca
Rupert Murdoch
Ron Perelman
Sumner Redstone
Martha Stewart
Donald Trump
Ted Turner
Jack Welch
Steve Wynn

Politicians: 12
Hillary Clinton*
John Edwards
John Ensign**
Rudy Giuliani
Al Gore

Gary Hart**
John Kerry
John McCain
Chip Pickering
Eliot Spitzer**
Mark Sanford
David Vitter**

Singers: 18
Sarah Brightman
Diahann Carroll
Sammy Davis, Jr.
Jerry Garcia
Judy Garland
Michael Jackson
Billy Joel
Jennifer Lopez
Madonna
Bob Marley**
Dean Martin
Paul McCartney
Luciano Pavarotti
Elvis Presley
Jessica Simpson
Frank Sinatra
Britney Spears
Barbra Streisand

U.S. Presidents: 5
Bill Clinton**
Warren G. Harding**
John F. Kennedy**
Ronald Reagan
Franklin D. Roosevelt**

---

* Did not divorce.
** Did not divorce but
   messed around.

CHAPTER ONE

What Went Wrong:

WHO, WHERE AND WHY?

Why do we marry in poetry and divorce in prose? The answer may be found in *Anna Karenina*, the classic 19th century novel about a family ravished by adultery. Today, Leo Tolstoy might well write, "Happy *marriages* are all alike; yet, every unhappy *marriage* is unhappy in its own way." In 2010, in the United States alone, well over one million divorces were granted. Most of them, however unique, are played out under an umbrella of mutual misery and shared stresses, frequently festered by rejection and rage.

Having filed or having been served with divorce papers, you will suffer. You'll experience the emotions played out in the opera *Tosca*, and as with Floria Tosca, many other women will ask, "Why, Lord, why do you reward me like this?" Most of the men may have already responded as in another great Italian opera, *Pagliacci*, where Canio lamented, "While I'm nearly delirious, I don't know what I'm saying or what I'm doing!"

Divorce often brings anger, betrayal, and even fear. Salvos of unbearable hurts and toxic stresses can suddenly besiege you. Unfortunately, this step is merely the first act of a difficult and extended process known as *Divorce Stress Syndrome* (DSS). Social scientists across the land have studied the individual causes and injurious consequences of DSS; their cogent findings and conclusions are now included in academic and medical publications. In their 1996 book, *The Good Marriage: How and Why Love Lasts*, Dr. Judith S. Wallerstein and Sandra Blakeslee report that about 54 percent of first marriages end in divorce. They classify the remaining 45 percent of lasting marriages as follows:

- Fifteen percent are romantically married and truly happy.
- Fifteen percent are coexisting as resentful roommates.
- Fifteen percent are actually miserable, but stay together.

The "romantically married" spouses are the Ron and Nancy Reagan-like couples who still openly express affection and strong appreciation for one another. The "resentful roommate" spouses are the Edith and Archie Bunker-like couples who stay together, in spite of having long ago lost the romantic spark that once passionately united them. The "miserable but married" pairings are the Peg and Al Bundy-like couples, the least contented of married couples. These estranged individuals have lost all love and affection for each other to the point that they are almost arch enemies, yet, they, too, stay together. Thus, we see that throughout America today, increasing numbers of couples who elect to stay together, are compelled to practice marital détente (and usually much more), to survive their stressed unfulfilled unions.

While Ron and Nancy have been well-loved, it's easy to understand why all four sitcom characters remained so very popular for so long. However exaggerated, they seem to reflect our reality as we too often see ourselves in those roommates and miserable characters. Looking back, divorcing couples are certain to see unfolding events of what was once their similar saddened status. We empathize with them because our situations parallel theirs, and we recognize similar actions and reactions. The large percentage of unhappily married people provides "fair warning" to engaged couples as to what may lie ahead for them.

Three Phases of DSS

This syndrome has three inter-related phases: pre-, present-, and post-divorce stress. The first, pre-divorce stress concerns the questions and realizations about whether to divorce or make one more good-faith effort to save a dying marriage. This phase encompasses cumulative past problems, the hurt and anger suffered by the person who wants to leave the marriage, and, not least, the shame and rejection experienced by the spouse who may be left behind.

The second phase, present-divorce stress, deals with the anguish and agony of the divorce process itself, including scheduled court appearances (which are always continued) with your soon-to-be ex-spouse and your spouse's support group. Protracted emotional exchanges—like depositions under oath and mandatory settlement conferences with the one you have elected to leave or who has left you—can be exhausting.

The third phase, post-divorce stress, covers the secondary proceedings and annoyances that surface after your divorce. This involves returning to court for unfinished business and the frightening process of starting over on your own. Thoughts of possible reconciliation, post-divorce dating, or moving in with a new partner, and even considerations of remarriage may all come your way after you're divorced.

You may not be impacted by all three phases of DSS. Some individuals are spared one or two of the Syndrome's phases, while just one overpowers others. The important thing is to realize that you can live through a range of unexpected and unwelcomed emotions. Once acknowledged, however, overwhelming emotions and their accompanying stresses will be easier to endure. Rest assured, you will steadily heal and recover from the shame and rejection of being left behind or from the guilt of deciding to leave.

Guilt and Grief

One of the primary pre-divorce stresses is the realization that you can no longer live with your spouse and must end your marriage to survive emotionally. Alternatively, you may have just been told that your marriage is over and that you must file for divorce or your spouse will. Either conclusion (or the resulting actions) must be viewed as a learning experience and not as a miserable mistake. We should all learn from life experiences, and our future decisions should be made with acquired wisdom. Still, for the spouse who has been told that her or his marriage is over, the anger, sorrow, and humiliation may be devastating. These emotions are also experienced by the spouse who has elected to end the marriage, albeit often to a lesser degree and for a shorter duration.

Elisabeth Kubler-Ross's 1969 book, *On Death and Dying*, lists the repeated stages of grief experienced by individuals facing death.

Most people in the process of dying go directly into one of five phases of grief. Interestingly, these same five stages are present at the death of a marriage (parenthetical comments are my own):

- Denial (*he/she will be back!*)
- Anger (*Why me? What did I do?*)
- Bargaining (*If only I could have …*)
- Despair (*Hopelessness and helplessness*)
- Acceptance (*Well, perhaps this is better… NEXT!*)

It's important to realize that your marriage has died. As with the death of a loved one, you'll likewise encounter [divorce] grief. There seems to be no established schedule or set season for experiencing these compulsory phases. They are all individualized, unique, and exclusive. They occur randomly, without any particular pattern; some repeat their unwelcome visits. Acceptance is the last and healthiest emotion of the five. This is our goal; nevertheless, for some divorced persons, acceptance may be delayed or just never come. The information provided here will assist you in finding acceptance and embracing its healing benefits.

Do not allow yourself to fall into a dark tunnel of endless depression. Acknowledging that denial, anger, and despair are normal and related divorce emotions is a good place to start. These separation human feelings will line the gateway to your recovery. Once you begin to understand their associated causes, cumulative consequences, and self-perpetuating cycles, you're on your way to overcoming them. Your sadness will lessen and one day ebb. Keep forever in mind that divorce affects us emotionally, mentally, and physically beyond our wildest expectations. Persistent bad feelings or continuing physiological or physical abnormalities may require prompt professional attention.

It is now common knowledge that fifty-five percent of all first marriages, two-thirds of all second marriages, and seventy-five percent of all third marriages are interrupted. The tsunami wave of divorces used to come in mid-life (45 to 55), usually after children leave the nest. Although mid-life has now been extended to the ages of 55 to 65, the foregoing spousal exit years remain; recent data suggest that these exit periods may have even been pushed back several years (see Appendix).

Why We Divorce

Scholars and clinicians report that marriage interruptions are caused by internal, external, and collateral factors. Internal marital problems deal exclusively with issues between a wife/husband and her/his respective husband/wife. External and collateral interruptions will be addressed later. Experts report that money, sex, and ineffective communication are today's three most common internal marriage interruption causes. Nevertheless, once a spouse elects to bail out of a marriage, the other spouse can do little or nothing to keep things together.

Money

> What's mine is mine;
> What's ours is mine; and
> What's yours will be mine.

Money is the number one reason people divorce. Low-income spouses often lack the necessary resources to meet basic needs. If basic expenses cannot be covered, there are no funds available for discretionary spending. Occasional and necessary diversions—like vacations, travel or other stress-reducing activities—cannot be enjoyed when there are insufficient funds. The prolonged inability to enjoy stress-releasing activities can lead to marital discord; however, lower-income spouses sometimes have greater family cohesiveness than wealthier couples. Closer family ties often aid low-income spouses through their marital difficulties; nevertheless, they are still impacted by divorce.

Middle-income spouses often differ over individual as well as joint spending priorities. Who brings home the bacon and how many pounds often determine who has authority to spend money and on what. Still, there are usually pestering questions on whether each spouse is actually making his or her contribution for the betterment and welfare of the marriage. Sudden shifts in income, earnings, and fortuitous financial windfalls—like an inheritance, gift, or even prize money—can cause new marital problems. Who gets control, where is *our money* kept, and how and when will it be spent? These new developments now become the vital questions of the day, night, and week.

A quick review of *Forbes's* 400 Wealthiest Americans list indicates that even the very rich are not immune to divorce; in fact, their rate of divorce is greater than those of the U.S. general population, for they certainly can afford the expensive lawyers and other related costs required to obtain their treasured freedom. Some have paid millions, and several have paid hundreds of millions, to end their stale marriages.

Rupert Murdoch is said to have divided $1.7 billion in communal assets with Anna Murdoch, his second wife of 31 years. Anna received a large payout because there was plenty to go around. Some 17 days after his divorce was final, Rupert, at the age of 68, married 31-year-old Wendi Deng, one of his employees.

Sumner Redstone, CEO of Viacom, was perhaps second in dividing marital assets. Phyllis Redstone, his wife of 55 years, allegedly received $1.4 billion of their accumulated fortune. Soon after the divorce was final, Sumner, then 79, married Paula Fortunato, 40, in April 2003. Unfortunately, their divorce papers were filed in October 2008, following a 66-month marriage; nevertheless, Paula divorced well. It is reported their prenup purportedly provided $1 million for each year of marriage; thus, she received $5.5 million. Remember, he was twice as old as Paula. Wealthy older men marrying younger attractive women, and younger women divorcing them, has become a familiar pattern, for it seems that (for both) age does matter.

Both Rupert and Sumner divided substantial assets to end their long marriages, yet, some will pay more while others will suffer in comfortable surroundings. Still, the beat goes on. Billionaire Jim Clark, founder of Netscape, married his fiancée Kristy Hinze, a 29-year-old *Sports Illustrated* cover model, in March 2009. Jim was making his fourth trip down the aisle on the eve of his 65th birthday.

Sexual Interruptions

Sexual-related problems between spouses are the second major cause of divorce. In the 1977 Woody Allen movie *Annie Hall* (voted best picture that year), Woody, while in session with his psychiatrist, tells him, "We almost never have sex anymore." In the following scene, Annie, while in session with her psychiatrist, says, "All we do is have sex."

These clever juxtaposed scenes illustrate a common gender difference in attitudes about sex and its desired frequency. Men and women also have different sexual arousal operating systems, which lead to divergent sexual starting times that can add to their frustrations.

John Gray (*Men are from Mars, Women are from Venus*) said it best:

> When it comes to being sexually
> aroused, women are like crock pots,
> men are like microwave ovens.

A couple's sex life is said to be the ultimate window into their relationship and with each other. Like homes, some couples come with large windows and others with smaller windows, yet many couples seem to have one-way windows when it comes to sharing their sexual needs, established limits, or true erotic desires.

Sexual intimacy problems are troublesome, and sometimes silent saboteurs affect sexual desire, performance, and the much-anticipated afterglow. Men and women are both troubled by stress, fatigue, and involuntary age-related conditions that impede and impact their sexual relations. Loss of desire and age-related abnormalities seem to head the list of women's silent sexual saboteurs; men, on the other hand, are troubled with issues of concern and panic:

> Concern is the first time a man
> cannot perform a second time;
> panic is the second time a man
> cannot perform the first time.

Additional saboteurs include having a picture of your former spouse or lover on the nightstand, your mother-in-law staying in the next room, and a lack of knowledge about basic sexuality (*Where does my leg go?* See: *Sex for Dummies*). Ineffective sexual communication can arise from an inability to acknowledge one's eroticism in front of his or her spouse. This lack of lust and trust, coupled with past episodes of betrayal, can also impact sexual desire, performance and satisfaction. Acts of selfishness on the part of a partner—such as repeated requests or suggestions to be satisfied first, or not reciprocating in enjoyable pleasures—can all take their toll on the other spouse.

Pre-existing medical conditions and prescribed medications, with their unforgiving side effects, often contribute to painful sex or no sex at all. Sometimes accidents or the onset of a health-related event can cause lasting sexual problems: a woman returned to see her doctor after suffering a recent heart attack and asked, "Can I still have sex?"

Her doctor responded, "Yes, but just with your husband." Still, men seem to have more health issues, performance problems, and shorter life spans than women.

> Why do married men die sooner than
> single men? It's because they want to!

Actually, the reverse is true: married men live longer than single men. It's because their loving wives politely pester them to go to the doctor when they are not well. It's also true that men are generally healthier, but die sooner, while women are generally less healthy, but usually live longer.

Lack of Communication

Ineffective spousal communication is the third major cause of divorce. As several of my university colleagues in the Interpersonal Communications Department often remind me, it is not the words per se, but rather the tone, voice, clarity, body language and vocabulary used—all intricate parts of the message that affect relations between spouses.

Most couples know how to communicate. Do you? The following incident drives home this point. One afternoon, when they were three miles from home, a couple started arguing. He said, "Stop the car. Let me out, right here, right now!" She immediately pulled over and let him out. He exited the car. She drove home. Somewhat shocked that she left, he walked home. He never argued with her again while she was driving.

In the example above, both spouses knew how to communicate and how to respond; however, they both failed to communicate effectively (he by asking to get out of the car, she by leaving). The problem is that sometimes a spouse does not want to hear what the other has to say and tunes that spouse out. As this becomes habitual, effective communication deteriorates further. Soon spouses become sarcastic and can predict the other's response in confrontational situations: "I knew you would say that!" Then, regardless of the issue, the ability to communicate is lost.

Women and men are like phones:
They like to be held, talked to, and
touched often. But push the wrong
button and you're disconnected!

Unsuccessful communication can lead to anger and resentment. Sometimes anger stems from family conflicts. Spousal/family feuds over the holidays are common. Occasionally the problems are simple, yet the solutions seem difficult. These strenuous disputes often worsen over time, usually starting small and almost always ending big. Initially small problems may place the pressed spouse on a slow burn mode, until pent-up resentment explodes into a marital blaze, with only the divorce ashes of a once viable marriage remaining.

Years ago I had a good friend named John. He designed and built a large, beautiful house overlooking the ocean, with only one bedroom. John enjoyed his friends but wanted no overnighters. John later married JoAnna, a PhD candidate in psychology (third marriage for him, second one for her) after their seven-month engagement. Months after their wedding, JoAnna wanted her adult son Fred to spend two days/nights with them while in town. JoAnna was insistent that Fred stay with them, even though John had expressed his strong objections. There were five-star hotels in the area; John even offered to pay for Fred's lodging. Still, JoAnna insisted: "It's just for a couple of nights."

Reluctantly, John agreed. While inconsequential to most, this deeply troubled John who had been accustomed to living alone for more than 10 years. His solo late-night and early-morning reading took place in his heavy reclining chair in the area where Fred was to sleep on a nearby couch. Fred was there the two full days and nights as requested. Months passed, and then JoAnna wanted Fred to stay for four days and nights. Again, John strongly objected; he pointed out that he had never allowed his own two sons or anyone else to spend the night. Over John's greater objections, Fred was allowed to stay again. The following year, JoAnna requested a six-day stay for Fred over the holidays. This was the proverbial straw that broke the camel's already overloaded back. It led to a major argument.

The problem was not with Fred; he was only the *spilt milk*. One cannot blame him, because had no idea he was adding to John and JoAnna's problems. How could innocent Fred have known this when JoAnna kept inviting him to stay? JoAnna had frequently told John that she knew him like a book, yet, surprisingly, she did not pick up on his serous discomfort with overnight guests.

Perhaps she did understand John's wishes and was just as stubborn as he was. Possibly JoAnna may have felt that John's strong resistance to letting immediate family stay in *their home* was unreasonable. Perhaps she thought that once John gave his approval, his later objections were forever waived.

Prior to marriage, JoAnna did say she wanted Fred to feel welcome, and John strongly agreed, but John's definition of welcome (as in *to visit*) was far less intimate than JoAnna's (as in being comfortable *to stay* for several days and nights). Interestingly, spousal struggles often involve issues in which both sides feel as if they are right and neither spouse is willing to negotiate a reasonable compromise (three night stays – six times a year?).

While John was very clear that he didn't want Fred to stay, JoAnna seemed simply to ignore John's wishes. Perhaps instead of saying 'no' or insisting that he didn't want overnight guests, John could have better expressed how he felt, that JoAnna was putting her son first by ignoring his feelings and that he was hurt because of it. With a better sense of this problem, she wouldn't write it off as his being silly. JoAnna could also have worked harder to help John appreciate why it was important to her that Fred be in their home, rather than at another impersonal hotel, instead of *insisting* that Fred stay with them.

As married couples, both spouses have an obligation to respect each other's privacy wishes, and this relates to repeated requests to have the other spouse's children spend two, four, or six nights in their home. As in many marital situations, initial requests are frequently increased over already stated objections. Increasing the scope of the request (staying for longer visits) seems unreasonable and could be construed as taking unfair advantage of the other spouse. An inability to discuss sensitive issues effectively only makes matters worse for both spouses.

Marriage, though never perfect, is about husband and wife, and not about stepchildren, parents, or pets. Still, some spouses don't know when to back off, and others feel they don't have to when discussing these issues. John and JoAnna never settled Fred's overnight stay problems. JoAnna eventually left for good. John (obviously still nursing a sore spot) later said, "Now that JoAnna has her own place, she can have Fred come over more often." Thus, even when you feel you know someone like a book, effective communication can still be a problem.

Following their marital explosion, I met with John and attempted to counsel him. I told him that when he married JoAnna, it was a package deal and that Fred was a part of the package. John refused to listen. Then again, he did acknowledge that JoAnna was as stubborn as he was and that there were other issues involved. As we will discuss later, some individuals should not marry. Perhaps a mutual premarital test on the stubborn-o-meter would have been a good idea for both of them.

After they separated, JoAnna continued her study of the male brain, and completed her dissertation. She later ran into John at Dobson's Restaurant in Chicago. After exchanging pleasantries, JoAnna told him that after her extensive study, she had come to realize that she *may have* mishandled their past problems. JoAnna said, "I should not have put my son ahead of my husband." Still, John was gracious, acknowledged his comparative fault of being stubborn, and thanked her. Acknowledging fault after such exasperating events is good for the soul. Accepting apologies without an "I told you so" is good for the other person. As you can see, sometimes (in addition to already knowing someone like a book) it sometimes requires earning a PhD to realize what went wrong.

The necessary restoration and repair of a marriage suffering from communication problems should be easy to remedy these days. First, however, both spouses must agree to resolve these disruptive issues. Long walks together, anger management classes, and seeking professional help— couples therapy with communications coaching if necessary—are effective.

Failures to communicate can also lead to resentment. This consequence, combined with apathy and indifference, becomes marital kryptonite. Once implanted, it is difficult to remove and can affect even super-wife or super-husband. But wait! What is resentment? Where does it come from?

Resentment

Resentment is like a small pebble in your shoe; at first it is only an irritation. If not removed, it causes only minor discomfort because it hurts just a little. If still not removed, it continues to bother you more. If allowed to remain, soon the skin will break and eventually, if still not extracted and the wound cleaned, infection sets in. If still not addressed, the infection spreads, and amputation may be required.

> **Resentment** n. Indignation or ill will
> felt as a result of a real or imagined
> grievance.

The same is true of marital resentment. It always starts off small. Sometimes the resentful conduct is repeated. This repetition adds to the original resentment, and the totals are compounded. Just as in the inhalation of mercury vapor, added amounts over long periods of time can lead to central nervous system damage, endocrine system disruption, and can even result in death [divorce].

Once implanted, marital resentment continues to grow and soon begins to affect even small, everyday spousal interactions. Combined with pre-existing resentment, new events can loom and overflow the often-petty precipitous cause into greater resentment. Resentment can also be caused by a meek person's repeated failure to object to offensive spousal behavior, because timid spouses are often apprehensive about bringing their objections to the attention of their partners. This behavior cannot last long for, sooner or later, this pressurized resentment will erupt as a lethal overexposure of marital kryptonite.

Resentment can also be founded upon baseless or groundless beliefs that are just not true (an imagined grievance). Suspicious spouses sometimes leave, or have been driven to the tipping point to do so, because of bogus believes, imagined incidents, or speculative suspicions which had no factual basis whatsoever. I am certain that you, too, have heard all kinds of unbelievable, bizarre cases like: "My spouse had sex with a werewolf, again!" Then there are cases where one spouse seriously, but mistakenly, believes the other is attempting to poison him or her, or have imagined some other odd, groundless claim.

Still, there are countless situations based on false premises that can cause legitimate resentment. Many a mistaken spouse, for example, has feared or believed that his/her spouse may have been unfaithful. These erroneous beliefs can lead to harsh punishments against an innocent spouse and his or her justified resentment. We see, then, that even an imagined grievance can create legitimate resentment, which is sure to increase over time. The unfaithfulness example above is based on mistaken perceptions, yet the retaliatory consequences to the innocent victim spouse are real.

Dealing with *compressed* legitimate or imagined grievances requires a sophisticated skills set. First, you must identify and separate ordinary, extraordinary, and super-extraordinary grievances. Ordinary grievances are usually based on mundane events: for example, your husband, realizing that you have worked all week, suggests taking you out to Friday dinner. You are tired and say, "No." The next day you ask your husband to join you for a trip to the mall. Recalling your refusal to go to dinner yesterday, last week or last year, your husband says, "No!" Offended that he will not join you, you go off to the mall alone. While there, you come upon a co-worker, classmate, neighbor, bank teller, priest, or other man. This person is polite, pleasant, and compliments you on your dress, and invites you to join him for lunch.

Remembering your resentful husband back home, you return the attention and the compliments. Second glasses of wine are ordered and unexpectedly, you and your newfound friend are sitting closer together than ever before. After six glasses of wine, no food and a little handholding, he politely asks if he can walk you to your car and you agree. All of a sudden, the two of you are walking together, holding hands, and being openly affectionate.

Arriving at your car, he leans over to give you a peck on the cheek. You recall the old, grumpy, resentful husband back at home and, that just because of your innocent refusal to join him for dinner yesterday, last week, last year, he refused to go with you to the mall today. Now you embrace your new admirer even tighter, offer a second lasting kiss.

Now it's as if the two of you were back in high school, and you both jump into the back seat of the car. Hastily clothes start flying off.

Soon both of you are stark naked, and the sex starts. You finish, and you each light up a cigarette (you don't even smoke) and talk about the old spouse back at home. Out of the blue, the mall police arrive and you're arrested for being naked and having sex in the car at the mall. You and your new friend are taken off to jail.

What now? What do you do? Just like *ET*, you too must phone home. But you must get your resentful husband to post bail to get you out of jail. You see? It does not pay to be resentful because sometimes even the slightest act or omission can set off unbelievable results. Not taking out the trash, not walking the dog, or not dropping off or picking up the dry cleaning all could lead to World War III. Missing a birthday or anniversary date or forgetting his/her mother at the airport might yield a similar result.

Just as a fuse does not determine the force of an explosion, it is the same thing with resentment. While the lit fuse (the event) sets off the charge, the force is determined by the consequences to the parties involved. There are no differences among ordinary, extraordinary, and super-extraordinary grievances because they are all super-extraordinary. All can lead to super-extraordinary results like being arrested naked in the mall parking lot and going to jail just because you refused to go to dinner and your spouse refused to go to the mall.

External Antagonists

External marital interruption problems involve issues over which one or both spouses have strong degrees of control over precipitous causes. The top three are:

- Extramarital affairs
- In-laws (all four of them)
- Children and stepchildren

Spouses who can't say no to others subordinate the health of their marriage and the welfare of their spouses by paying attention to others first. Extramarital affairs head the list. A detailed discussion of extramarital infidelity would require an entire book, Volumes I, II, and III. But wait! Why do so many married persons stray and have extramarital affairs?

What are the common causes for adultery? Some spouses may feel that it is because their spouse is not taking care of their [sexual] business at home, and this frequently leads to rationalized affairs or other marriage-compromising activity. Not surprisingly, these feelings include a sense of not being loved, respected, or appreciated by a spouse, as well as generic boredom, Tuesdays, and the missing essential validation (not received from their spouse) that they are still a desired person.

Others claim that extended marital intercourse is like going to the same restaurant, sitting at the same table, and being waited on by the same waiter, who brings you the same appetizer followed by the same meal you always order. Others say there are various menu appetizer (foreplay) and entree selections (positions), tables (rooms), and waiters (sexual aids) at the same restaurant, and everyone should try something (not someone) new, now and then. Need I say more?

Every day, somewhere, select husbands/wives are having sexual intercourse with someone other than their [respective] wives/husbands. Frequently unfulfilled and unappreciated spouses will look elsewhere for what's already at home, but which is no longer being served on the marital menu. This topic will be further addressed in later chapters. The foregoing listed causes for adultery and ensuing infidelities often lead to divorce, because unfulfilled spouses become distant and resentful or often get caught while seeing someone else.

In-laws (known by some as the crabgrass on the lawns of matrimony) are the second major external interrupter, and the couple's children or stepchildren are the third. Marriage partners often let *life* set their priorities. In first marriages, it's often the parents of the other spouse, their children, or career that are in first class, while the other spouse is placed in coach. In second, third, and even fourth marriages, it's usually placement of stepchildren (as with JoAnna and John) or the in-laws again who are placed ahead of their spouse. Remarried spouses who fail to replace their parent/child bond with their mature adult spouse may be sabotaging their own marriages.

Most spouses do not like being in coach while others enjoy first-class. This arrangement is not good: the marriage must always come first, wives/husbands, second. Your/her/ his children are third/fourth, followed by parents, in-laws, careers, pets, and others.

Additional external marital antagonists include stressed situations where one spouse insists on keeping in contact with past paramours. The other partner may be uncomfortable with this arrangement and have already expressed his or her objections. Still some spouses continue to keep in touch with past lovers secretly, while others do so openly. Even if there's open and *mutual acceptance*, this pernicious practice should be avoided. It's not good for the marriage because it can erode an already fragile intimacy, due to diminished confidence or marginalized trust felt by the other spouse.

There's no question that the Internet, with its diverse offerings and private viewing, has impacted marriages worldwide. This invention has spawned a superabundance of new marital challenges. Online chat rooms, private email accounts, and extramarital dating sites, along with self-proclaimed cheating sites, soft- and hardcore porn sites, and a host of other hostile marital websites are affecting marriages everywhere. Now it's just you at your computer, in your room, in your home. It seems as though this *viewing* comes within the periphery of reasonable expectations of privacy, as guaranteed by the Fourth Amendment. This *privacy*, of course, would not include your spouse (unless he or she is seated next to you enjoying the show).

The Internet has increased marital challenges because it offers covert alternatives for spouses to maintain secret relationships and have access to extramarital sexual stimulation through porn (which may be normal for many, but can be nauseating to others). For select married individuals, questions may arise when concealed activity is discovered by the other spouse. To some, catching one's spouse fantasizing at the computer or self-enraptured in viewing porn may be examples of such harmful activity; to others, these are meaningless, innocuous acts. Still, these activities can be damaging to some conservative or insecure spouses. How might you feel if you discovered your spouse self-absorbed at the computer with hidden autographed pictures of some fantasized lover? For sensitive, married persons, these activities can cause feelings of rejection and humiliation and may further erode an already compromised spousal intimacy. To many others, "it's no big thing," and sometimes these activities are appreciated and even welcomed by their spouses.

Collateral Interruptions

The last of the three internal marriage interrupters is collateral marital problems. These can be collectively described as difficult situations in which spouses have no ability to control or to eliminate the underlying causes. Leading examples include:

- Repeated loss of employment
- Unsolvable financial problems
- Serious sickness, disease, or lasting addictions

Many spouses cannot cope with their partner's repeated loss of employment and continued inability to find and hold meaningful work. Financial ruin brought on by protracted litigation, bad investments, or other such economic calamities can all be disastrous to marital bliss. Incurable sicknesses and disease, as well as lasting addictions to alcohol, drugs, or gambling can also impair marriage survival. Additional collateral factors, like unexpected adverse business fluctuations or even natural disasters (in-laws and their dogs moving in with you) may stretch a marriage beyond its limits and cause a spouse to leave. Any of the preceding can, and often does, lead to divorce.

Latent Causes of Divorce

Some spouses are unaware of the underlying causes of their marriage interruption problems. A common example involves incompatible stealth couple dynamics, as in the example that follows. Betty is particularly physical, and she gives and needs repeated touching, sporadic samplings of affection, and gentle expressions of love. Her husband Bob, on the other hand, is appreciative but is just not at the same level of physicality as his wife. To Bob, who may be more cerebral than physical, her needs seem unimportant or insignificant. He does not reciprocate with similar affection, attention, or other loving acts as provided by Betty. Thus Betty sometimes feels rebuffed and rejected, while Bob remains oblivious of a problem obvious to any trained observer. These issues intensify with age, are *compressed* with resentment, and other hurts, as feelings of being unwanted or summarily abandoned continue to increase.

Today's troubled marriages have many affection-deprived spouses. I've sat and talked across my desk from probably one hundred individuals who have told me they wanted to divorce their spouse because of a continued lack of affection. I once had a woman named Ruth tell me that her husband rarely touched, kissed, or held her during their eight years of marriage. She told me how she was starving for intimacy that never came and that she hungered to be held, kissed, and touched, but never received any of the foregoing from her cold, distant husband. Ruth then informed me that she had become involved with a fellow church parishioner who initially greeted her with warm handshakes and left her with departing affectionate hugs. This was far more than she ever received at home. As Ruth and her new married friend became closer, they would secretly meet just to talk. This increased closeness was followed with mutual disclosures of their common lack of fulfillment needs, which gradually led to cherished moments with mutual loving affection.

Ruth's marital concern is a common issue among discontented spouses. Months later I met with a man named Ralph who was in the same sad predicament. His wife, it turns out, was somewhat aloof, cold, and not physical. Ralph told me how he wanted and needed affection from his wife but never received what he longed for at home. As humans, many of us innocently look elsewhere for what is not received at home; this innate biological need (sex/affection; along with the other vital requirements for water, food, and sleep) manifests itself in several ways. Some are out subconsciously looking for someone to hold, touch, and love them, while others are vulnerable to appreciated advances from others. I was later informed that Ruth and Ralph were an *item*.

There are many Betty wives, and perhaps even more Bob husbands, who seem to march to different drummers. These dissimilar spouses can sometimes benefit from professional help, via discussions and alternative solutions regarding their desires and requests. These needs and wants should actually be discussed and discovered during the one-year minimum dating, and one-year required engagement (cumulative two-year period), as mentioned in coming chapters. Similar problems are likely after the fourth, fifth, and sixth anniversaries (because supposedly, the *marriage-glow* typically lasts for only three years).

Early stages of the foregoing marriage interruption factors can become later justifications for a disappointed spouse to look elsewhere. It seems as if today, when it comes to looking elsewhere, all is fair and unrestricted. Case in point: Woody Allen and Soon-Yi Previn. Woody and Mia Farrow were together for 12 years (1980 through 1992), but never married.

Their relationship ended when Mia allegedly discovered nude photographs Woody had reportedly taken of Soon-Yi, Mia's adopted child with André Previn. Since Woody was not Soon-Yi's father, he could marry her and did so in 1997 (he was then 62, she was 27). The pair has since adopted two daughters. At least everyone already knew everyone else.

Don't feel bad; many of us may be walking on thin ice. Did you know that only 51 percent of married persons would marry the same spouse again? It gets even worse because 43 percent of married women have had serious thoughts (this week) about leaving their present husbands. Obviously, many have already left. Married men, on the other hand, seem to be more satisfied and content in their marriages, because only 29 percent of married men have thought about leaving their wives (this month), but most stay married. Despite the stereotype that women want commitment while men don't, in reality men seem to be happier in their marriages and with their lives than women.

Perhaps you or your spouse had an affair. Was it disclosed? Whether it was emotional (intimate conversations), physical (hugs, kisses, and heavy petting), or sexual (new positions and fresh techniques), there are many factors to be considered. Several commentators consider all of these behaviors a breach of fidelity. Most reporters acknowledge that seeking emotional, physical, or sexual intimacies elsewhere are all repugnant to marital trust and fidelity.

Living with someone brings innumerable stressors; nevertheless, couples manage. Cumulative years of struggling with bills, children, and careers can compromise intimacy. The *romance* may be gone, but the relationship still provides a sense of identity and safety to both partners. Disclosure of a past affair can instantly destroy domestic stability and security. These consequences require thinking things through carefully; you'll need to step back and take a good look at your partner and her/his level of emotional fragility.

The conventional wisdom among psychologists was that a married person should reveal any infidelity to their spouse. That said, we acknowledge that others hold contrary views. Today, an increasing number of psychologists feel that disclosure of an affair may not be necessary. This is a topic of avid discussion. Questions seem centered on infidelity and monogamy studies, about whether affairs are natural/unnatural, and why "confessing" seems to be more about guilt than a true desire for intimacy. Guilt can be a double-edged sword: for many, guilt can make or break an affair. Guilt is there from the start, making you think about the consequences of what you're doing or about to do. Is it really worth the shame you will face and the hurt you will cause?

The traditional view was that the unfaithful party must confess the affair, because honesty is of the utmost importance, and that will help both spouses make a fresh start. This approach embraces the reality that the victim spouse unwittingly may have been a contributing or related factor in the unfaithful spouse's indiscretions (perhaps because of a general lack of interest in sex, not allowing the use of sex toys, viewing porno movies together, or "*dressing for the occasion*"). Each couple's situation is unique, and each has its own constellation of distinctive symptoms.

You must also consider the foreseeable fallout and collateral damage, because, your spouse will more than likely be devastated by your confession. All trust and respect your partner once had in you will be gone in an instant ("You did what with _____?"). Revealing your affair will alter both of your lives in ways that you cannot predict or control. There will be deep anger and severe hurt. Your spouse may leave you. Your marriage may end in divorce.

If you elect to disclose your affair, keep it simple and brief but at the same time answer any questions your partner may have. You must be prepared to make it clear you realize you have made a mistake. You don't have to give *exact* details of your affair but be honest with your partner. Some detail-giving will be appropriate (some spouses will insist on all of the details). Do not get into past gift-giving or anatomical comparisons, as doing so will surely make your partner's healing process more difficult. Answer questions asked, because silence may infer that you are continuing the affair and/or protecting the affair partner.

Give yourself time to prepare for this step; you may even wish to seek professional guidance and support. It is also important to remember that although you may have behaved badly, you are not a bad person. There is a fine line between taking responsibility for your actions and becoming self-destructive. It's important to remember this because your partner might not agree in their initial rage. Your injured spouse may do everything in her/his power to make you feel awful about yourself. This is a natural response. Express how sorry you are and how much you regret your unfaithfulness. Emphasize that you have ended the affair and that you want to work on saving your marriage. I recommend reading: *After the Affair: Healing the Pain and Rebuilding Trust When a Partner Has Been Unfaithful,* by Janis Abrahms Spring, PhD.

Be sensitive; your partner will likely not be able to give you an answer on the spot about where they wish to go from here. Repeat your hopes for a future together (if that is what you truly want). Be realistic and considerate in giving your spouse the necessary time to work things through and evaluate alternatives. The innocent spouse should be aware that 70 percent of affairs last only two months, and only 30 percent of affairs last more than a year. Only approximately 3 percent of affairs result in marriage, and are subject to second marriage 67 percent divorce rates.

The non-disclosure school of thought suggests that you take this secret with you to the grave, as there is no need to cause your spouse unnecessary anguish. Still, keeping your misguided activities a secret won't be easy either. You'll likely feel guilt and shame. If you had unprotected sex or left hotel receipts in your car, clothing, or elsewhere, you may not have a choice about the affair being revealed. If you have had two, four, or eight affairs, you may need to think about your reasons for disclosing the incident before you say anything to your spouse. You do have the right to remain silent. If it was a one-time incident, and you have broken it off, and the guilt is enough to keep you on the straight and narrow, perhaps keeping it to yourself may be the better. Be extra careful if you talk in your sleep, use credit cards, or wear shoes, however. Whatever you decide to do, you must carefully weigh the alternatives.

WHAT YOU NOW RECOGNIZE, UNDERSTAND, AND ACCEPT

1. Fifty-five percent of first marriages end in divorce.

2. Sixty-seven percent of second marriages end in divorce.

3. Seventy-four percent of third marriages end in divorce.

4. Only 15 percent of married people are truly happy in their marriages.

5. Fifteen percent of married people are roommates and just cope.

6. Fifteen percent are actually miserable, but stay married for various reasons (emotionally forgotten, but not physically gone).

7. Divorce is like a death; you need to grieve it, before you can get over the loss.

8. The Internet has negatively impacted marriage and will continue to do so.

9. Money, sex problems and ineffective communication cause the majority of marriage interruptions.

10. Brothers and sisters, you are not alone!

CHAPTER TWO

Divorce Diplomacy:

DEPARTING WITH DIGNITY

ITALIAN SECRET FOR
MARRIAGE DIPLOMACY

At St. Cecilia's Italian Catholic Church they have a semi-annual husbands' and wives' marriage retreat. At the session last week, Father Ricardo Capra asked Signora Stefana, who was approaching her 50th wedding anniversary, to take a few minutes and share some insight into how she had managed to stay married to the same man all these years.

Signora Stefana moved to the front of the room and replied to the assembled couples, "Well, I've tried to treat him with respect, spend money on him, make him think he is in charge; but best of all is, I took him to Italy for the tenth wedding anniversary!"

Father Ricardo Capra responded, "Donna Stephana, you're an amazing inspiration to all the wives here! Please tell us what you are planning for your husband for your fiftieth wedding anniversary?"

Signora Stefana proudly replied, "I'm going back to get him."

As noted above, *"Absence [sometimes] makes the heart grow fonder."* All that's well does not always end well, however. Nothing, it seems, begins with more excitement and optimism than romance, and more often it consistently ends in disappointment and distress. We already know that most marriages end in divorce. We further realize that the majority of married individuals are not romantically happy or emotionally fulfilled. Many divorce for medical reasons: *they get sick of each other!*

Class, Dignity, and Respect

Spousal disappointments and blame for a faltering marriage are common, as are most of our unenlightened responses that precede them. Rather than offering acceptance, forgiveness, and wisdom, we often react with bitterness and choose to become the victim. Instead of questioning our own shortcomings about love, many of us blame our spouse for not living up to our expectations or validating us as partners. Sometimes we make only minor efforts to resolve the underlying problem and put even less energy into bringing a troubled marriage back to good health. Other times we censure our spouses with resentment and indifference for that which should have been accepted and forgiven. It is no wonder then that so many people are unhappy in their marriages.

Whatever happened to you is history; somehow your love lapsed. Unexplained, annoying dissatisfactions between you and your estranged spouse festered beyond your tolerance threshold, and one of you decided it was time to leave. Leaving, or receiving the ominous news that your marriage is over, must be handled with dignity, diplomacy, and without further hurt or pain to the spouse you once loved, treasured and adored.

The important word here is [divorce] diplomacy. Divorce diplomacy can be defined as the art and skill of ending a marriage or accepting your spouse's decision to do so, with sensitivity and respect. Difficult as this may seem, there are mutual benefits to be gained. Many of life's decisions are difficult; nevertheless, we are frequently called upon to go the extra mile and do more than situations warrant. Saying farewell to a spouse or acknowledging that your marriage is over certainly rank among the most traumatic and hurtful of adult experiences.

When the time comes to leave your spouse or to acknowledge their departure, why not do so with class, dignity, and respect? Someday your words of kindness and care will bring beneficial reciprocal returns. The same is true when you say something mean or spiteful. You'll get the same in return, and it always comes back compounded. Negativity puts you in a bad light. Others will lose respect for you, and there's no dividend earned. There's no need to be mean and hurtful, and cause further pain. Would you rather be remembered as a Jackie Kennedy or a Tonya Harding; compared to a Cary Grant or some other noted opposite?

First, a few interesting words about Cary Grant and Jackie Kennedy, our standards for excellence. Their stormy marriages and troubled lives were extremely difficult. Cary Grant was born Archibald Alec Leach (name change: obvious). Cary had five marriages: first there was Virginia Cherrill. Then there was the ultra-wealthy socialite, Barbara Hutton; the couple was sarcastically nicknamed Cash & Cary. Hutton had extensive prenuptial agreements, and Cary refused any financial settlement when they later divorced. Cary always ignored accusations that he married for money. He said, "I may not have married for very sound reasons, but money was never one of them."

Cary then married actress Betsy Drake, then the much younger Dyan Cannon. These four were followed by marriage to his long-time companion, British hotel PR agent Barbara Harris (his fifth wife, who was 47 years younger). She was with him when he died in 1986.

What is there left to say about Jackie Kennedy that has not been said ten times? Even though she was widowed by both of her adulterous husbands, she had ample cause to divorce them both. In Chapter 7, I list some of JFK's known escapades that were consistent with the reputations of Jackie's openly unfaithful father (her parents divorced), father-in-law, and brothers-in-law, and properly focus on her following quote: "I don't think there are any married men who are faithful to their wives."

Recently discovered was the fact that her marriage to Aristotle Onassis, 23 years her senior, was troubled from the start to its 77-month end. They spent most of their time separate and apart from each other.

Besides, when you own a shipping line, finding an extra pleasure yacht to entertain a lady-friend is never a problem. Still, Jackie kept all of her personal sorrows and private unhappiness to herself, and she remained the epitome of elegance and sophistication. Even though Jackie was well aware of Jack's extramarital activities, she always stood by his side during the entire ten-year marriage, and she was buried next to him. She never aired her hampers of dirty laundry about either of her two unfaithful husbands.

Cary and Jackie had six troubled marriages (two for Jackie and four for Cary). Both had profound individual challenges, keeping closeted secrets and carrying heavy burdens, yet they still remain the gold standard for class, dignity, and respect toward others today.

How to Leave A Spouse

If you're the spouse who has decided to leave, here is what you must do. For the ladies, think of something special you did for him. Perhaps it was a surprise birthday party, a special dinner, or even just a regular dinner for a special event, where you put in extra time planning and preparing. Most male spouses will still recall the manner in which they popped the *"Will you marry me?"* question. The bottom line is that you made a significant effort to make it special. Why not spend a little extra time now to ease the pain and foreseeable hurt about to be delivered?

Reading and studying the tone of departing messages may inspire you to use such compassionate, soft loving words such as Lord Byron's "When We Two Are Parted," where you'll find at the next chapter's opening. You must realize that you'll be long remembered for your exit and especially for your departing words. Why not take a few days to think through and prepare this important farewell? By all means, do not practice or make a video of your farewell address before your mother-in-law or others (this can result in embarrassing consequences: YouTube!). Bear in mind that your estranged spouse will soon tell everyone near and far about how she/he was treated. Your departing farewell address will linger on for time immemorial; divorce farewell addresses are always repeated to others and remembered by many.

Mack Trucks

Each one of us has exclusive control over our character-development; in fact, we improve or diminish it as we go. Every ethical and moral decision adds or subtracts to the mosaic that creates our character. Why not add a couple of diamonds to your character mosaic by exercising exemplary behavior in giving your divorce notice, or in accepting your spouse's decision, with class, dignity, and respect?

At the time of telling your spouse of your decision to leave, try to be a Jackie Kennedy or a Cary Grant. Tell him/her how you enjoyed your life together and that the time has now come for both of you to go your separate ways. Remind your spouse of his/her good qualities. Assure your spouse that he/she is a good person, but not the right husband/wife for you, as you are just not the proper wife/husband for him/her. Remember, you've had ample time to review, plan, and prepare for what will happen. Responding to such news is far more difficult. Being the recipient of this upsetting news is like being hit by a Mack truck. Then, while going through the divorce process, the Mack truck comes back and hits you yet again—with no warning or preparation time.

Honor your spouse's requests for reasons or answers; however, don't discuss details at this time. By all means, do not get into the YOU, YOU, YOUs; instead, use I, I, I and stand tall. If necessary, take the hit yourself. Yes, you can take responsibility for what happened. Acknowledge your own faults and deficiencies. Certainly, no one can criticize us when we take responsibility for what went wrong.

Besides, you must have contributed to the interruption of your marriage to at least some degree. It takes two to have an argument or a breakup. Divorce is a delicate process and must be handled with extreme care. If you leave your spouse as a Jackie Kennedy or a Cary Grant, you will soon discover that cumulative dividends and compounded returns will be earned from these altruistic acts.

Having heard the crushing human reactions to this shocking news from clients and others, I tender this noteworthy advice. Even if your spouse is prepared and expecting divorce news, you still need to be caring and show class, dignity, and respect in telling/accepting this notification and during the entire divorce process and thereafter.

If you are the recipient of these terrible tidings, there's no need to get mad or abusive and start throwing dirty dishes and the kitchen sink at your spouse. Perhaps your spouse still has last-minute doubts about whether to stay or leave. Any explosive or violent reaction will only validate his/her decision to leave. A better choice, and an interesting human experiment, is to accept the news with empathy, sympathy, and love for the other person. This approach will be difficult, if not impossible, but clearly worth it, for it will definitely help both of you.

Try this and see what happens:

- You say you realize how difficult it must have been for them to tell you (continue).
- You say you realize how difficult it must have been for them to live with you (continue: bite your tongue if necessary).
- You say you will help them in every way to make this transition as easy as possible for both of you.

What do you have to lose? Nothing that's not already lost. Why not take the high road? Here is what you do:

- Show you accept their decision to leave.
- Show you are not a vindictive person.
- Show you're a person of class and dignity.
- Show you'll not grovel and beg them to stay.
- Show you are like Jackie Kennedy/Cary Grant.

I've actually seen this result in a change of heart. It may even work for you. If you have not yet recognized this approach, it's called (first) kill them with kindness. Once again, I ask you to put yourself in the other person's shoes. Given the choice, to which alternative would you be more receptive? If your spouse has even one scintilla of desire to stay married, perhaps this one scintilla could be turned into two, three, and then more. Less turmoil and trauma from you may convince your spouse that perhaps she/he is wrong. This may lead to a, *Can we try again?* Yes, it happens. Sometimes people do fall back in love with each other. So, don't throw out the towels just yet, because he or she may be back.

Ending a marriage can be a harsh and trying experience. This quandary will bring anger and apprehension to both spouses. Being told that your union has ended will ignite instant feelings of hurt and deep rejection; it's really painful being told that you are no longer loved and that you will be left behind. Spouses who elect to leave their marriages will frequently feel guilt and shame, even though they are sometimes filled with compressed anger and collected bitterness. Both spouses will experience sadness and a sense of mutual loss. Still, as difficult as it seems, departing spouses and partners left-behind need to be sympathetic and comforting towards the person they once deeply loved. As you will read throughout this book, you and your soon-to-be ex-spouse will get through your divorce less emotionally scared and financially battered, and you will both recover faster, by being companionate, civil, and cooperative.

Assuming that you have tried counseling, therapy, and other alternatives, I offer the following advice: after you have thoughtfully made up your mind to leave, follow through. Do not second-guess yourself and do not change your decision, for this will cause both of you added stress and turmoil. Being hit once by a Mack truck is bad enough; there's no need to be hit yet again making matters worse.

The next item is a two-step process. First, you need to disassociate yourself slowly from your spouse. You must stop doing things together and let your spouse do things without you. This approach includes everything: shopping and anything else you used to do together. Repairs and fix-it items should all be delegated to the local handyman. Both must do their own laundry and other necessaries. This arrangement will help both of you prepare for the coming change.

You must also become less available. I remember leaving home earlier and returning much later. Go to a movie, church, bookstore, or anywhere else, but go alone. You should also move into a separate bedroom or use the sofa to sleep alone.

If you'll be moving out, take the necessary time and care to ensure that all moving matters are completed beforehand. Mail forwarding, utility hookups, and furnishings, if necessary, should all be completed well in advance of your anticipated departure date.

If you fail to address these nuance matters in a timely manner, they will cause both of you added stress and tension. Joint accounts and credit cards must all be closed out. You must open new checking, savings, credit card, and other necessary accounts in your individual name only. Insurance beneficiaries should be changed as necessary. All these actions must be completed before you file or are served with divorce papers. Most state divorce forms contain restraining orders, effective upon filing or service, prohibiting such actions thereafter. Assuming the foregoing is completed in an appropriate manner, the next thing to do is to thoughtfully provide your spouse with notice of your decision to move out.

In planning their divorces, many spouses rely on the advice of *experts*. The prevailing thinking among these *specialists* seems to be: "Tell your spouse you want a divorce at a public place to prevent possible violence, physical attacks, or emotional outbursts." I recall a former client named Heather telling me she followed this expert advice. After a heated argument one afternoon, she told me, her husband Henry followed her to a park that she frequented. There in the park, Heather told Henry she wanted out of their troubled marriage and that she was going to file for divorce. Henry responded, Heather said, by yelling at her. She responded in the same manner, and soon a small audience of onlookers and passersby took great interest in their discussions there in the park. Well, so much for *experts*!

Another client told me she and her husband were at home when she told him she wanted a divorce. There, my client said, she patiently listened to her husband's findings of fault and conclusions of cause. She allowed him to vent, gave no retaliatory comments, and did not ratchet up the volume of their conversation; she agreed with him whenever possible, and politely ended their somber discussions with: "This is no way for us to live. It's not healthy for us, and it is causing us both great hurt and deep pain. We certainly both deserve better."

Some might consider holding back the bad news to be a deliberate failure to communicate. Others might call this passive-aggressive or even controlling behavior (what else is there?), yet continued civility and compassion toward your estranged spouse quashes such specious concerns even after the bad tidings are finally delivered.

Notice: When and Where

Given the severity and likely consequences of your *bombshell* notification, you may have also accepted the reality that there's no good place to deliver this hurtful news. Based on years of client feedback, discussions with psychologist, and other experienced individuals, I have concluded that the best place to give this news might be at home or other private place. There are also good days and bad times to present you notification. The best days to deliver your planned and rehearsed farewell address may be on a Friday evening or Saturday morning over a three-day weekend. Giving notice over a three-day weekend gives her/him an additional day to cushion the impact of the news prior to returning to work or to other responsibilities on Tuesday. Never ever on his/her birthday, your anniversary, or on a day that would be forever spoiled because of the news tendered. Only a sadist would deliver the word on New Year's Eve/Day, Christmas Eve/Day, Valentine's Day, Mother's/Father's Day, Thanksgiving Day, or other such days.

Again, stop, think, and consider what you can do to make for a softer landing for your spouse. For unknown reasons, many divorcing persons give notice on New Year's Eve, their children's graduation, or on the other days listed above.

Noted Farewells

I once had a client who told me how she had thought long and hard about how to tell her husband that she wanted out of their nine-year lifeless marriage. For three months, she secretly wrote considerate letters, addressed to both of them, but mailed just to her. Finally, on the date she had selected to give her husband the news, they sat together. They took note of the aged postmarks, and then opened and read her letters.

In her first letter she told him how she still loved him and how she had agonized over her decision to leave. Her second and third letters mentioned her personal struggles, her faults, and her efforts to overcome them. As reported to me, soon they were both crying. Somehow their shared sorrows and mutual thoughtfulness made the menacing news less difficult for her to deliver and easier for him to accept.

Carly Fiorina, former CEO of Hewlett-Packard and recent California senatorial candidate, may not have left her marriage with a good farewell address. She first married Todd Bartlem, her Stanford classmate in 1977. The marriage did not go well, and they were said to have been estranged since late 1979. They divorced in 1984. Allegedly, Carly's farewell address amounted to: "I will never see or talk to you again in my life."

Carly is said to have left without a forwarding address or any other means of contact. She reportedly has never seen or talked to Todd again. Jackie Kennedy might have said, "I want to thank you for the good years and wish you the very best. I am truly sad that things did not work out for us. You can reach me via email." This alternative would have been a far better farewell address; however, such eloquence is difficult when giving or receiving word that a spouse wants out of her/his marriage.

Your farewell address must be made in person, not by email, carrier pigeon, press conference or any other insensitive manner. America's Mayor Rudy "9/11" Giuliani did not. Rudy first married Regina Peruggi in 1968. They divorced in 1982 when Rudy *claimed* that Regina was his second cousin, and also discovered that she was left-handed. Was it because of news from a recent family reunion or DNA testing? Whatever!

Next, Rudy met Donna Hanover (who had been previously married to writer Stanley Hanover) on a blind date in Miami in 1982. Rudy proposed six weeks later and Rudy and Donna married on April 15, 1984. Six years later, it was reported that Rudy may not have exercised divorce diplomacy by allegedly airing his dirty laundry in telling members of the press, city staffers, and the viewing public (including Donna) that their marriage was over. Donna didn't waste any time; she married Edwin Oster (no more Italians) the following year.

Elin Woods (see Chapter 6) certainly had justifiable cause to air Tiger's over-stuffed hampers of *dirty laundry*; however she did not. She instead demonstrated divorce diplomacy. "Elin dealt with the scandal and the divorce in a way that makes people respect her even more," said Magnus Alselind, managing editor at the Swedish newspaper *Expressen*. "She has held her head high."

Reciprocal Altruism

Being on good terms with your ex-spouse can bring numerous rewards. Joe DiMaggio handled Marilyn's funeral and had roses delivered to her final resting place twice a week for 20 years. Frank Sinatra paid for Ava Gardner's $50,000 medical bills and left first wife Nancy and third wife Mia Farrow sizeable cash bequests in his will. The Donald graciously hosted Ivana's (his first ex-wife) fourth wedding at one of his houses. My first ex-wife edited my manuscript (I carefully checked; she did not change anything). The list of reciprocal courtesies, altruistic acts, and continued acts of random kindness between ex-spouses can be endless. Yes, even for the wealthiest man in America who already has earned cumulative dividends and compound interest, this is still true.

In April 1952, Warren Buffett married Susan Thompson. They had three children and remained in Omaha, Nebraska (why?). Apparently their marriage, like many others, seemed to have possibly lost its steam and they, too, may have slowly drifted emotionally apart while remaining physically together. Susan reportedly took extended unaccompanied trips to San Francisco to work on her singing career. Long before Susan started her solo sojourns to San Francisco, she had met Astrid Menks at a restaurant in Omaha where Astrid was the hostess. They soon became good friends. Susan later introduced Astrid to Warren and they, too, became good friends.

In 1977 Susan moved to San Francisco by herself. Before leaving for San Francisco, allegedly at Susan's request, Astrid moved in with Warren. After supposed in-house dating, Warren and Astrid became an item. Susan highly approved of Warren's relationship with Astrid and he was obviously comfortable with the arrangement. Once again, we have another one of these wonderful situations where everyone already knows everyone else. Meanwhile, Warren was fully supportive of Susan's goals and helped her in every manner possible. Susan and Warren remained good friends; they talked frequently and even vacationed together. Warren was at Susan's side at the time of her death, in July 2004.

Twenty-seven years after their introduction by Susan, and two years after Susan's death, Warren and Astrid formalized their long relationship and were married on August 30, 2006—his 76th birthday.

It was a brief civil ceremony held at the Omaha home of Warren's daughter Susie. Warren purchased a wedding ring for Astrid from a local jeweler. After the (free) home ceremony, the reception (sit-down) dinner was held at the Bonefish Grill, where they all had the early-bird special. Daughter Susie allegedly commented: "It's her only and his last wedding, but certainly not their last early-bird special."

Good heavens. How many of us would have married at home, taken the entire wedding party to a local fish restaurant and ordered the early-bird special in lieu of a grand wedding, an extravagant reception, followed by a formal dinner? How many of us are among the most prosperous people in America? Perhaps that's why Warren is the wealthiest person in America and we are not.

Thus we see that many divorced individuals (Ava Gardner, Marilyn Monroe, Ivana Trump, Susan Buffett, and others you'll soon read about) have benefited from their graceful exits and divorce diplomacy, via reciprocal altruism. There are many others who neither profited or were later chastised for their neutral divorce exits. There are those finally, who have taken the low road and resorted to mean-spirited maneuvers and tasteless tactics by being cruel, clever, and cold.

For those who consider themselves to be cruel, clever, and cold, please do not make a spectacle of the situation. No video cameras, no one jumping out of a cake, and no other act that would bring further pain or sorrow to your former spouse. If you harbor thoughts of this nature, think how your loved ones might feel being subjected to what you are considering doing to your former spouse. If you still entertain thoughts of retaliatory or vindictive actions, then call 1-855-I-PSYCHO or 1-855-I-AM-SICK; both are toll-free calls.

After the marriage-ending news has been delivered and after someone moves out, continue to be civil, polite, and responsive to your estranged spouse. Emails are a good way to communicate about divorce questions and issues. Keep it friendly, because soon you and your estranged spouse, and their attorney, will be in extensive settlement discussions over unresolved issues. You do not need or want to come across as a classless person without dignity or respect before, during, or after your divorce.

Your attitude plays an important role in facilitating settlement of remaining divorce matters. If you have found someone new, keep that new person totally out of the picture. Bringing Mr. or Ms. Replacement with you to court or other meeting places will only irritate, hurt, and inflame your ex (especially if that person is thinner, stronger, and younger). If you really wish to make a statement or an "I told you I could do better," you can always rent an escort or a model to accompany you to various appearances.

Acknowledge your former spouse's birthdays, Mother's Day, and Father's Day with modest greeting cards. Again, keep it friendly and keep it nice. Remember, too, that others will soon hear about your departure and your exit thoughtfulness or lack thereof.

Additional divorce footnotes: keep your decision to file or the fact that you have been served to yourself. You do not want to become the center of the gossip farm at work, church, or elsewhere. You will already have enough on your agenda. You do not need additional activity from others who may care, but have no immediate need to know.

For some strange reason people often think that talented and successful individuals are immune from the hurt and pain experienced when divorcing. We wrongfully conclude that because of their fame and fortune they do not bleed when cut, they do not cry when hurt, and they do not suffer as we do. Such is not the case. We all suffer the same slings and arrows of divorce.

Countless examples have been provided, and additional cases will follow to demonstrate that it pays to act civilly when divorcing. Here are additional examples of celebrity divorces with accompanied diplomacy.

Sarah Brightman, the eldest of six children, first married her music manager at the age of 18, while advancing what later became a great career. This marriage lasted three years, and they later divorced on good terms. She later met and married Andrew Lloyd Webber while performing in *Cats*. Their marriage lasted six years, and they pleasantly divorced in 1990. At last report they remained on friendly terms.

Later, Sarah became involved with Frank Peterson; this relationship lasted for several years. In 2004, Sarah and Frank elected to go their separate ways, although he continues to produce her albums (See? It can be done).

Even if you're from one of the richest counties in America (Nassau County/Long Island) and you're already known as the *Piano Man*, all of this does not ensure success in marriage. Billy Joel first married his business manager, Elizabeth Weber Small; after nine years they agreeably divorced, and Billy kept Liz on as his business manager.

Billy then met Christie Brinkley in 1983 on the island of St. Barts in the Caribbean. Even though she was an uptown gal and he was a backstreet guy, Billy proposed and she accepted. They married in March 1985. Things did not work out. Billy and Christie divorced amicably in August 1994.

In October 2004, 55-year-old Billy married 23-year-old Katie Lee. Billy and Christie's 18-year-old daughter, Alexa Ray, served as maid of honor. Christie also attended the union and gave the couple her blessing. It was just another one of those splendid situations where everyone already knew everyone else. Then in June 2009, Billy and Katie announced their separation: "Billy and Katie remain friends with admiration and respect for each other." Weeks later, Billy may have read Chapters 11 and 12.

Reportedly Billy announced that he was now dating Alex Donnelley, who will soon turn 51 and is much closer to his present age of 61. Thus we see that short dating cycles, followed by shorter engagements, often lead to "short" (relatively speaking) marriages. Individuals who marry and remarry after limited post-divorce recovery periods frequently divorce again.

Difficult Beginnings and Harsh Endings

The following true stories are right on point. Years ago I had a former divorce client named Luke who met a wonderful woman named Lucille. After dating her for two years and living together for an additional year, Lucille insisted they marry. Luke gave in, and they were to be married on February 14th of the following year. In mid-January, Luke fractured his right femur and left arm in a skiing accident four weeks before they were to be married. At the time of their scheduled wedding Luke still could not walk or stand. His "wonderful" Lucille suggested that her Luke, who had been fitted with a *spica cast* (from his mid-chest down to his right ankle), be carefully loaded onto a rented hospital gurney, and that he be rolled down the aisle by the twin Cantors who were to perform the wedding ceremony.

Lucille was going to spend the night at the hotel where the wedding was taking place and drove there in her new SUV. Lucille individually arranged for her nephew Flash to bring Luke to the wedding in his truck, for Luke still could not drive. After the wedding, Luke would be loaded into Lucille's SUV, and she would drive them home.

Lucille was fully aware of Flash's well-known reputation for being late to everything. Meanwhile, Luke had no knowledge of Flash's propensities. Despite Flash's habitual lateness, Lucille arranged for Flash to pick up Luke at 4:00 p.m. in order for them to be at the hotel by 5:10 p.m. The wedding had to start at sunset at 5:43 p.m. that day. As fate would have it, Flash arrived at 4:30 p.m. rather than at 4:00 p.m. as arranged. Already behind schedule, Flash had to stop to get gas, put air into his under-inflated rear tires and then pick up a friend along the way.

En route to the hotel, Flash received a frantic call from Lucille at 5:10 p.m. when they were still some 20 minutes away. When asked where they were, Flash quickly passed his cell phone to Luke. He told his wife-to-be that they were still 15 minutes away and would be there soon. Lucille became so upset that she hung up on him. Luke then told me how they arrived exactly 15 minutes later. Luke was loaded onto the waiting hospital gurney and pushed into the wedding hall. Luke had tears in his eyes when he told me the next part. Lucille immediately confronted him.

Mercilessly, Luke was berated and belittled in front of Flash, his two friends, a waiter, and others. Lucille let innocent, hospital gurney-bound Luke have it with both barrels. She contemptuously proclaimed that he could never be serious or trusted to do anything right, and she went on and on. Then she stabbed him in his right arm with her four- inch hat pin. As Luke said, "Lucille was really mad at me." He went on: "My bride-to-be was obviously mad at the wrong person. She was the one who made the transportation arrangements, not me, and she was the one familiar with Flash's lateness, not I."

After the verbal lashings and a heartless stabbing to his arm, Luke told me he was rolled to the front desk. There he asked for a bandage for his bleeding arm and a limo to take him home. He just wanted to go home, but soon realized that this was Lucille's special day. Luke said that he thought at the time, "I should be more concerned about Lucille than about my hurt feelings and injured right arm." He stopped the bleeding and had himself rolled into place before the start of the wedding. Lucille made her grand entrance and Luke said, "I do!" Innocent Luke had been lambasted and stabbed for something that wasn't his fault, all the while on a rented hospital gurney, and on his wedding day. Then weeks later, Luke filed for divorce.

Luke's decision to divorce Lucille must have included other issues. Spouses rarely drive down to their lawyer's office to file for divorce because of one explosive event or oppressive occurrence. Of course, being verbally abused in public and stabbed while seated on a hospital gurney just before your marriage ceremony may certainly qualify. As with most divisive matters, Lucille should have lovingly acknowledged her fault. She should have sincerely apologized to Luke for the embarrassment, the stabbing, and the hurt she had caused him on their wedding day. Telling your partner about your pain and hurt must be done in a kind, mild manner. If you're angry, furious, and sarcastic, the other person will become defensive and the matter will escalate into a battle that may lead to war.

It is inappropriate to get into open warfare with your-spouse-to-be, child, or even a subordinate in public. All of these (especially the spouse-to-be one) necessitate private settings where just the two of you can discuss the issue at hand. Whatever the issue or problem, civility must be exercised. It appears that Lucille mistakenly attacked Luke for Flash's errors (misguided anger).

What could be worse than what happened to innocent Luke at the beginning of his marriage? The ultimate marriage-ending pre-divorce malicious act has to be the Lorena Bobbitt "cutting" incident of 1993.

After an evening of heavy drinking, John and Lorena supposedly ended up in bed and reportedly had a series of wild (are there any other kind?) sexual encounters; she later claimed that John raped her. After their aggressive sexual episodes, Lorena allegedly went to the kitchen and came back with her brand-new deluxe French carving knife and (using a deep-lateral cut) proceeded to cut off John's penis; she then left with penis in hand, to get new knives (more cutting?). While driving, she threw John's remains out the window. She later returned, called 911 and after a detailed penis search, they found it, and it took two doctors ten hours to reattach it. Wow; what else? Thank goodness that Lucille was not as mad as Lorena.

Both Luke and Lorena ended their marriages abruptly. These stressed couples should have been discussing their feelings and issues and attempting to work things through. If your spouse knows of your unhappiness and realizes that things will not get better, then the news is not a shock. It certainly would not seem difficult to be forgiving after being stabbed with a hat pin; however, it is likely impossible after having your manhood cutoff.

A Smooth Transition

Your first and last divorce actions should be handled with civility, compassion, and consideration towards your ex. Remember, you and your ex likely shared some good years, close memories, and pleasant experiences. While your time together has ended, there is no need to remain resentful, repulsive, or ruthless in your future days or lasting years. Doing so will only hurt you and you will end up being the biggest loser. Remember the past-page lessons on *Divorce Diplomacy* and *Reciprocal Altruism*. You, too, may one day be the recipient of such benefits and goodwill. Recall also that the listed beneficiaries in both categories were diplomatic and cooperative in their divorce partings and post-divorce lives, and they all remained in good favor with their ex-spouses.

Becoming a Jackie Kennedy or a Cary Grant can be fun; once one of you starts, the other will likely follow. Whether it's the manner in which you communicated with him/her or it's because of her/his own self-development, personal growth will benefit you both.

WHAT YOU NOW RECOGNIZE, UNDERSTAND, AND ACCEPT

1. The first step is to take the next step; take the first step.

2. As difficult as it is, why make it more hurtful, painful, or worse?

3. Remember: you, too, can be a Jackie Kennedy or a Cary Grant.

4. It's easier to show some class than to be a jerk.

5. Practice your farewell address and give it your very best.

6. Three-day weekends are good times to give the news.

7. Don't become argumentative, defensive, or sarcastic; be compassionate and respectful.

8. How would you want your parents and siblings to be treated?

9. Departing with dignity requires class; show your class to your ex and to others.

10. Do not start or end your marriage in poor taste.

CHAPTER THREE

Healing Yourself: Getting Over Him or Her

"When We Two Are Parted"
by
George Lord Byron (1788-1824)

When we two parted
In silence and tears,
Half broken-hearted
To sever the years,
Pale grew thy cheek and cold,
Colder, thy kiss;
Truly that hour foretold
Sorrow to this.
The dew of the morning
Sunk, chill on my brow,
It felt like the warning
Of what I feel now.
Thy vows are all broken,
And light is thy fame;
I hear thy name spoken,
And share in its shame.

They name thee before me,
A knell to mine ear;
A shudder comes o'er me ...
Why wert thou so dear?
They know not I knew thee,
Who knew thee too well ...
Long, long shall I rue thee,
Too deeply to tell.
In secret we met
In silence I grieve
That thy heart could forget,
Thy spirit deceive.
If I should meet thee
After long years,
How should I greet thee?
With silence and tears.

Even though Lord Byron's poem is over 200 years old, yet it remains relevant today. Although many things have changed, the human heart still aches after the loss of a person once deeply loved. Byron's insightful words impart a meaningful message to all. Getting over a former spouse can be a painful and prolonged process.

The death of a spouse is said to be the greatest of all human loss experiences. The loss of a spouse by divorce has to be second. In both cases, you lose your lover, partner, and best friend, and this can leave you broken-hearted. We've all recalled favorite poems and soothing songs in times of sadness or sorrow. "Long, long shall I rue thee, Too deeply to tell." While dramatic poems have waned in popularity, today tender lyrics and soft melodies heal our broken hearts. Listening to favorite songs helps to ease our pain and comforts our sorrows.

No matter how difficult your interrupted marriage, there must have been some good years, months, or at least days. Recalling shared intimate moments, like being sheltered in someone's arms, can bring tears to even those with a glass-eye. Such fond memories will continue to flash through our minds. Sometimes we cry as tender moments are recalled, and at other times we laugh when remembering something funny once shared with someone special.

As humans, we store painful events and hurtful episodes. We also retain pleasant memories and treasured experiences. Don't consider yourself frail or helpless when a delightful event surfaces. Allow these pleasant recollections to pass through; they are gifts from your past. Do not, however, dwell on them or attempt to recall them, for that will surely delay your recovery.

As separation and divorce time passes, we often declare ourselves healed while still silently bleeding on the inside, sometimes harboring resentment, anger, and even lasting hate. Often, these toxic emotional salvos are directed at the one who has left; other times, we include ourselves as intended targets. These lethal feelings can become self-destructive and will certainly impede your emotional recovery.

Carrying a torch fueled with venomous emotion for a spouse who has exited and will never return will hurt you. Healing requires total forgiveness for your former spouse and you.

Acceptance and After

Recognizing and accepting that emotional pain and physical suffering are ordinary divorce responses helps us rise to the next levels of healing and recovery. With hope and a willingness to move on, you can launch the necessary self-help healing processes and thereby shorten your anguish and eventually end your torment. I must tell you that one day you'll look back, as I've done twice before, and wonder why in the world you spent countless hours and pounds of emotion getting over them. When you can make that admission, you'll be on your way back to emotional good health.

The best way for you to start is to sit down and have a good talk with yourself regarding the twelve listed realities here below, for it is a sure way for you to get over "your departed" spouse:

- Accept that separations usually lead to divorce.
- Respect yourself and do not grovel for his/her return.
- Accept that there's nothing you can do now.
- Stop repeatedly blaming yourself for what happened.
- Forgive yourself for what you have done or failed to do.
- Don't allow yourself to wallow in the past.
- Don't allow yourself into the Poor Me Syndrome (PMS).
- Forgive him/her for leaving you and hurting you.
- Let him/her go and say goodbye.
- Avoid "chance" attempts to see each other.
- Get involved in new activities with new people.
- Keep a firm, positive, and forgiving attitude.

Once these 12 interrelated actions are implemented, you will be on your way back to emotional normalcy. Below I've provided sound reasons for you to start your 12-step recovery and relief program today.

Number 1:
Accept that separations usually lead to divorce.

Separation is the second station of divorce, preceded often by ill-tempered and vindictive behavior, stresses, and events that brought you there as a result of Station One. You already know that most separations lead to divorce; still some marriages survive (Bill and Hillary Clinton's). Separations frequently ignite into full-divorce mode because of offensive responses or objectionable conduct that surfaces during this hurtful period. During this time you must be cordial and conciliatory. Again, you must be a Jackie Kennedy or a Cary Grant. Trial separations and counseling sometimes work.

Separations can provide couples the necessary time and space to calmly evaluate their futures. Marginal advice from friends, mixed signals from partners, and attention from new suitors, however, can confuse couples, and frustrate their goals. Effective separations require:

- Duration: a set-period (three to six months and no more) of time.
- Rules: mutually acceptable rules (what-is-and-is-not acceptable).
- Intimacy: (with each other) you must have an agreed yes/no plan.

Number 2:
Respect yourself and do not grovel for his/her return.

Good heavens, if you don't respect yourself, how do you expect your spouse or anyone else to respect you? Pride, confidence, and self-respect are attributes of healthy individuals. The absence of these traits is frequently found among the stressed and unhealthy. How do you expect to be a good partner to someone else when you cannot even be a good person to yourself? Take into account that a relationship can only be as strong as its weaker member. Were you the weak one? Even if you were, this acknowledgment does not justify demeaning or judgmental behavior by others.

No one wants to be with an emotionally unfit, stressed individual. Anyone who pleads for forgiveness and repeatedly begs to be taken back does not come across well. Such people are difficult to be with, and others may find them exhausting. If the foregoing paragraph describes you, then do one of these three things: call, buy, or download and then listen to Aretha Franklin (1.855.RESPECT).

Be sure that you have a circle of close friends who support you and are reasonably sympathetic to your situation. The last thing you need is a group of friends who put you down. So-called friends, who beat on you via deep-seated criticisms and blame, are not your friends. Never allow yourself to become anyone's punching bag. If that is the case, you need to do two additional things: first, avoid and stop seeing these toxic individuals; second, go out and make new friends.

Sometimes I feel as though my children are still upset with me for divorcing their mother. Perhaps their frustrations are the result of the other women I've introduced to them after my two divorces. We can always find new friends, but family is forever. Be prepared to recognize and forgive collateral family criticism. Be patient, for often this family cleansing takes time, patience, and lots of love.

Number 3:
Accept that there's nothing you can do now.

Just as in any other catastrophic life experience, there is usually nothing that can be done after the event has taken place. Most divorcing individuals initially find themselves shocked and in a state of denial. Often this contradiction includes a failure to acknowledge repeated behavior over prolonged periods that suddenly caused your spouse to leave. Perchance it was the cheesecake or the many pizzas and extra beers at the game, and the added pounds that followed all three. It's not as if you can instantly lose thirty-five pounds by simply cutting off your left leg! If you find yourself in such a place, you may need prolonged periods of introspection to help you realize that there's nothing you can do now.

Still, you must look back and determine what went wrong; if it was something you caused, you must take the necessary steps to identify it, understand where it came from, and fix it.

Then again, perhaps your spouse just flipped out and without comparative fault or contribution from you, he/she just unilaterally elected to leave. It's rare but it does happen. Often there is some underlying emotional pathology or undiscovered problem that may have triggered the separation. Mid-life crises are not exclusive to men. Women have been known to wish simply to leave a marriage for inexplicable and irrational reasons (country music?) as well. While you may not be able to do anything about the already-filed divorce, this time affords a great opportunity for personal growth, self-improvement and other self-empowering exercises. You now have time to focus on yourself, and you don't need anyone's permission to do what you've wanted and may have put off before.

Number 4:
Stop repeatedly blaming yourself for what happened.

Reread Numbers 2 and 3 again. Why kick yourself when you're down? Why degrade and insult yourself with unfounded conclusions and hurtful criticisms? First of all, no one, not even your tax person, likes being around someone who constantly blames herself/himself for what went wrong. Would you have dinner with such a person? Would you go on a 10-day cruise with that individual? Then why keep berating yourself? *Let go!*

Relentlessly re-living the past and reminding yourself of what has already happened will not help you get over it. Constantly feeling sad and sorry for yourself does not help, either. If you have been acting this way, you may have unwittingly become an individual suffering from Poor Me Syndrome (PMS). The road to recovery and emotional good health requires that even PMS individuals have a sensible recovery. Sure, a year or two is a reasonable and understandable amount of time, but then enough is enough!

Suicide, manslaughter, and even homicide are third cousins not far removed from divorce. Divorce-related death rates are higher than the norm. All you have to do is to watch the evening news (NBC: Nothing But Crime). Anger, hurt, and rejection can rapidly turn into rage against yourself, your spouse, his/her new lover and others.

If you find yourself contemplating the foregoing, seek professional help. Sadly, there are certain divorce situations that end up with dead spouses, dead family members, and incinerated family homes. Such was the case for a divorcing, distraught southern California husband who killed his wife and eight of her family members, set his in-laws's house on fire, and then killed himself over the 2008 Christmas holidays. It happened again in Miami, in March 2009, when a scorned divorcing husband killed his estranged wife, three others, and setting the family house on fire, before killing himself. As we have seen before, divorce can be a devastating and even deadly event. Perhaps they should put Prozac in the water supply, in local vending machines, and offer it at all Starbucks. "Give me a decaf latte with double Prozac to go!"

An article in the *The Wall Street Journal* during 2006 reported how the legendary Diahann Carroll had once checked into the Waldorf-Astoria Hotel in New York to commit suicide over a lost love. She talked about her pain and her decision to end it all at a classy place. The best part of the article covered how Diahann regained her self-respect and changed her mind. Sadly, Diahann's successes on stage and set did not follow in her four marriages. Her first marriage lasted seven years and ended in divorce. In 1972, Diahann was engaged to Sir David Frost; she frosted him when she broke off their engagement to marry Fredde Glusman. Their marriage lasted only six weeks; she divorced again. Diahann married again and was left a widow. Her fourth marriage was to singer Vic Damone; that marriage did not last either.

Number 5:
Forgive yourself for what you have done or failed to do.

Someday, somehow, you must forgive yourself for whatever it was you did or failed to do. It may have been not taking her dancing, not spending more time with her family, or not dressing up when she came home. Then again, it may have been due to her being too critical, complaining excessively, or making cookies for the pool boy. What's done is done! Life has no undo button. "Oh, if only I hadn't made cookies for the pool boy. I know, I'll just push the undo button and that will never have happened." Wrong!

Whatever you may have done, you were the one who did it or failed to do it. It's not as if someone held a gun to your head and said, "If you do not make cookies for the pool boy, you'll be shot." Take responsibility for your actions; it's a sign of maturity. Contrition sends a clear message that you realize you that screwed up. Pencil manufacturers are still placing erasers on pencils because people still make mistakes. Mistakes are so commonplace today that new computers will soon come equipped with two undo buttons: one for the computer and one for the operator. Just as the cobbler's kids have no shoes and the lawyer has no will, many of us schooled in specific academic disciplines fail to follow our own advice given to others for a fee. Some of us, like me, make repeated mistakes: my one-month and two-month marriage proposals. I finally acknowledged my mistakes. You've heard it said before: "To err is human; to forgive is divine." Why not be divine? *Forgive yourself.*

Number 6:
Don't allow yourself to wallow in the past.

President Nixon once said, "We must not wallow in Watergate." You, my friends, must not wallow in the empty hallways of your interrupted marriage, which may have been vacated months or years ago. Wallowing in the past is unhealthy. It hurts us psychologically and physically. How do you stop wallowing? Perhaps you can use the classic rubber band trick recommended by therapists for behavior modification (i.e., you wear a rubber band around your head and snap it every time you start wallowing). This practice helps you to catch yourself when it starts and eventually to stop it altogether; the rubber-marks on your forehead also will fade in time. It's like the "I could have had a V-8" commercial.

Whatever it was that caused your spouse to leave, is in the past. A wise woman once said, "People who live in the past cannot enjoy the present today or the future tomorrow, because everyone knows that we can't be in two places at one time." Letting go of the past will free you from your self-imposed enslavement of seeking to recapture what you once shared with your former significant other.

Letting go of the past allows you to enjoy the present today and the future tomorrow. They are great places to visit, especially when you have not been there for a while. Both are far better places to go to than the one in which you may have been trapped. Realize and accept that the past has passed. It's gone forever, and there is nothing you can do to go back to the past, not even with Michael J. Fox and his speedy DeLorean, because there's no Netflix movie titled Back to the Past.

Number 7:
Don't allow yourself into the Poor Me Syndrome (PMS).

Sometimes we feel just a little too sorry for ourselves. We get into PMS. "I knew this was going to happen to me." "Oh, poor me!" "Why me?" Many divorcing and divorced individuals seem trapped as PMS victims. Why Me? Everything happens to me: "I went to the Grand Canyon and it was closed." If you're not laughing, perhaps it's because you were not a geology major ("*closed*," not as in admission, but as in "being filled, as to make it totally disappear"). Oh!

Some, nevertheless, are justified to ask, "What did I do to deserve this?" As mentioned in the opening of Chapter 1, Puccini's Floria Tosca asked the very same question in her beautiful aria *"Vissi d'arte:"*

> I lived for art, I lived for love,
> I did no harm to any living creature!
> With a secret hand
> I aided all the misfortunates I knew.
> Always with sincere faith
> My prayer rose to the holy tabernacles.
> Always with sincere faith
> I gave flowers to the altar.
> In the hour of sorrow
> Why, why, Lord,
> Ah, why do you reward me thus?
> I gave jewels to the robe of the Madonna,
> And gave song to the stars, to the sky,
> Which smiled all the more beautifully.
> In the hour of sorrow
> Why, Lord, why you do reward me thus?

Floria Tosca just could not accept that she had to sleep with opportunistic Scarpia to rescue her beloved Mario. Somehow Floria Tosca mistakenly believed that her altruistic acts, benevolent behaviors, and charitable contributions would insulate her from all misfortune. Life's theater always presents such predicaments as hers. Even if we are not as benevolent, compassionate, and civic-minded as Floria Tosca, bad things can and do happen to good people, even to you. If Floria Tosca, who seemed to have done all the right things, still had to endure humiliation and dishonor, why can't we accept our divorce situations with such elegance and grace?

Feeling sorry for ourselves for months may be natural, normal, and even necessary; however, we cannot make careers out of it. We cannot condemn ourselves and those around us to a life sentence of self-imposed self-pity and self-inflicted despair. We, too, should acknowledge and accept that given our individual circumstances, no matter how painful, no matter how hurtful, there are always others whose situations are far worse. Constantly crying about your situation only fuels the fire burning within you and annoys everyone around you. Take responsibility and admit that you, too, were not perfect. Start your 12 steps to recovery today by going forward with a new way of life filled with new positive attitudes and affirmative goals.

Number 8:
Forgive him/her for leaving you and hurting you.

Repeatedly telling others of open wounds and lasting hurts only delays recovery and forestalls your healing. This behavior adds weight to your already heavy burdens, and it aggravates your sadness and extends grief. It has been said that the recovery period for an interrupted marriage can be measured by the duration of the marriage. I disagree. You hold the get-out-of-jail card. People sometimes hold on to and nurture their past resentments, thereby unknowingly extending their sadness and sorrows. Granted, we all go through a grieving and recovery period during and after divorce; however, the duration for both periods is up to us, not the other person, your boss, or anyone else.

The longer you hold the grudge, the longer you'll experience the pain and sorrow, and the longer you will suffer. Just let go, and you'll be freed.

You certainly would not hold onto a burning match; why then hold onto a burning grudge? Both ways, it is you who will be burned. Once you forgive yourself and your former spouse you will start to heal. Eventually you will forget and thereby steadily rid yourself of inner demons and emotional toxicants that have attacked your mental and physical wellbeing. Thus to heal: you must first be a healer and forgive; only then you will successfully forget. Try this; it will work for you.

Number 9:
Let him/her go and say goodbye.

This part is really tough. After reading the previous eight suggestions, this one is perhaps the most difficult. It comes in two parts, and both are mandatory. First, let go of "your departed" spouse and be either a Jackie Kennedy or a Cary Grant. This course of action means departing with class, dignity, and respect. No street fighter or guerrilla tactics, and no knee-capper antics. Part of letting go successfully is to do so amicably. Be affable, not awful.

Hello out there, this is your brain (and the author) telling you that your spouse has left and is not coming back! It's not as though your dog left (then again, there may be some similarities). Granted, you used to be married, but soon you'll be divorced. Your soon-to-be ex has his/her own life. Each, too, has the absolute right, privilege and freedom to make independent decisions. One of those decisions may have been to terminate their marriage with you.

Accepting this fact is important; nevertheless, be patient with yourself. It's okay to falter. Don't give up. Keep trying. Feelings heal with each passing day. Days turn into weeks, and then become months, and finally years will pass. You will get through this passage but you must endure. You have to try. It's as though you were playing the lottery; you must first purchase a ticket. How else do you expect to win?

There comes a time when you have to let go. This is the time to give up the torch. Some, however, just cannot let go. I've had clients who were compelled to seek and obtain restraining orders to keep a pernicious past spouse away from them at home and at work. No one needs a stalker lurking around him or her, and no one should engage in such spiteful behavior.

Take the high road and show your departing spouse that you're still a good person. Thank your spouse for the good times you have shared. Take responsibility and admit that you, too, were at fault. Wish him/her the very best. Be forever gracious, kind, and consider how you would want your loved ones treated in these difficult circumstances. One cannot show too much class.

Number 10:
Avoid "chance" attempts to see each other.

I can still recall a futile high school practice related to a girl I once really liked but who did not feel the same about me. I discovered where she lived and I would repeatedly—morning, noon and night—drive by her house hoping to catch a glimpse of her. I even had delusions of grandeur that somehow she would suddenly run out to greet me.

Most of us are past high school. Few would think about doing something as ridiculous. How many divorced persons, however, return to the same banks, churches, and markets, as well as the usual parks, performing arts centers, and restaurants formerly frequented by them and their former spouse? These actions are human, but are not part of moving on. Perhaps you should not allow yourself to frequent such places; there are alternatives. Then again, your former spouse may also be frequenting alternative places as well, and the two of you may meet there.

If you are out one day with a new friend and serendipitously run into your ex with his/her new friend, what should you do? I suggest being polite and pleasant, exchanging introductions and then going on your way. Perhaps it would only be human also to check swiftly the new friend's shoes, waistline, and possibly take a quick wrinkle check.

But what do you do if your *ex's new friend* is the *ex of your new friend?* What? But wait, for divorce does bring us entertaining moments that can be long appreciated. As mentioned before, these are unique interesting human events, where everyone already knows everyone else. Perhaps the four of you can go for coffee and have a compare-and-contrast session? Yes, you can determine who ended up with the better deal. Obviously, I am being facetious and allowing you a needed laugh, but these things do happen. Be prepared!

Number 11:
Get involved in new activities with new people.

A further distressing consequence of divorce is that one spouse frequently takes the friends once shared and enjoyed by both. Friends are not community property. They cannot be divided between former spouses. Most friends are like cats; they go where they want.

Even worse than losing old friends altogether is an evening with former *friends*, followed by an immediate detailed report back to your former spouse by your *friends*. Frequently, these comprehensive reports include an assessment of your current status, weight, and healing progress, as well as whether you're dating again (and whom), along with all of the other personal information just provided to your friends in confidence.

You know the old saying, "With friends like that, who needs enemies?" If this has happened to you, go out and meet new, interesting, non-double-agent friends. This is a great time to blend new interests with fresh acquaintances, and to rid yourself of others.

Meeting new people is an exciting and enriching experience. Start off on the right foot. Don't bring out your PMS dirty laundry and start overloading new friends with all of the intimate, boring details about how he/she dumped you and left you behind for someone else or even joined the Sons/Daughters of Italy in Sofia, Bulgaria. Gradually, the time will come for you to disclose slowly details of your past without dropping a full wheelbarrow load onto some new, innocent soul.

Wait for your new acquaintances to share a little of their past as you slowly unfold short installments of your own history. Do not turn these gradual get-acquainted sessions into formal presentations of all the tedious tidbits of your failed relationships and boring unhappiness; doing so will surely scare them away.

I recall once telling a colleague about my recent separation from my first wife. She comforted and embraced me. Wow! Then I told her that my dog had died and my cat had run away. She soon realized I was pulling her leg, even though I could not reach it. As she later said, "You seem to be handling all three experiences very well!"

Number 12:
Keep a firm, positive and forgiving attitude.

Please, for your own wellbeing and those close to you, set the rules of disengagement and stay the course. That's right; don't even allow yourself to think about him/her anymore. It's just not good for you to keep climbing back into that emotional sewer. Only you can control you. You may need to place and snap the rubber band around your head again. Your attitude is *your* call. It sets your course either to stay in the sewer or to sail on past it to higher and healthier places. I admire and salute both of my ex-wives for not wanting to get back into our past divorces by writing a chapter for this book (I had invited them both to write a chapter about being married to me for this book; they both graciously declined).

Moving On

But the question remains: *How do you move on?* Basically, "moving on" means to stop thinking about him/her and to acknowledge and accept that each is forever gone and will not return. Moving on is achievable and can be accomplished through the recommendations found in this and other chapters. The foregoing 12-step recovery recommendations will help you, for as they now say in China: 一個 100英里的旅程的開始 12個步驟。 "A journey of a hundred miles begins with twelve steps." Getting over a former spouse/lover is a process that takes you through several cumulative emotional seasons. It's not as though you can just flush him/her out of your life. I recall when my first marriage fell apart I was really crushed. I still loved this woman, but we both realized that we could no longer live together. I was so upset that I looked into joining the French La Légion Etrangère (Foreign Legion), and no, she was not French! I did not meet the Legion's entry requirements. Besides not meeting other requirements, my French was not good: "Oui"—yes, it is the only French I knew then. I was also not crazy about French food, but have long enjoyed their great cheese, breads, sauces, and of course, bordeaux wines.

It was even worse when my second marriage collapsed. I was totally crushed; I still love her as well. I decided to change my life in some profound manner to help rid myself of my lasting hurt.

I thought I'd become a Buddhist monk; however, I soon discovered I could not sit in the lotus position. I could not endure the two-day fast, and they didn't have 12 EE sandals. Well, so much for those two great ideas. I am certain that many others have considered something as radical and profound as my two recovery ideas.

Complaints and Dislikes

As forsaken, divorced individuals, we are compelled to live without the one we once deeply loved. *But wait!* It's not all bad; there will be some peace of mind and freedom from past torments. Still, we see our former partners infrequently at best. Widows and widowers, on the other hand, never see their loved ones again. Years ago I dated a widow who had lost her husband when she was only 45. We frequently discussed her late husband. It allowed her to vent and me to learn more about her successful handling of this serious loss. For most who lose a spouse by death, the recovery period is similar to that of those who lose a spouse by divorce. Many of the same human dynamics and emotions are present, albeit without the rancor associated with divorce.

It seems as though widowed individuals frequently make better recoveries and are far healthier afterward than those of us in the divorced group. Perhaps we should realize that anger and the associated smorgasbord of malevolent divorce emotions should be controlled and eliminated. Elimination of these troublesome emotions will help bring quicker and better recoveries for those still languishing at hell's gate. Remember that forgiveness speeds recovery. The sooner you forgive and accept your situation, the faster recovery will come to you. Still, it is important for you to acknowledge your progress in the grieving process and to accept it without judgment or fault. This, a little dark chocolate and a glass or two of good red wine will help you to move forward toward your prior state of emotional good health.

Divorce recovery can also be impacted by attitude and expectations. If you regard your loss as an unalterable tragedy, your present days and future nights will conform to your expectations. Alternatively, if you accept what has happened, take responsibility for your contributive share of your interrupted marriage, and work towards becoming a more loving, concerned and caring person, this experience will be good for you. Others are sure to notice. Your desire to find fulfilling companionship and lasting happiness can also become a self-fulfilling prophecy. Why not let your changed attitude, improved behavior, and positive expectations help you to achieve these salient goals?

Like Popeye, I too love my spinach, albeit with *liquid olive oil* and bits of garlic. Like Popeye, I realized that "I yam what I yam." Long ago (about the age of 14) I also recognized that I was not perfect. As I matured, I noted additional deficits; nevertheless, I accepted myself for who I was and noted that, with hard work, I could improve. It's been a life-long effort and an ongoing process, but it has certainly been well worth the investment.

Divorce is also a life-learning experience that can bring realized benefits and positive life changes. This unwanted, yet common event now brings a variety of choices and alternatives. Take your time to make the proper decisions, address your deficits, and work on becoming a better person. Start by forgiving "your departed" spouse and yourself for what has happened to both of you. Ultimately, healing yourself is up to you and you alone. Jack Daniels or his close friends Jim Beam and Jose Cuervo can only do so much, for you'll never find lasting happiness at the bottom of an empty glass. Remember, and reread if necessary, the lessons learned about self-defeating PMS restrictions and other self-imposed recovery limitations.

Too often the fear of being alone is the glue that keeps unhappy people in miserable marriages, for many would rather be with someone than be alone. Even to the mistreated, unfulfilled, or unappreciated, loneliness seems a greater burden than remaining married. Recall that 15 percent of married individuals become roommates and another 15 percent are miserable. Still, like so many others, at least Edith and Archie and Peg and Al, had each other. The above figures clearly support the conclusion that 66 percent of first-marriage people (two-thirds of the 45 percent that remain married) are not really happy. Surprisingly, there are marriages where both are miserable; however, they each fail to take the first move to leave. Alternatively, you may have already left, or your spouse left you; thus, you're no longer trapped in an unfulfilled dead marriage.

Perhaps it was that:

- You ran out of love or commitment.

- You married "for better or worse" and you figured that it had to get better because it could not get any worse. But it did.

- Your spouse started listening to country music, and that was the last straw (pun intended).

Sometimes spouses run out of love, while others lose their sense of commitment. It's not like running out of gas or losing your keys, where you can easily buy more gas or find new keys. I've represented many divorce clients who one day, out of the blue, announced to their spouses that they no longer wanted to be married (to them), that they now wished to be alone. Often no reason is given, but for their simple, exiting statement; the likely unspoken matters that could no longer be tolerated are frequently never mentioned. Now that you're alone and recovering, you can reflect and recall if there were things you could not stand. There are several things most people will usually not put up with.

They are:

- Being criticized
- Being criticized
- Being criticized

These are the top three things that men and women cannot stand and will usually not tolerate. Being subjected to endless criticisms could erode even Tony Robbins's and Dale Carnegie's confidence! Beneath our complex images, we are all sensitive and fragile. Women, just like men, cannot stand to be criticized, especially by our spouses (or any person of the opposite sex). Women who criticize their spouses become their mothers. Men who criticize their spouses become their fathers. As these behavioral patterns continue, you became antagonistic, and these practices cause your love to sour.

I remember frequently telling my first wife to stay out of the sun. Her response: "You're not my father!" My second wife was always after me to exercise. The more she reminded me, the more I resisted. Men and women do not like being told what to do. Continued criticisms often lead to further hostile commentary. I admit that I used to be the one who was always telling others what to do; I finally stopped, unless they ask for my specific help.

I must have heard the listed laments below at least a thousand times from men and women.

First from women:

- We never talk anymore.
- He watches TV, then we go to bed for sex and he falls asleep.
- There's no romance left in our marriage.
- He never does what he did when we were dating.
- We never go to nice places anymore.

I hear the same critical commentaries from men:

- She never wears sexy clothes anymore.
- She never cooks anymore.
- She never does what we used to do when we were dating.
- She's critical and extremely judgmental.
- She does not like sex anymore.

Looking back, you may recall comparable whining about what was wrong. The foregoing harsh commentaries are endemic among both men and women and common in most marriages. Such is life between two individuals who attempt to live as one. Based on decades of my own experience and the recollections of other divorce lawyers, post-separation and divorce comments are even worse. Listed below are the top-ten complaints being heard today.

Women's top five criticisms and complaints about their estranged or former husbands:

- Bullying
- Selfish
- Self-centered
- Cold and insensitive
- Cruel and controlling

Men's top five criticisms and complaints about their estranged or former wives:

- Self-centered
- Dull and boring
- Cold and unresponsive
- Critical and judgmental
- Manipulative and controlling

Whatever it was that caused you to leave or to be left, you no longer have to put up with it; now, it's about mending yourself and moving on. Most divorced individuals will eventually find new spouses, partners, or lovers. Keep in mind that your children, no matter what happens, will have only one father and one mother. Because you have children with your ex, you may never be completely rid of each other. Refrain from using your children as therapists, for doing so will permanently harm them; remember also that as long as the two of you are alive, you and your ex will come up in your children's conversations. But wait, it becomes more complicated. Surely, you and your ex will attend birthday parties, graduations, and weddings, as well as funerals, holiday functions, and other celebratory events where you will see each other, and then the cycle starts all over again with grandchildren.

Your behavior sets an example and permanent imprint for your children to follow. Whatever, wherever, and whenever you do something hurtful or in poor taste to your ex, you're hurting your children's mother/father. It's just as if someone did something spiteful to your mother or father. How would you feel? How do you think your children feel?

WHAT YOU NOW RECOGNIZE, UNDERSTAND, AND ACCEPT

1. When we lose someone we once loved, we grieve over that person's absence (someone who is never there).

2. This healing phase is normal and a required part of our divorce recovery.

3. Accept and respect the farewell decision and go forward without groveling.

4. Forgive yourself for whatever you did or failed to do.

5. Forgive him/her for leaving you and for hurting you.

6. You must start a new life for yourself, with new people, activities, and different places.

7. You are a good person, just not a good husband/wife for him/her.

8. Do not get into a PMS mentality. No one will want to be around you.

9. There are many good men/women out there who would love to be with you.

10. The sooner you let go, the sooner you will recover.

CHAPTER FOUR

Looking Back and Looking Forward

Donatello went to confession with Father Apollonio and said,

"Forgive me, Father, for I have sinned. "I had sex with a girl."

"Who was it, Donatello?"

"I cannot tell you, Father"

"Was it Antonella Buenofuto? Was it Stefena Vaccherino?"

"No, Father, please forgive me; I cannot say who it was."

"Was it Simona Montefeltro?"

"Father, I cannot tell you. I promised never to tell anyone."

"Okay, Donatello, say five Hail Marys and four Our Fathers, my son."

Donatello walked out to the pews where his friend and co-conspirator Clemenza was waiting.

"What did you get?" asked Clemenza.

"Five Hail Marys, four Our Fathers and three good leads."

The court's entry of your Final Divorce Judgment (usually a year or two after filing) will complete the legal aspects of your divorce. While you will then be legally divorced, the emotional aftermath continues. Grieving the death of your marriage and the loss of your partner requires additional time. You must not rush your recovery passage. It is important to make all the necessary stops along the way as you regain your emotional footing. Your first big milestone will appear when you start living in the present and leave the past behind. Graduation occurs when you once again see yourself as a person of significance and self-worth, and no longer as the dependent half of a former union. This may also be an appropriate time to look back into your interrupted marriage for missed flawed fundamentals that can now be recognized.

Looking Back

Initial attraction aspects can be misleading. While exterior *features* are obvious, interior characteristics take time to be discovered. Even the passage of time, however, cannot insure long-term consistency or certainty of another's character, personality, or commitment to marriage.

Married persons continue to change as they learn to adjust, blend, and compromise with each other. Even tenured partners, though, will often act or react differently in ordinary or stressful settings. While shocking when first experienced, you may have wished you had asked: "Were these reactions predictable?"

Your past dating experiences may have been your billboard of coming behavior attractions. Early break-up and make-up patterns most likely revealed which partner was first (and last) to forgive past disputes or reconcile new differences. Did you select your former spouse wisely?

Finding a spouse is said to be our second most significant lifetime decision (career choices are first). For the most part, there are two popular spousal connection alternatives (romantic and arranged); is one really better than the other? But wait! Are we really *hard-wired* to be with just one person for a lifetime? Pervasive atypical marital behavior, the increasing global divorce rate, and new scientific research suggest that we may not be so inclined.

Romantic Marriages

Western countries primarily have romantic marriages. Critics suggest that these unions are founded upon early childhood expectations that romantic love will bring lasting happiness. Elementary concepts of mutual love and lifelong marriages are said to originate in youthful fairytales. Many will include matched themes, like a confined beautiful princess being rescued by a handsome prince on a white horse; they marry, move to the suburbs, and live happily ever after.

These positive prospects are later promoted in popular adolescent romance novels with related endings and further sponsored in endless *dreamy* motion pictures with comparable conclusions. Thereafter, we are presented with fabulous fables of a tranquil family life in a suburban home with a white picket fence. Commentators maintain that for many individuals, these romantic themes and wishful messages become the basis for the unsound belief that romantic love provides a solid base for lasting marriages and continued happiness.

Romantic love marriages were frequently founded upon fortuitous meetings or peer introductions. Today, partners are also romantically connected via online dating and commercial introductions. For many marriage-minded couples, these *chanced encounters* result in love at first-sight via instant chemistry or lightning lust. Many of these accidental unions lead to exclusive dating, early engagements, and eager marriages. Over the years, escalating divorce rates and severe financial losses by divorcing spouses have brought prenuptial and (later) postnuptial agreements into Western marriages.

Generally romantic marriages start off hot and chill with time. Current U.S. divorce statistics mentioned in Chapter 1 reveal that most romantic marriages do not last. Conceivably, marital expectations founded on fairytale themes and forged in artificial anticipations may not provide a solid foundation for lasting marriages or continued happiness.

Note that today, many couples choose to cohabitate, to test their compatibility and respective comfort levels. Even though cohabitation arrangements are increasing throughout the world, these partners experience greater break-up rates (72-82 percent) than married couples.

Arranged Marriages

Several cultures throughout the Eastern world still have arranged marriages where respective parents (or family elders) screen and select spousal candidates for newlyweds-to-be. Either person can usually reject a suggested spousal selection. Eastern marriages are said to start off cold and become warmer. These marriages foster falling in love gradually as mutual attraction and appreciation continue to develop over time.

Perhaps our impression that romantic love and its primary tenet that impulsive love will continue to provide lasting happiness needs to be questioned. Perhaps we have unwittingly set the lasting-marriage happiness expectation bar too high. Perhaps our Western marital visions are unrealistic, given the divorce data presented here. This may also help explain why Western world divorce rates have always been higher than in the East. Do arranged marriages have better selection platforms than the romantic marriages alternatives described above? Perhaps not! Data presented in the Appendix documents that Eastern world divorce rates are increasing as never before. The bottom line is that all marriages are not perfect, because all marriages are unions between two imperfect individuals. Western and Eastern marriages may one day become more alike, as our mass media and communication networks continue to shrink the world.

There are three major takeaways in this section. The first is that in all marriages, couples seem to increasingly become oblivious to the reality that their love needs to be nurtured. Once married, many spouses seem to lose interest in their mutual need to love each other. Rather than practicing their primary mission to focus on loving their significant other, many world spouses become obsessed and preoccupied with their individual goals and objectives (and some with their insecurities). Suddenly, everything else in their lives becomes more important than the need to express and expand their love for each other.

As time passes, their unions become more uninteresting and stale. Still, many *love-lethargic* spouses will exert little time, energy, or finances to advance or promote happiness in their marriages. Sadder yet, is that most of these unfulfilled partners are often unmindful of the shared lack of attention that caused their disappointed status.

The second lesson here is that Western and Eastern merging marriages need and require continued validation, love, and attention, along with intellectual and social improvement. Again, our utmost concern should be for our spouse; this commitment must be continuous, unselfish, and bonded with total acceptance of our partner's faults, imperfections, and other shortcomings. (No one is perfect and we all have our defects.)

If you were bored in your last marriage, it was likely because you were a boring person. Who is there to blame if you were a *homebody, a couch potato,* or *do-nothing* individual? All marriages need balance. Taking turns in selecting new things to do together, along with shared activities, will keep couples together and make them interesting persons to be with. As with other relationships, marriages also require occasional diversions from the humdrum boredom and mundane patterns of daily life. Keeping your marriage interesting and exciting keeps it together.

The third helpful lesson is the need for effective *conflict resolution skills.* We discussed ineffective communication in Chapter 1. Revisiting this concept here is timely because the causes of divorce are now better understood. First, acknowledge that no one gets married to get divorced and that that no one intentionally sets out to hurt or injure his/her spouse. Admit also that all spouses-to-be truly love each other (in the beginning) and that they, too, are expecting to live happily ever after.

Now, an undisputed reality of all marriages: each and every single marriage will sooner or later experience discord, disagreement, or disapproval. In addition, as complicated humans, we each come with our own unique bundle of complex feelings, bruised egos, and childhood traumas. In turn, we each act and react differently to conflict, criticism, or censure. Many of us also lack the necessary skills to lovingly articulate a legitimate compliant or justified rebuttal.

Hence, in expressing criticism or responding to conflict, we often innocently injure our love ones. Again, these inappropriate salvos are not intended to hurt anyone, but they always do. Worse yet, most injured spouses store their hurt feelings as compressed resentment, to have it one day erupt, much like a dormant volcano that explodes violently. Interestingly, the "triggering" cause that sets off the emotional eruption is usually an unrelated mundane factor.

Why Some Spouses Stray

Social scientists have long held various theories as to why married spouses stray, cheat, and end their marriages. These theories were primarily based on expert opinion, antidotal findings, and other empirical evidence. These conclusion all lacked scientific proof.

The advent of brain-scan imaging now brings scientific validation to these longstanding beliefs (see *The Compass of Pleasure* by Dr David Linden). This new book and a plethora of journal articles that followed corroborate these long-held conclusions. Social scientists can now scientifically confirm that in many aging marriages, spouses lose the zeal, pleasures, and erotic excitement enjoyed in earlier days. Brain-scan imaging can now record declining activity associated with romance, passion, and sexual excitement. These changes are now tractable to diminishing levels of dopamine, serotonin, and norepinephrine, all of which are consistent with natural aging. Still, many spouses want what they once enjoyed and several [mistakenly] believe they can recapture lost passion with a new partner.

While love and attachment remain in most marriages, recollections of lost romantic excitement and sexual pleasure can be troublesome. For many distressed spouses, fading romance and the loss of passion can spawn accompanying desires to look outside their marriage for replacement ecstasy and missing excitement. It seems that the loss of sexual pleasure or emotional delight can also be viewed as justification to engage in a romantic relationship. For others, these losses provide an excuse to end a *lifeless* marriage. While an affair or a new spouse might bring recaptured passion and new excitement, soon familiarity

sets in again, to recreate the same situation previously exited. Now, it's a new person, new sheets, all in an old bed.

Psychologists and other clinicians now conclude that romantic love (with its short life-expectancy) may not provide a sufficient foundation for lasting marital bliss. But wait, loss of the foregoing physical and emotional marital benefits are not intact; after all, there are millions of lasting marriages. But wait again; recall the research findings and three classifications for lasting marriage set forth by Dr. Judith Wallerstein and Sandra Blakeslee in the opening pages of Chapter One.

The information above supports new academic findings that affairs may be normal and natural human responses to formerly unrecognized love addictions. As with other dependencies, the gradual loss of an addictive element can disrupt mental, physical, and emotional balance. It can actually make you crazy. While newfound love can suddenly make the skies bluer and the grass greener, its unanticipated loss can bring withdrawals, obsession, and other prominent personality changes that can also lead to bizarre, erratic, and mean spirited conduct.

Spouses caught up with new *hot* lovers can become euphorically intoxicated with instant lust and engage in reckless behavior. Affected spouses can lose restraint; others lose sexual self-control. Shocking at first, abnormal marital behavior has now become the norm. Spouses sending sexually suggestive emails or sexting (sexual messages sent with attached photos or erotic videos) are now common events. It's everywhere: government officials carrying on as if they were still in high school, diapered astronauts driving cross-country to confront priority lovers, and actors involved with live-in domestic employees.

When these reckless acts are discovered, all hell breaks lose; some spouses go off the deep end and resort to homicidal actions when an affair is admitted or exposed. Incidents involving multiple homicides and other criminal acts have also been noted when separation or divorce are mentioned or initiated.

Acknowledging romantic love as addiction may help us understand why infidelity is pervasive and why its consequences are so extreme. But how can you tell? Sudden attention to dress, appearance, or abrupt weight-loss may all be telltale signs of a fresh romance. Remember, most extra-marital *escapes* are short-lived, while others can be the first of sequential hookups with a variety of rotating partners.

My Flawed Fundamental Factors

Looking back, I discovered my flawed fundamental factors; I must admit that I actually made the same marital mistake twice. Here is a quick summary of my marital hits, runs, and errors.

First Marriage

I met my first wife (let's call her Apollina) in a romantic restaurant. I asked her to dance. While dancing, I told her that I had lost my phone number and asked if I could have hers. The following Thursday we had dinner together. We each ordered three large crab-stuffed shrimp. We ate, talked, and laughed. She then asked, "Would you like one of my shrimp?" The following month I proposed, and she accepted. We shared 22 years together. Most were great, some were average, and (toward the end) several were stressful. Like other marriages, ours had cooled down. Here I will share with you some of the major episodes that led to the interruption of our troubled marriage.

As our daughter started high school, my law practice really took off. I was promoted to full professor. We had made some wise investments; it was time for a big house high on the hill. I designed our palatial new home myself. Without realizing it, however, I had become obsessed and possessed with the design, construction, and furnishing of this great house, which never became our home. Somehow, during the construction of this 8,302-square-foot temple, I had become a monster. Apollina and I had several disagreements about house issues: for instance, she wanted the dishwasher on the right side; I wanted it on the left because I often helped with the clean up and I am left-handed.

We argued about the dining room configuration, then about a sunken seating area in the master bedroom. Finally, Apollina threw in the towel and said, "You always want everything your way. Why not just do it all yourself?" It took two years to build and furnish the house; it had two dishwashers (one on the left and one on the right), an elevated dining room, and a sunken seating area with a small refrigerator and a bar sink in the master bedroom. My unreasonable demands and inadequate communications led to the destruction of our 22-year marriage. All this I had brought upon us. I did not allow Apollina to participate in the design or furnishing of OUR house; I acted as if it was to be only MY house.

Our divorce followed. I am, however, happy to report that Apollina and I have remained good friends, fifteen years after our divorce. I've frequently taken her to and from the airport (1-800-EX-HUSBA).

Second Marriage

Eight years after divorcing Apollina, I met my second wife (let's call her Aida). We met at a Harvard Parent Appreciation event (our daughters were Harvard grads) held at the Il Fornaio Ristorante in Manhattan Beach, California. Ricardo Capra graciously welcomed everyone. I carefully worked the room and made mental notes on the available women I found to be interesting.

Dinner was set for eight o'clock. I secretly enter the dining room and changed the seating-cards to placed Aida, the woman who remained number one on my list, to sit across from me. Dinner with Aida was delightful. We discovered several common interests and exchanged email addresses. After two months of almost non-stop dating, I proposed to her. We married seven months later and filed for divorce 27 months there after. First, let me state that I take full responsibility for this incomplete marriage, for I rushed into it faster than a firefighter charging into a burning building, without following my own alarms or advice.

I had again married someone I did not know, and someone who did not know me. Mistakenly, like many others overtaken by the forces of love, we missed warnings of what later become unacceptable behaviors. The missed *red-flags* that impacted us the most were the mutual beliefs that once we each made up our minds, our decisions were forever set in concrete. As with our other decisions, when it came to our marital ending there was no discussion, review, or anything else. Looking back, I realize that perhaps my failure to respond to Aida's silent treatment may have been a subconscious control maneuver, thinking that somehow she would apologize for not communicating or initiating reconciliation discussions. She did neither! As I reviewed the carnage, I felt that her response, though never communicated to me, might have been, "Fine, if that's what you want, I'll show you." Well, what can you do after knowing someone for two months before asking her or him to marry you?

Given our super-stubborn and incompatible personalities, we could never find common ground on material issues. Even though we truly loved each other and shared significant similarities, we interacted like mineral water and olive oil. Here is a brief summary of how our incompatibilities played out.

Six months after marrying Aida, our marriage was on the rocks, and it was ebb tide. We had failed to resolve cumulative stressful occurrences that exploded one-year later. One day after a brief discussion, Aida left by herself for a few days, and, as could be predicted, neither one of us called the other. Three days later, I came home find her wedding ring inserted on to a short-stemmed red rose. My credit cards and the diamond earrings I had recently given her were also on the table.

Her symbolic message was clear: our marriage was over! Then Aida suddenly entered the condo, stating that she had returned for her family pictures and that she was leaving. I tried to comfort her and lovingly asked her to sit and talk with me. I felt that we could get things back on track. It was a hot July day, but a definite frost had entered with her. These sudden cold spells are common events in broken marriages; they frequently last for the remainder of the marriage, as it did for us. Aida stayed for 36 additional days; however, neither one of us made any effort to discuss our dispute or vent our seething sub-surface anger.

Things did not get better; they became worse, and then, apathy and anger all moved in with us. As strained events followed, there was less conversation or contact between us. Nothing, not even a white flag was raised by either of us. I (finally) discovered that Aida was as stubborn as I was, and like me, she knew little about being conciliatory and less about apologies. We both had long histories of having others bend to our will. This *perfect match* had become an ongoing power struggle. Neither of us had the couple-conflict resolution skills to get us through our dilemma.

My mother used to say that husband, wife, and their marriage were two; that is to say, the marriage was first and the wife AND the husband (together) were second. Between husband and wife, their marriage always had to come first. Husband and wife had to agree, concede, flip, split, or do whatever was necessary, to keep the marriage together. Even though we were both reared by loving, secure, and never divorced parents, Aida and I did not learn their valuable lessons. Both of us were used to winning; thus, we both lost. It's depressing to see your marriage die before you. These deaths, however, can be followed by personal growth and expanded emotional development, as in the reforestation of a severely burned woodland.

Looking Forward

Divorce need not lead to economic ruin. My wise father used to say that God was an accountant, and that everyone is given his/her fair share of debits and credits. While women and men will both experience pressed divorce-driven financial circumstances, these costs can be manageable. Chapter 8 provides detailed explanations of child and spousal support issues, lawyer fees and costs, and other divorce related expenses.

For most women, things will definitely change; their lifestyles will likely suffer and they may face (what may seem to be) insurmountable financial challenges. Women cite loss of financial security and personal identity as their greatest losses. Even so, they will survive. In fact, their situations unusually improve via more suitable partners and a life free of past stresses and inescapable pressures.

For men, child and spousal support payments, along with monthly checks to two lawyers (hers and yours), will haunt them; yet, these annoying expenses are usually not permanent and will likely be paid-off in the distant future. Children eventually become adults and support pay ends when they turn 18. Today, most married women are already working; after divorce, most will continue their employment, or return to school to get a better job. Their earnings will reduce or may even eliminate their support. While most women will generally swear-off remarriage after divorce, many remarry after three years. This event will also terminate their spousal support.

Men (without prenups) are usually most affected by the loss of one-half of their net-worth and vested retirement benefits. Still, most men will continue working, and have ample time to replenish their reduced retirement accounts, and rebuild their depleted net-worth (men usually remarry four years after divorce).

Divorced spouses may also need help with personal despair or what may seem to be endless depression. Regaining lost self-respect or weakened self-confidence, and avoiding self-deprecating conduct or self-destructive behavior may require professional help. Again, these topics will be further addressed in later chapters; however, the information that follows is also helpful in dealing with these emotional issues.

With marital errors and behavioral mistakes behind you, they are no longer subject to your (or anyone else's) consideration, correction, or criticism. Still, these past experiences must be viewed as sound lessons learned and remembered for future reference.

Most divorced individuals will gradually reenter the dating venues they visited long ago. As will be explained in later chapters, protocols in this arena have significantly changed. Successful emotional recovery will be the forerunner to your reentry to the singles scene and move into the world of modern post-divorce dating. Chapter 11 deals with the overall mechanics of these ventures. Here we will review vital psychological factors that may hinder your progress or delay advancement in finding a meaningful relationship and lasting love.

Thresholds and Transitions

Divorce will bring new thresholds and involuntary transitions. You may have already classified the first as Shock and Awe. As mentioned in Chapters 1 and 2, giving notice that you want to end your marriage, or being told that it's over, was like having three coordinated bombs going off in your heart, head, and soul.

Next, you dealt with relocation and economic survival, followed by your forced return to single status. Months later, you finally came to accept what had happened and that you were getting divorced. You gradually enrolled in Divorce Recovery College and made good progress in healing yourself from [almost] mortal wounds. These topics have been partially covered in previous chapters and will be expanded here and in coming chapters.

Post divorce dating will likely bring back previously conquered personal challenges that you overcame years ago. Rejection, social activity, and intimacy apprehension will be back, along with what many referred to as Peter Pan Syndrome (commitment anxiety). In addition, dating practices have changed and will require familiarity.

Dating has always included the above five pressures. As would be expected, however, post-divorce dating brings these forces back in greater frequency and with higher levels of apprehension.

First, dealing with rejection: we have all been there and have likely experienced both being rejected and rejecting others. Coming across as being super needy, overly horny, or still bitter will all work against you. Mocking your ex puts you in a bad light and signals that you are not a forgiving person. This hints that you have not moved on. Instead, speak positively about your ex and champion his/her good qualities. It will not hurt to mention your own human errors and past faults. Also, losing a few pounds, wearing new cloths, and having a fresh hairdo may help.

Social involvement merely requires that you circulate and not sit at home, at the office, or other such retreat. Your apartment, condo, or the office can become a tomb and you can socially die there. We all need to "get out among them" and, as they [should] say in baseball, in order to get hit on, we must first take a swing. Reality requires that we be available to meet others and that we do so with an clean slate, free of resentment, lingering negativity, and other menacing conduct that would scare off others. Frequent places you enjoy to meet others with similar interests, education levels, and values. Go to church, lectures, plays, and places where you will have active and dynamic interactions with others.

Intimacy apprehension deals with the inherent fear of being close or uneasy in becoming amorous with a new lover. Many will fear the terror of getting naked (with the lights on) with someone new. All of this may stem from the loss of a former spouse. Excessive guarded behavior will impede romantic progress; take these steps gradually; get help if needed.

Conquering Peter Pan Syndrome requires great care and careful attention. Many of us receive intra-body messages or gut feelings on what to do and not to do. Frankly, if you feel hesitant or doubtful about saying yes; perhaps you should do a Rip Van Winkle and sleep on it for a year or two. Why not wait an additional year, two, or even three; what's the rush!

Two of the overstated mandates mentioned throughout this book are the requirements that you have a meaningful dating duration and an extended engagement period. How else can you possibly get to know your spouse-to-be? Thus, spending a year or two with your beloved will provide necessary and required opportunities to witness and experience moods, behaviors, and other conduct that you can later expect and accept. "One day as a couple equals a hundred days of experiences!"

A full year after my second divorce, I realized that in spite of the many positive things that Aida and I shared and admired in each other, and that no matter how much we loved each other, she and I should never have married. "Why," you ask. Well, it was just not going to last because some two individuals should simply not marry each other! After all, just look over the list of interesting divorced persons in the front of this book.

Perhaps marriage license applications should require a test *behind the wheel*, in the kitchen and in *other rooms*. Most are familiar with many of the great love adages, like, love is blind, true love conquers all, and other such memorable sayings. In the real world, however, such inspiring sayings are merely "sayings" and are mostly poetic prophecies, wishful thinking, and writings found in Hallmark cards.

Given today's pervasive improper marital behaviors and worldwide escalating divorce rates, is it fair to ask: "Are there certain individuals who should just not marry each other?" The answer is clearly yes!

Take Joe DiMaggio and the Marilyn Monroe. These individuals were a total mismatch. They were opposites in significant areas and had several conflicting personal traits. Marilyn spent most of her childhood in foster homes and orphanages. She never had a stable and loving family life. Marilyn constantly sought attention, affection, and applause from her fans, friends and the press. Joe, the eighth of nine children (five boys and four girls), was reared in a warm, loving home, where his mother, eight siblings, and father were always with him.

After their brief courtship (sound familiar?), Joe and Marilyn were married at the San Francisco City Hall. Joe had just ended his career; Marilyn was just starting hers. Next, they were off to Tokyo for their honeymoon. Marilyn's mere presence in Japan caused a near-riot.

Marilyn loved and needed the attention; shy and serious Joe preferred his privacy (Joe did not like the press or his ball fans). Marilyn, against Joe's strong objections, took time during their honeymoon to perform for the U.S. troops stationed in Korea, where thousands of men were ogling his new bride. Joe was understandably uneasy with this, for he just wanted to be alone with her. As later reported, this event *killed* their marriage; it lasted only 272 days. Most were spent apart from each other, and nearly all were filled with quarrels, tears, and severe stress.

Chiefs and Indians

Successful marriages seem to require coordinated combinations. One that appears to work is the one-chief, one-Indian combo. Marriages lacking this combination are sometimes destined for stormy seas, separations, and eventual divorces. My first marriage had one chief (me) and one Indian (Apollina). Interestingly, though, my psychology colleagues have told me that it is the Indian who usually has the power. My marriage with Aida had two chiefs and no Indians. Granted, there are selective, successful marriages with two chiefs and perhaps fewer with two Indians, where both follow and lead together. Many marriages with two chiefs, like the combustible six-year stormy marriage between Frank Sinatra and Ava Gardner, are just not likely to last; even though these two individuals truly loved each other, their union did not survive.

After Aida and I separated and the smoke cleared, I realized that we had been on the same bus with Joe and Marilyn, Frank and Ava, and many other couples who were simply not meant to be married to each other. Again, just review the long list of divorced celebrities at the beginning of this book; look at your family, friends, relatives, and other acquaintances, and you'll see more! While Joe and Marilyn seemed to be total opposites, Frank and Ava shared several similarities. Aida and I, it seemed, had innocently combined a lethal combination of accelerant attributes, bookend backgrounds, and combustible characteristics that likely prevented us from ever staying together. As I mentioned before, when we are in love we are blinded and cannot see or hear what should be avoided. It's even worse when you rush into a short engagement and then marry someone you do not really know.

It's not uncommon that what attracts us initially (like powerful magnets) can also become the same forces that later destroy a marriage. It's as if the same powerful magnets that once pulled you together were suddenly rotated. Unexpectedly, these *attraction forces* later present as repelling incompatibles that are now pushing you away and apart from each another; moreover, similarities in attributes, backgrounds, and characteristics (as with Frank and Ava, who were also both extremely stubborn) can yield the same disappointing results. Aida and I were simply too much alike!

Ask and Answer

As you move into the dating scene, take the time necessary to truly get to know the people you date. Pay attention and be aware of their habits, lifestyles, and relationship expectations. Look into the back seat of their cars and you will see how they keep their living quarters. As you visit their abodes, you will learn more. The best thing to do is to ask as many questions as you can; you should do likewise and give answers to the same question you ask them (fair is fair).

During my two-month courtship with Aida, I asked her endless questions and she had honestly answered them all. I answered reciprocal questions, and I, too, gave honest and complete answers. We asked and answered more questions than an entire floor of ambidextrous hourly-paid lawyers could have asked in one month of non-stop depositions. We had more settlement discussions than all of the Arab-Israeli conflict negotiators combined. Many an evening we shared a good bottle of Napa Merlot while talking into the wee small hours of the morning. We discussed and examined various marriage scenarios, plans, and life expectations. We had 44 years of marriage between the two of us. We both knew what we were looking for and what we expected.

Today, I am here writing this book about how to overcome the stresses and traumas of divorce, and not *The Joys of a Second Marriage*. In my continual premarital discussions with Aida, as with Apollina before, I asked repeated questions about her childhood, about her family and about her expectations for the future. We talked excessively about her interesting father, loving mother, and several siblings. Psychologists still suggest that we avoid individuals with damaged or difficult familial relationships: "You may one day end up on the same disapproval list; you may one day become the replacement piñata for her/his residual anger from a passed failed family relationship," they tell us.

That said, there are many good people who have developed strong character by dealing with family difficulties. These tested individuals come with an awareness of their family challenges, insight into their own weaknesses, and the wisdom to forgive. The only way to discover hidden treasures is to ask many questions of your soon-to-be spouse.

There is no *Fifth Amendment* right to remain silent, no right to counsel, and no right to refuse to answer any question when it comes to talking about spending your future with one person. Ask, ask, and re-ask! Start with the ABCs of it; then get right down to the XYZs of everything. I was really good at asking probing questions and getting down to the underlying factual predicates regarding each one of the three (childhood, family, and future expectations) topics.

Even so, my legal experience and skilled interrogations were of little value. Why did my detailed questioning and her truthful answers not work? It was like many of you, I was also bewitched, bothered, and bewildered. When we are in love (or infatuated), our outlook gets a little hazy; we get a little crazy, and our common sense goes right out the window. We are just not rational or realistic. Sometimes our children warn us; other times, it's our parents or our co-workers that tell us of likely problems. Again, we just don't listen! Several have confessed to me that they did not listen to parental disapprovals of former spouses.

Admonished and forewarned that we are about to make a mistake, we turn a blind eye and a deaf ear to those caring people who try to alert us. Many discover significant inadequacies, obvious inconsistencies, and evident imperfections in the suitors that pursue them, as well as in the ones they pursue. Still, with this material information in hand, they marry these affected individuals. This pattern is especially true for us men, who do not think with our heads or our hearts.

Life always brings latent disappointments and resulting changed plans are common in all marriages. All of us are compelled to accept changes brought on by illness, disease, and other forced physical challenges that life deals us. These involuntary hands must be played out. Such events are not our choices, but spouses are frequently forced to make the best of bad situations. Then there are the poorly played hands created by our own free choices that are not accepted by our spouses. The wants of one spouse conflicting with the likes of the other can cause severe marital disharmony, stress, and lasting resentment. But these conflicts, too, must be reconciled and resolved to retain marital harmony. As you may have already discovered, too many times such unresolved and uncompromised choices (like clashing travel agendas) can force a marriage into the tank.

Divorce need not be a series of Greek tragedies (even if you were married to a Greek). Just as in childbirth, divorce has its agonizing pains, hurts, and extended discomforts. Growth and improvement are also accompanied by agonizing pains, hurts, and extended discomforts, yet lasting rewards and permanent enlightenment can also follow.

Since we have mentioned Frank Sinatra in this chapter, we end and list his four wives and three children:

LAST WILL AND TESTAMENT

of

FRANCIS ALBERT SINATRA

I, FRANCIS ALBERT SINATRA, also known as FRANK SINATRA, declare this to be my Will and revoke all former Wills and Codicils. I am a resident of Riverside County, California.

FIRST CLAUSE: Marital Status And Family.

I am married to BARBARA SINATRA, who in this Will is referred to as "my Wife." I was formerly married to NANCY BARBATO SINATRA, to AVA GARDNER SINATRA, and to MIA FARROW SINATRA, and each of said marriages were subsequently dissolved. I have three children, all of whom are the issue of my marriage to NANCY BARBATO SINATRA: NANCY SINATRA LAMBERT, FRANCIS WAYNE SINATRA, and CHRISTINA SINATRA. All of the above-named children are adults. I have never had any other children.

Time Heals All Wounds

Interestingly, Sinatra left large cash bequests to ex-wives Nancy and Mia (whom he obviously still remembered and cared about), as well as to his widow Barbara. Finally, recall that time heals all wounds, and all wounds heal with time. Take the time and make effort to be extra nice and super considerate to your ex-spouse. These welcomed acts of reciprocal altruism will accelerate your healing (as well as his or her recovery and healing) even more. It's not as though you're trying to get back together with him/her, but then again, no one knows for sure.

Perhaps it may be a good idea for you to put down on paper your present divorce feelings, heartaches, and discomforts. Make two copies and mail them to yourself. Open one on each yearly anniversary of your divorce and see how your outlook has improved. You'll note that much of your heartache and discomfort has dissipated. Write a new description of your one-year post-divorce feelings and how your life has improved. You can list what still troubles you and why. Mail this to yourself for opening the following year. You can now compare the noted changes from two-years ago and last year. As you will see, time heals all wounds and brings new wisdom. This insight can be the gift you give yourself following your divorce.

As I finished my book, I sent Aida a pre-publication draft for her review. Five days later I received this email:

> Dave,
>
> I just finished reading
> your entire book.
>
> I am speechless!
> I am touched!
> I am grateful!
> I am also in tears!
>
> This is going to be an
> emotional week, weeks … .
>
> Love,
>
> Aida

WHAT YOU NOW RECOGNIZE, UNDERSTAND, AND ACCEPT

1. Consider the people you have dated and married.

2. Look for repeated patterns and attractions that may not be healthy for you.

3. What stands out; is she/he a clone of your last spouse?

4. Remember, when we are in love we do not listen to the advice of others.

5. There are certain individuals whom we should not marry.

6. Do not despair: new people come in and out of our lives all the time.

7. Be wary of someone who has opposite views, values, or needs.

8. Be wary of someone who has the same views, values, or needs.

9. Look at your ABCs to be certain that they are compatible and cool.

10. Discuss travel needs, wants, and preferences—perhaps take a trip or two together before marriage.

CHAPTER FIVE

Spending Time with [Just] Yourself

One morning an ex-wife decides to take out her ex-husband's fishing boat. She motors out a short distance, anchors, puts her feet up, and begins to read her book. The peace and solitude are magnificent. Then, along comes a fish and game warden (who happens to be her ex-husband) in his official boat. He pulls up alongside her and says, "Good morning, Emilia. What are you doing?"

"Reading a book," she replies (thinking, isn't that obvious?).

"You're in a Restricted Fishing Area," he informs her.

"I'm sorry, Emilio, but I'm not fishing. I'm reading."

"Yes, but I see you have all the equipment. For all I know you could start at any moment. I'll have to take you in and write you up."

"If you do that, I'll have to charge you with sexual assault," she tells him.

"But I haven't even touched you," says Emilio. Emilia responds with, "That's true, but you have all the equipment. For all I know you could start at any moment."

"Have a nice day Emilia," said Emilio as he left.

Divorce recovery can be a painful, prolonged process, and, unfortunately, most of us do not have a genie to help us navigate the course. The good news is that divorce is a period of transition that will bring change, recovery, and wisdom, along with a newfound freedom perhaps never experienced before. You'll soon discover that this is the perfect time to re-examine yourself from an outsider's perspective; you can reassess your personal, vocational, and recreational interest to determining if changes are necessary. Now that you're alone, it will be easier to make desired adjustments to achieve new goals or desired objectives.

Looking back at the course, you may still recall the all-night discussions, arguments, and negotiations following the reality that you had serious marital problems. You recall bargaining with your spouse, yourself, and with God. You and your spouse explored various ameliorative actions, including counseling sessions, trial separations, and other suggested alternatives. Both of you tried, but the problems could not be reconciled, resolved, or repaired. For others, there were no negotiations or reconciliation efforts whatsoever; instead, all rescue and settlement efforts were skipped and someone moved out, and the thunderbolt hit: divorce was imminent. Forced economic and social adjustments followed, as survival became your chief concern. Earlier, marriage had been an adjustment to a new way of life; your sudden divorce-turn now brings you to finding yourself single and alone.

Coping and Getting By

In navigating the course, you considered how others coped with their marriage-ending ordeals. You may have read or recalled that many going through divorce became antisocial and retreated inwardly to deal with their anguish and sorrows. Others you observed became super social and searched for audience with anyone willing to listen to their tragic, sad stories. Some solo flyers sought medical attention and were ethically medicated to deal with their depression and loneliness. Several going through the process elected to self-medicate with alcohol, drugs, or other harmful substances, behaviors or persons to help themselves overcome their personal painful problems.

Numerous divorcing individuals sought validation about still being a desirable person, via rushed sexual encounters with newfound partners. These hollow sexual experiences, they later discovered, left them disappointed, empty, and still alone. They subsequently realized that *transitional partners* couldn't be used as pleasure units to fill their emptiness and continued longing to be loved during this phase of involuntary desertion or voluntary departure.

Married life brings bonding life experiences. Once you were an inseparable team of two, sensitive to each other's needs. Your previous magical marriage that once bonded you and your former spouse has ended. Your former partner, lover, and best friend will not be home tonight, tomorrow, or next month. Perhaps, as did I, you, too, may have anticipated that everything would stabilize and suddenly become rebalanced after his, her, or your exit; however, such is not the case, as you found yourself alone.

Now silence and sadness fill the empty chair once occupied by "your departed" spouse. Now you can better appreciate the applicable words of F. Scott Fitzgerald's *Tender Is the Night*, "Being alone in body and spirit begets loneliness, and loneliness begets more loneliness." Yes, living alone is frequently equated with being alone, yet it does not have to mean being lonely. Living alone has value and virtue.

In the last chapter, we discussed missed fractured fundamentals, reviewed crossed thresholds, and looked at forced transitions. Here we'll touch upon modern remarriage, its unfolding realities and material myths. As noted, continued discussion on previously introduced topics is a great teaching technique, for it reinforces what has been learned, and allows for cumulative content. While some sing that *Love is Lovelier the Second Time Around*, second marriages have much higher divorce rates than first marriages (76 percent vs. 55 percent). Second spouses don't always come with enhanced communication skills, dispute resolution flare, or improved marital maturity. Many new husbands, however, do come with ex-wives, minor children, and court-ordered support. Some also have ailing parents, business or personal debts, and other generic baggage. Second wives can also bring similar baggage and obligations. Chapter 12 has listed remarriage audiences that will be helpful in dealing with these issues.

Given the increasing number of remarriage high hurdles, it's no wonder that women and men everywhere are postponing remarriage (see Appendix). As global cohabitation continues to gain acceptance, this may become the new living together arrangement (LTA) for the future. Is this new living together model right for you?

Evaluating remarriage and other LTAs is important. But wait! Can you accurately consider these alternatives fairly when out on your own? While being alone may provide optimum *settings* for reviewing relevant facts and foreseeable demands, these commitments must be looked at objectively. These are difficult calls; choices must be made free of any and all economic pressures, emotional needs, and social prejudices.

Before making any decision on these selections, perhaps you should first answer the following:

- Who were you?

- Who did you become?

- Who would you like to be?

The first question is easy. Your adolescent-persona was likely shaped by family and peer dynamics. These early interactions were instrumental in the development of your personality, dating patterns, and educational objectives. The second question is answered by reviewing post-marital events, choices, and responsibilities. These likely included selecting a career path, deciding where to live, and starting a family; your partner joined in these decisions. As the years passed, you continued on this pathway until divorce disrupted your previously tranquil life.

As you look back, you realize that most decisions regarding who you were and who you became were made either by others, or with others. Perhaps your expectations and goals were overruled and denied. But wait again! Were you a victim of your parents' or siblings' vicariousness? Did you become a clone of your mother or father? Were you constantly seeking the approval, attention, and affection of an oppressive spouse?

As bad as divorce is said to be, it also brings opportunities for positive change and personal growth. This sets the stage for answering question three.

Yes, now you can reevaluate your *past life* and make necessary adjustments or desired improvements, if you care to do so. You can start a new career, date new and interesting people, or even move to a desired location. You can now evaluate each of the listed queries, make adjustments or changes you deem necessary, or maintain the status quo. All of this can be done without the bossy impute or aggressive counter demands of others. Many, of course, appreciate the guidance and direction from others, and there is absolutely nothing wrong with this alternative. The key is to feel at ease in your personal decisions and living a life in which you have had a say. You have an absolute right to participate in such matters and relationship decisions must include welcomed impute, fair challenges, and rebuttal commentary from both partners.

Further emotional, economic, and social challenges will surface as you continue your individual journey through the divorce process. Helpful solo suggestions and individual activity recommendations follow that will keep you occupied in your future days.

Do not Panic

Divorce can bring depression and sadness. You must step back and realize that this is normal and an expected human response to what has occurred. Women and men are said to react and deal differently to divorce-depression; women experience excessive guilt, sadness, and a sense of worthlessness. While women generally become more sociable with family and friends, men usually react in the opposite manner, becoming loners and keeping to themselves. Men will likely turn to their work, drugs, or alcohol to deal with their depression and onset of fatigue, sleeplessness, and anger.

For many, the sudden exit of a spouse can bring an accompanying loss of their identity and security. Women and men often experience mood swings, lapses in their thinking, and even episodes of reckless and irresponsible behavior. These activities are components and consequences of DSS. These impulsive behaviors will come and go, however, you may need to seek medical attention if they persist.

Being alone is not that bad; it can actually be beneficial for us after periods of great difficulty, and especially after filing for divorce or being served with divorce papers. This is the proper time to look back into your marriage and reflect upon your requirements and requests and those of your now-absent spouse. You could review each other's needs and wants fulfillment ratios to determine who had the better deal, or perhaps just plan for next time. You could explore alternatives to keep the home fires burning with a new partner. You could also use this precious time to develop your character further and regain the confidence you may have lost along the way.

Don't waste this valuable time. It can help prepare you for whatever greatness lies beyond self-imposed limitations. These solo periods can nourish the spirit, lay the groundwork for great things to come, and help prepare you for future experiences. Look at it this way: your separation and divorce may be part of a master plan. These passing events could be stepping stones toward that place where you're destined to be.

The gateway to your future can be discovered through the process of introspection, which may best be achieved with the help of a competent psychologist or strong friend. If you select the latter, be sure to find one who will not fear being honest with you, even if your feelings are hurt. Look back into your marriage and recall that it takes two to tango and two to argue. Ask yourself: Was I too critical, demanding, or unreasonable? Did I habitually make more withdrawals than deposits from our emotional savings account? Did I become apathetic? Be honest, but be gentle with yourself. Remember, you, too, are only human and no one is perfect.

Remind yourself that leaving, or being left by a spouse, is a far more complicated life-changing experience than one might initially realize. Many of us have been with the same spouse for years and may have simply become a *single-unit* of two. Now that one has left, both must accept that the absent person will be missed in the other's heart and by their side. Being alone will bring difficult adjustments. Sleeping and waking alone, eating alone, and not having your former best friend anymore can be strenuous. Constant reminders of your past will occur and these flashbacks will add to your loneliness.

In time, however, you will continue to adjust to your new way of life and passing thoughts of *yesterday* will diminish and become less frequent.

Even so, many exiting or forsaken men, and less similarly situated women, will rush to seek and find a caretaker companion or a rebound romance (see Chapter 11) to help them deal with their grave loneliness. This proxy person will become their source of temporary support while they struggle to regain their emotional equilibrium and lost confidence.

Most transitional relationships, however, do not last. Once the hurt has abated and the healing is completed, the recovered person is off to search for (what they may consider to be) new meaningful partners.

To overcome your single-status sadness effectively, you must find wholesome and rewarding things to do. Fill the vacuum in your heart and mind with interesting solo activities that you can enjoy alone. Whether you realize it or not, one of your major problems is that now you have too much free time on your hands. You also no longer have anyone to do things with you, as you were accustomed to with your *now-departed* spouse. Assuming your ex, his/her attorney, or your attorney has not taken all of your funds, here are several suggestions for things you can do alone!

Twelve Inspiring Things
To Do When Alone

1. Consider a pet

Tired of coming home to an empty house? What about a used dog or cat? Used dogs can be a pleasure because they are already over the unruly puppy stage and sometimes even housebroken. In fairness to cat lovers, I'll be the first to acknowledge that cats are just as loving as dogs. Still, cats can be aloof, but they're far more independent and require less attention. If you do elect to get a pet, be sure you have the time to take proper care of its basic needs: food, water, daily walks, and a monthly bath, as well as an occasional trip to the vet and, of course, love and attention from you. Fortunately, pets make no demands, don't smoke, snore, or watch sports over the entire weekend and holidays or Oprah in the afternoons. Dogs especially are always glad to see you. The later you are, the more excited they are when you return (unlike you know who). Also, a dog's parents never visit or call and tell you what to prepare for dinner.

2. Go see a psychologist

This is an excellent time for guided introspection because you're at a vulnerable low point in your life. Go now and get answers to all those nagging questions you always wondered about. I went to a great psychologist named Ayle. My sessions with her were super productive; these lessons helped me to become a better person.

Why not have a psychological purging? We usually get rid of unnecessary items when we move. Well, you've just moved again (from married to divorced). My house design, construction, and furnishing monster personality traits were revealed to me in my therapy sessions. I did not discover them on my own, though I did recognize them through the consequences of my past oppressive behavior. In sessions with Ayle I realized that I had become a combative contractor. I guess it was a survival mechanism that helped me deal with others who were confrontational (me) and unreasonable (me again). I learned how to overcome this bad side of myself (my Igor construction monster personality). I became my own exorcist and removed toxic alter-ego contaminants from my persona. Had I not done this, my ugly behavior would have followed me.

Many of us who have done battle in divorce court may have subconsciously created our own *survival monster personalities* to fight off evil, oppression, and tyranny in handling the ex, his/her parents, or their attorney. These battles are now over; there's no need to bring your Igor and his confrontational behavior with you to new suitors or old friends.

I used to say that to dream of the person you would like to be was to waste the person you are; nevertheless, sometimes the person we are needs change and renovation. We all take our cars in for required oil changes and scheduled tune-ups. Why not have your *emotional oil changed* and have your attitude tuned up a little? If it helps your car run better and longer, perhaps it can do the same for you. Just think: a few sessions may bring modifications that can make you a better and more enduring you.

Undergoing therapy was a wonderful learning experience. It was half of what my lawyer charged and is sometimes covered by medical or health insurance and included parking. Unlike going a couple of rounds with my expensive lawyer, I always felt better after sessions with Ayle.

3. Take tango lessons

Among the many differences between women and men is the reality that most women usually love to dance, while men do not. If this was an issue in your last marriage, why not take dancing lessons for next time. Tango?

Argentine tango, not American tango; this is a wonderful and exciting dance to learn and enjoy. You can have fun, meet new and interesting people, and open up an entirely new activity. It will take practice, lots of practice actually, and a commitment to follow through, but, as with life's other challenges, the rewards are well worth the effort. Just think, ladies, perhaps Arnold or Al (*True Lies* and *Scent of a Woman*) will ask you to tango one day. Be ready, for the men, Helen Tasker or Juno Skinner (characters in *True Lies*) may be in need of new partners.

Check out and watch the movie *Assassination Tango* a time or two; Amazon.com carries no less than 12 other tango DVDs for your viewing, practice, and enjoyment. After you feel comfortable with your moves, consider a solo trip to Argentina, where everyone tangos! Perhaps you'll see Governor Mark of South Carolina and his soul mate out on the dance floor.

4. Take some interesting classes

Select a ceramics class, and as in the movie Ghost, you, too, can master the pottery wheel. Take an art, music or a cooking class: Indian, Japanese, or just general cooking classes are great. You'll be amazed at what you'll learn. While eating is a biological necessity, it can also become a great social event. This can be the perfect time to up-grade your diet, cooking presentations, and community involvement. Invite your family, friends, or neighbors; many will reciprocate and invite you over for a meal, two, or three (you can also find individual video cooking instructions by merely Googling: "How to make Spanish rice," or "How to prepare eggplant," and anything else).

Check online for cooking classes. Major malls usually have a Williams Sonoma, *Sur La Table* or other major stores that offer enjoyable cooking classes. Besides, you get to eat the prepared meals. There are usually restaurants close by where you can purchase a glass of wine to bring back to class and enjoy with your meal. Better yet, bring a bottle (glasses and a corkscrew) to enjoy with others.

5. Work on a hobby or try acting

Find someone to work with you to improve your skills and knowledge. If you've been interested in woodworking, find a tree. Hey, it's a place to start, and look what it did for George Washington. Home Depot and many other stores offer special home improvement classes taught by women, exclusively for women.

Several local cities have playhouse performances featuring local aspiring actors. Why not get involved in a minor role—perhaps it could grow into a leading role. Then again, you can get involved in the production, directing, or other aspects of local theater. Everyone has to start somewhere. If you never start, you'll never get there.

6. Get your shape in shape

If you anticipate reentering the dating scene, losing a few pounds (on each side) couldn't hurt. Join a gym and sign up with a personal trainer. Work on what needs work. This will improve your looks and energy levels. You'll feel better instantly due to increased endorphins, which have been shown to reduce depression and relieve stress.

Change your diet and eat better. Make this a part of your new routine. Learn the art of walking. Start a rigorous exercise program today. If you haven't already noticed, many of these suggestions go hand-in-hand. Your exercise program could include tango lessons before or after seeing your psychologist. Better yet, find a psychologist who tangos, and do three new things at once!

7. Remodel your living quarters

Take some remodeling classes. Subscribe to *Architectural Digest* or home improvement magazines. If you're not the handyperson type, you can always design or duplicate a new entertainment center, table, or wall modification. Have a local contractor build it for you (always get three bids). Visit new model homes, hotels, condominiums, or even boats. Get new design ideas from the best experts in the field.

Make a mess. Paint and, if you're not pleased with the new color, repaint your walls. Look into new furnishings to improve your surroundings and elevate your comfort zone. Mirror a wall, or two, or three.

8. Take a cruise by yourself

Do something you enjoy. Why not take a cruise? Several leave daily to Alaska, Mexico, or Asia from the West Coast and to Europe, the Caribbean, and South America from the East Coast. There's nothing better than the lure of the open ocean. Most ships have excellent libraries, lectures, and learning activities up the wazoo, they also have Internet access, gyms, and a limitless supply of fantastic food paired with wonderful wines. You'll meet new and interesting people and go to exciting places you may never have seen.

National cruise retailer Cruise.com recently announced a series of cruises dedicated to the "divorced and single again" market. This special cruise could be exciting. (Be sure to check with your ex to be certain that you don't end up on the same cruise ship.) There are appealing river and sailing cruises, too. Again, go for the adventure, meet new friends, but don't go looking for Mr./Ms. Replacement.

9. How about a road trip

Fly into or out of Seattle, San Diego, Boston, or Atlanta. Rent a hybrid car and head back home. Stop along the way to smell the roses. See the local landmarks as you go. Stop and see your favorite rock group. Mine is in South Dakota: *Mount Rushmore National Monument* [rock group]. Oh! Look up old classmates, relatives, or even past places where you've lived. If it's good enough for Oprah, it's good enough for you!

You can break it up. Take a train ride for a few hundred miles. Why not rent a Corvette, Ferrari, or Aston Martin that you have always fancied? Be Jane or James Bond for a few hundred miles. Try a Rolls Royce or a vehicle you may have always wanted to drive. Better yet, go totally green and ride a hot air balloon part of the way. Fond memories are sure to follow new and exciting activities. Again, check with your ex to be certain you both do not end up in the same gondola.

10. Be more sexual

If you were previously boring in bed, get some help now. Learn how to become more exciting. Enrich your romantic side; dress for the occasion. Victoria's Secret has made millions selling its expensive peek-a-boo items for women to entice men. Hey, an old JCPenney tee-shirt with two mid-chest circular cutouts will do! As for the men, you could wear tights; you can be Mikhail Baryshnikov for the night (if you elect to use the rolled-up pair of socks *enhancement*, be sure you place them securely in the front).

You can become a new *you*; you could talk dirty. Yes, you can say, "A woman fell in the mud. She entered the house and tracked mud all over the house. Next, she looked in the refrigerator and left her dirty handprints on the door." If you're seriously following the last paragraph, you may really need help.

Sadly, most people don't realize or appreciate that, in most cases, our brain is our largest sex organ (some have sex organs larger than their brains). Talking dirty to the one you love (or even just the one you're with) is inexpensive. Many still do not realize the inherent shared value of talking dirty and its welcome pleasure and eroticism. Several are burdened by sexual inhibitions that deny them and their partners the benefits of this mutual pleasure. Some seek these experiences from others and frequent those who sell their services by the hour to enjoy what could be available at home, but perhaps is not on the current marriage menu. Like anything else of value, learning how to let loose and be comfortable talking dirty takes time and (reasonable) practice.

Here are three simple suggestions to improve your sexuality:

- Be yourself. Sex is like popcorn: you can see, smell, taste, touch, and hear it. For her/him to hear you, you need to talk. Being polite, proper, and professional just does not cut it. Many of us get turned on watching a sexy movie, reading a romance novel, or listening to Marvin Gaye singing "Sexual Healing." Others love watching Tina Turner (in that great little red dress) climb back up the stairs after singing "What's Love Got to Do with It?"

- Just like Hillary found her voice before the 2008 New Hampshire primary, you can find your talk-dirty voice. You need to find your own way of talking dirty; you can be Hillary, or be Barry White and use low, rhythmic "Barry" whispers.

- Just let go. Talking dirty is your opportunity to express yourself as never before. Avoid clinical terms (like penis); get as raunchy as you can. Enjoy!

11. Learn about human sexuality

Learn more about the opposite sex and have more sex. In her book *The Female Brain*, Dr. Louann Brizendine writes:

> Males have double the brain space and processing power devoted to sex as females. Just as women have an eight-lane superhighway for processing emotion while men have a small country road, men have O'Hare Airport as a hub of processing thoughts about sex whereas women have the airfield nearby that lands small and private planes.

Take a few classes in human sexuality. My students tell me that these classes are interesting and cover various topics that include the Biology of Sex, Cultural Diversity, Personal Points of View, Research Highlights, Sex in History, Sexual Health, and Society, Values, and the Law. One of the books they use is *Human Sexuality* by Simon LeVay and Sharon Valente. Every copy includes the interactive *Exploring Human Sexuality Study Guide* CD-ROM. This CD-ROM is keyed to the text. Class discussions also get into the use of sex toys, better bedtime communications, and other sexual improvement techniques on various subjects. They also use *The Joy of Sex*, which is still a top selling book. One student mentioned that these books are also popular at home and are frequently viewed by moms and dads.

12. You can help others

Why not help yourself by helping others? Several of my mature academic colleagues still teach for the mere enjoyment. One recently told me that she needs the job for her mental and social health, and not for her economic obligations. We have several retired business executives who wanted to teach so badly that, as part of their hiring agreement, they return their entire monthly checks to the university, just to remain in an environment of continuous learning. The only way to keep learning is to keep learning.

As mentioned before, divorce leaves many of us with too much free time, nothing to do, and no one to pass time with. It seems as though when we are busy, we are somehow extremely productive and everything gets done. When we have nothing to do, nothing gets done, even though we have ample time. Everyone has a unique interest and special skills that could be turned into a volunteer work assignment. If history is your interest, consider becoming a docent at a local museum or gallery. If you're good at raising money, why not help as a fund raiser for a local nonprofit? There are so many wonderful and interesting things to do. As many have already discovered, helping others has its value and virtue.

There's a major difference between being alone and being isolated. Even if we're living alone, we all still need human connection and interaction with others. Granted, you may have lost your spouse, but interactions with family, co-workers, and the rest of the human community are essential for your emotional and social well-being. This is a good time to become involved in church activities, community events, and other collective endeavors.

Various exciting solo activities are available for you to enjoy. Do them for the adventure, experience and self-improvement that follow. There's no reason to be bored or to stagnate from the mundane. Implementation of two or more of the 12 enjoyable things to do will bring you happiness and make you a more enjoyable and interesting person. Your boredom problem may have impacted your past, but don't allow it to injure your future.

Group vs. Solo Activities

Many people require continuous companionship. Are you one of them? Some persons need constant group stimuli: dinners, movies, and lectures, as well as plays, operas, and other entertainment events with others. It goes on and on. It's nonstop. These individuals seem to lack the ability to find solace within themselves. We all need balance between our necessary time alone and *activities* with others; still, the foregoing activities can be enjoyed alone. Being alone after the sudden loss of a spouse due to divorce need not be a difficult and painful experience.

Whether you're single, married, or divorced, happiness should always be your primary objective. Your individual happiness is the most significant dimension of your waking and subconscious experiences. Just as good feelings replace bad feelings, and vice versa, we should all avoid the pain and misery of unpleasant memories and move toward the sublime, pleasant, and joyful life experiences that await us all, especially when alone. When we are happy, our joy spills over into the lives of others. When you're smiling, the whole world smiles with you!

If you can function and socialize alone, you'll do much better with others. Knowing how to nurture yourself and socialize as a single person is important. It can be done; there's nothing wrong with being alone. Start your own solo spiritual journey and heal your mind, body, and sprit. Believe it or not, we all need periods of time just to be alone. It is part of the flushing process for us to rid ourselves of toxic thoughts and reap the sounds of silence, which is when we can recreate ourselves.

This reality is one of the fundamental reasons why carpooling is not more popular. For many deprived souls, being alone in the car is their only moment of peace, rest, and rapture from the toils of their otherwise occupied daily lives. When alone in the car, we are in charge. We can listen to *our* radio selections; we can sing solo, backup, or as a duet, or even conduct. We can cuss out the guy in front of us for going too slowly, or even wink at the lovely person stopped next to us. We can engage in a host of other personal hygiene activities prohibited by the presence of another.

Living alone for extended periods without social intercourse is not good for you. Several years ago, a research study was conducted in the Mission District of San Francisco that centered on men and women who lived alone in $20/day hotels for five or more years. The results were predictable and gave rise to "Single Room Occupancy Syndrome" (SROS). Persons affected by SROS had increased mental, physical, and social problems. Not surprisingly, being alone for long periods of time without social activity takes its toll. Once again, the combined adverse syndrome problems were far more severe among single men than single women. SROS persons had more frequent problems with alcohol addiction and drug abuse.

Increasing divorce rates continue to change our social landscape. Since 2005, unmarried couples are now the majority in an America previously dominated by married couples; in fact, 51 percent of women are living without a spouse. Interestingly, however, 54 percent of men are living with a spouse, girlfriend, or other female companion (mother?). Living alone does not mean being alone. Still, leaving a spouse or having been left by a spouse provides no reason to stay home drinking up Sundays and spending them alone. We are social beings and not meant to be alone for extended periods of time. We all need human companionship and the comforting camaraderie of others.

A word of caution ... be careful! Be on guard for associations of angry, bitter, and cynical groups who gather to wallow about their dissatisfied single status and disparage former spouses or lovers. These contaminated clusters of men or women should be avoided, for they are antagonistic to your return to good mental and emotional health. One doesn't get over unhappiness by gathering with pessimists, and you certainly do not want to become one of them by association or osmosis.

After Aida left, I continued my solitary morning and evening walks along the ocean. This time I did not feel the enormous emptiness experienced after my first divorce. I realized that my missing her would eventually ebb, that my pleasant memories of her would remain, and that I would again return to my previous state of good emotional health.

Whether it was your first or subsequent marriage, you know that marriages come with promises and perils, and pleasures and problems. For many of us who are now divorcing or already divorced, the number and realities of perils and problems may have surpassed the anticipated promises and pleasures that were delayed or never delivered. But wait! How much of your past marriage interruption had to do with an initial "poor choice" versus an inability to actively be in a meaningful relationship with another human being? If you married someone with extensive tattoos (Jesse James) and you do not have any markings of your own (Sandra Bullock), don't be surprised if your spouse later "hangs out" with someone similarly printed named *Bombshell* (while you are busy at work). Lack of shared interest may lead to other inevitable divides.

Whatever it was, something like this may have caused one of you to file or be served with divorce papers and, for now, to spend time alone. But wait; life goes on, as you must go on and complete your divorce and recovery. Your divorce time will pass and your recovery will follow. Remember, your times alone are like transitional single accommodation voyages, which are all self-booked. We are the ones who determine the mental destinations and durations of our stays in single status. We are the ones who can start a new way of life, where we elect to remain single but not alone. There are many interesting ways to spend your time and still make meaningful contributions in a community of giving to and helping others, while also helping ourselves.

Your single life may start anew. Post-divorce dating awaits you and there are many interesting people who would really appreciate getting to know you. Chapters 11 and 12 will provide helpful guidance on your new quest, be it dating many, cohabitating with one, or even later remarrying. No matter your choice, all of us will one day check out for good and will be left with only our final words on our burial epitaphs.

Here are interesting ones that sum up their positive life experiences:

- Mel Blanc: "Well, that's all folks."
- Jackie Gleason: "And away we go."
- Dean Martin: "Everybody Loves Somebody Sometime."
- Frank Sinatra: "The Best Is Yet To Come."
- Mine will read: "I knew I would end up here!"
- Anonymous: "She lived with her husband of 50 years And died in the hope of a better sex-life."

WHAT YOU NOW RECOGNIZE, UNDERSTAND, AND ACCEPT

1. There's a difference between being alone and being lonely.

2. Take this precious time to learn more about yourself and others.

3. Discover your deficits and start rebuilding your self-confidence, self-esteem, and self-worth.

4. Learn how to do and enjoy things on your own: movies, plays, books, and travel.

5. Remember: you are your own best company.

6. Take up a new hobby, interest, or activity.

7. Work on your emotional, mental, and physical health; they are all interrelated.

8. Take a trip, vacation, or a cruise just for the adventure of it.

9. There are many far worse off than you; however, they cope and still function as you should too.

10. Volunteer your time, energy, and spirit to help others; it pays well.

CHAPTER SIX

Reconciliation:

ANSWERS AND ATTITUDE ADJUSTMENTS

An Italian couple arrived for counseling with a prominent therapist. When asked what the problem was after 20 years of marriage, the wife went on a passionate, painful tirade listing each and every problem they'd experienced during their long troubled and loveless marriage.

She went on and on and on: neglect, lack of intimacy, emptiness, loneliness, feeling unloved and unlovable, an entire laundry list of unmet needs she had long endured.

Finally, after allowing this to go on for a sufficient length of time, the therapist stood up, walked around the desk and, after asking the wife to stand, he embraced and kissed her passionately as her husband watched with a raised eyebrow. The woman stopped talking and quietly sat down as though in a trance.

The therapist then turned to the husband and said, "This is what your wife needs at least three times a week. Can you do this?"

The husband thought for a moment and replied, "Well, I can drop her off here on Mondays and Wednesdays, but on Fridays, I play golf."

_____

Sometimes there is no hope! Some couples just cannot get past dead issues. In past chapters, I've repeatedly advised you to move on and get over "your departed" spouse. Still, many divorced individuals have had thoughts or even seriously considered reconciling their differences and returning to their strange, estranged spouse. I am neutral on this issue and address it here only to highlight critical realities and provide recommended guidelines.

Hence, this chapter carefully addresses the important issues and struggles faced by selected couples who have already filed for divorce or are contemplating filing on Monday, but reconcile their differences soon thereafter. We will also review recent reconciliation efforts (successful and unsuccessful) to look for common uniting threads, and missing required stitches. We will also examine triumphant reconciliations between those who divorced long ago but successfully reunited years later.

Men and women who have reached their individual marital breaking points often feel as though the deception, betrayal, and loss of trust are so great that nothing could repair damaged feelings. If you're one of those individuals, honor and respect your decision to divorce and realize that you are on the right track. Bear in mind, you're not a failure or a quitter. You merely realized the need to cut your losses and get out and away from your toxic past. All the same, if you're in the middle of your divorce or even if your divorce was completed long ago, you may still want to consider a possible reconciliation one day. One never knows. Two know even less.

There are only limited data on the number of filed divorces that are dropped or dismissed because of subsequent reconciliations. Anecdotal evidence supports the conclusion that the percentages are small. Post-divorce filing reconciliations may be in the limited range of 12 to 16 percent, with an estimated 6 to 7 percent becoming a successful reunion. The current number of successful reconciliations among those who *completed* their divorces is said to be even less, perhaps a 7 to 11 percent attempted rate with a much smaller success rate (3 to 5 percent). From the available statistics, it's clear that the rate of successful reconciliations continues to decline, while divorce rates increase or remain the same.

Only a small percentage of couples, struggling by themselves with their significant marital issues, are able to work through their problems to successful resolutions and remain married. Interestingly, Harrison Ford and Melissa Mathison, as well as Michael and Juanita Jordan, who were married 18 and 17 years respectively, found themselves in this situation. First Harrison and Michael each separated from their respective wives, then each filed for divorce. Next, both husbands reconciled with their respective wives, and both later separated again; soon thereafter, both completed their already-filed divorces.

Others attempting reconciliation are merely postponing the inevitable. Still others seek professional guidance and benefit from this help, but leave the marriage with noted improvements to be later shared with new partners.

Increases in marital stresses have greatly impacted the institution of marriage worldwide. One would think that corresponding increases in psychiatric and psychological clinical research would lead to improved marriage durations, as well as an increase in successful reconciliation ratios of interrupted marriages. Such, however, is not the case. Many claim these results are consistent with modern views that we live in a disposable society, where even marriage can be tossed out if no longer convenient to one of the spouses. This unpleasant reality is well documented in Andrew J. Cherlin's 2009 book, *The Marriage-Go-Round: The State of Marriage and the Family in America Today*, where he persuasively describes "Americans and their combinations of frequent marriage, frequent divorce and the great number of multiple short term cohabitation relationships."

Internal Reconciliations

As mentioned in Chapter 1 of this book, marriages are interrupted because of internal factors (strictly between the spouses), external factors (someone or something other than the other spouse), and collateral factors (events beyond the control of either spouse) — all of which are discussed below. We listed the three primary internal marriage interruption factors as money, sex, and poor communication.

Successful reconciliation prospects for internal factor marriage interruptions seem limited. Although money and communication problems are frequently curable by non-professional counseling, self-improvement classes, and other self-help alternatives, such is not the case for sexual intimacy issues. These deep-seated psychological problems often require professional intervention. Frequently, even professional assistance cannot resolve complex underlying causes.

While it's not rare to find marriages with money problems, sexual issues, and inadequate communication skills out of balance, is it possible to find marriages with all three factors out of kilter? This result raises the question: "How in the world did these people get together in the first place?" Granted, most individuals seek others of a similar type. We also choose people who complement our individual neuroses, yet it is possible to see marriages with imbalanced combinations of these three variables.

Perhaps a quick review of some of these combinations would be helpful for those contemplating reconciliation with someone who may have displayed the following.

- Money problems, great sex, and poor communication
- Money problems, bad sex, and good communication
- Money problems, bad sex, and terrible communication
- No money problems, bad sex, and poor communication
- No money problems, great sex, and great communication

Wow! What a list! It actually makes your head spin. It's like seeing *Death of a Salesman* three times in one day! We must slow down and look at these combinations individually.

1. Money problems, great sex, and poor communication

As good as the sex may be, and sometimes it is really great, it is still not enough. Life just has too many other demands and pressing necessities to carry it on great sex alone. Besides, you must pay the rent, buy lots of cigarettes (if you always smoke after sex), and also need to talk at least once in a while.

2. Money problems, bad sex, and good communication

Even if both of you were great communicators, this grouping is still not enough. An occasional good roll in the hay is necessary, and you no doubt have other things you would like to buy and do besides just talk, write, fax, or email each other.

3. Money problems, bad sex, and terrible communication

Good God! No money, bad sex, and bad communication is more than any individual should be forced to endure. This mixture is truly cruel and unusual punishment. Run, don't walk; get out of that situation. Wow, after all that, we need a cerebral bath!

4. No money problems, bad sex, and poor communication

Having money is great; however, it cannot buy long-term happiness (but you sure can have lots of short-term enjoyment). Having to live with someone with whom you cannot effectively communicate or enjoy in the bedroom, the kitchen, or other rooms, just makes life too difficult and often outright impossible.

5. No money problems, wonderful sex, and great communication

Hey, even if you do have all three, that still does not ensure that you'll enjoy your lives together. Divorce dockets are full of individuals with all three of the above who are divorced today (control issues can trump all three). Better yet, just look back on our celebrity list at the beginning and review what has happened to them. Again, look at the people you work with and your acquaintances. You're bound to see more of them there.

It seems that being out on their own works well for young single people, because being in charge of their own finances forces them to be more responsible. Perhaps being divorced and out on your own can also accelerate maturity and competence in communications and sometimes other areas, too.

Divorced spouses dating others realize that interpersonal communication can be difficult with new persons and not just former spouses.

Sometimes this realization helps divorced spouses appreciate what they had before. This awareness can also provide needed practice to help them better articulate what it is they need to say and want, and how to listen with attention to their partner's needs and wants. The communication-improved returning spouse may actually now actually be better suited for the former spouse than when married.

Sexual communication, performance, and satisfaction may sometimes improve and become less routine and robotic with new experiences. Post-divorce reconciliations occasionally achieve greater success where a spouse has gained knowledge which may help in filling in missing skills in their previous marriage. Being divorced can help with other problems, including drinking and gambling. Many a drunken spouse has benefited from their designated spouse driver. After she/he is gone, a DUI or two can help remedy the excessive drinking problems. Gambling is more expensive on a single income.

External Reconciliations

Of the three marriage interruption factors, it seems as if external-factor incomplete marriages present the best prospects for successful reconciliation. These incomplete marriages were deemed salvageable because one or both spouses had major control over the outside interruption cause. Remember, the still most common external-cause marital interruption is the extramarital affair, followed by in-laws and children.

Most marriages have external-factor distractions. Often couples have real problems lurking behind closed doors. Spouses are sometimes out of sync with each other's special needs or are oblivious to other spousal dependencies. Still, couples can have successful reconciliations without physical separations. Some couples have the tenacity to weather even the most difficult external-factor marital storms. Remember Hillary Clinton's public response immediately after the Monica incident? There was none! Oh, how we wish we could have been flies on the wall when Hillary let Bill have it, telling him how she really felt and not … .

This (*unprecedented* act of forgiveness) may have been the ultimate econciliation of them all, given the fact that:

- Everyone throughout the world knew about it.

- He went on national television and denied it.

- "It depends on what the meaning of 'is' is!"

- He said, "I did not have sexual relations with that woman [Hillary?], Miss Lewinsky."

- He later said, "Indeed, I did have a relationship with Miss Lewinsky that was not appropriate."

Unsuccessful Reconciliations

If the Clintons had the number-one reconciliation of all time, then the second unsurpassed reconciliation [attempt] had to be the John and Elizabeth Edwards effort. While running for president, and being watched by almost everyone, John Edwards engaged in conduct said to be an *infamia* (the Italian word for total disgrace involving scandalous and immoral wrongful conduct, like cheating on your spouse when she is ill) relating to a major breach of trust given the fact that:

- He repeatedly denied the affair on national television.

- He was later caught at the Los Angeles Hilton where his mistress was staying.

- He later admitted the affair, but continued to deny his child's paternity.

- On January 21, 2010, he said: "I am Quinn's father."

- On January 22, 2010, Elizabeth Edwards said: "That's it; I'm out of here!"

After repeated strong denials, former presidential candidate John Edwards finally admitted to the world that his extramarital affair was allegedly caused by his narcissism: $400 haircuts, removal of a facial mole, the devil ("Yes, the devil made me do it!") and, of course, all of those long-days working at the mill. He finally disclosed his love child's paternity 528 days later; this was the last straw for their reconciliation. Elizabeth filed for divorce. Thus we see that total honesty and full disclosure are reconciliation prerequisites, for nothing can make a bad situation worse than additional lies. Also noted was the fact that President Bill had the wise counsel of Jesse Jackson (who had his own recent love child experience). Perhaps John Edwards should have conferred with Jesse.

There are always numerous couples going through the reconciliation process; some spouses separate, while others never return from going to have their nails done or going out for a newspaper.

Tiger Woods and his wife Elin were not reconciliation candidates. One, two, and then four sexual companions seemed certainly beyond the pale! Five, seven, and then more (some report that Tiger confessed to over 100 sexual encounters) were far too much for anyone to bear. They divorced in August 2010.

Let's review their history. Husbands caught in *unacceptable behavior* must initiate immediate recovery action. Wealthy husbands usually do it via enhanced postnuptial agreements proceeds, a new car, or allowing their mother-in-law to move in with them. Tiger's multiple bogies in his now "mulligan marriage," resulted in an immediate offer to Elin. Ostensibly, if she remained married to Tiger for an additional two years, Elin stood to receive $60 million (existing $20 million payout, plus an additional $35 million, plus $5 million signing bonus) for staying with Tiger for an additional 24 months. Let's do the math: $60 million over 24 months yields $2,500,000/month, divided by 30 days, equals $83,333/day, which is $3,472/hour. How do you spell YES? A counteroffer, of course.

Next, Tiger made it abundantly clear at his late February 2010 press conference (she was not there with him, which was not a good sign) that he and his wife were working on his problems (she did accompany him to a few therapy sessions). Initially, media pundits suggested that Tiger allow his wife to file for divorce. As such, they surmised, Tiger would be viewed as just another professional athlete who faltered, tried to save his marriage, but was left by an *unforgiving* wife.

In my law classes, one of my students would surely have asked: *"What would you have recommended?"* I would have suggested a multipurpose Solomonic plan that would have accomplished several goals. First, I would have worked at saving their strained marriage; second to provide for Elin's future financial security; and third to sanction Tiger (in a corporate sponsor/ general public acceptable manner) that would not be an oppressive overkill of Tiger's valuable (but fading) name brand. While a $5 million "staying/ signing bonus" seemed significant, it was apparently less than one percent of Tiger's reported $600 million net worth. I would have recommended that Tiger offer a $100 million signing bonus, payable one-third now and the balance over the next two years. After all, Tiger earned an estimated $110 million in 2008. Still, $100 million is a reasonable and fair amount because it is more than fair to both. Tiger might have kept his marriage together, and still retained 83 percent of his alleged net worth after transferring a mere 17 percent to Elin.

Tiger would have appeared more sincere and contrite; Elin would have come across as being reasonable and not overreaching. This would certainly have helped shield his corporate sponsors from further criticism and would also have promoted forgiveness from a hostile public. Still, his corporate sponsors are public corporations with millions of shareholders, guarded public images and the obvious fear of being associated with someone as controversial. Several corporate backers have already severed their sponsorships with Tiger, others may follow; Nike, it seems, will stay.

Perhaps, rather than offering a fixed lump-sum payout for staying married as mentioned above, Tiger's legal team should have considered offering a "floating percentage-based payout" (10 to 20 percent, or combinations thereof) from Tiger's annual income to Elin for 10 years, or so long as they remain married. This it seems may have been a better choice for both. Tiger would not have been strapped with a fixed-figure payment in bad years and both would have benefited in good years.

Just as with Howard Hughes' unique spousal support payments, a floating percentage based on the consumer price index (see Chapter 8), Tiger could have comfortably shared his earnings with his wife. Elin would have been reassured that she'd be well provided for, and, most important of all, Tiger (a Buddhist himself) might have rehabilitated himself by adhering to total *arhat* (the Buddhists' term for enlightenment), and the acronym for attention, respect, honesty, affection, and trust. This alternative would have been more acceptable to his mother-in-law, corporate sponsors, and angry general public, as well as to antagonistic commentators, fans, and others who have attacked his multiple transgressions. The bottom line, Tiger should not have been oppressively punished for what he did, and Elin should not have received a windfall; nevertheless, Elin would have been expected to act as the dutiful wife, accompanying her husband to scheduled events and appearances in a state of loving normalcy.

At first, rumors estimated that Elin would possibly end up with as much as $360 to $720 million. Sure, Tiger became the first athlete to earn a cumulative $1 billion; however, that was before taxes and overhead expenses. Tiger's eventual divorce settlement was for a reported $100 million to Elin, their former residence in Florida, plus endless child support beyond the norm. This settlement likely was paid in a lump-sum spousal support settlement. Tiger likely paid all of Elin's income-tax deductible attorney fees and costs ($3 to $7 million range).

Tiger's 2010-11 lackluster performance on the greens may possibly be due to an orchestrated to keep his 2010-11 earnings at a modest level (greater earnings could trigger additional support payments to Elin?). Let's see if Tiger's late 2011 game suddenly improve and higher solo game earnings are won. Tiger's skilled lawyers likely negotiated a lower spousal support settlement by having Tiger forego available federal and state income tax deductions for paid spousal support (again, Tiger's marginal performances on the greens and recessionary earnings on his investments support the conclusion that Tiger did not need any 2010-11 income tax deductions). Elin, of course, would also have benefited from not having to declare her support as taxable income. Elin will still retain her strong public sympathy for not having come across as being a greedy, vindictive, and oppressive ex-wife. Still, it was sad to see a 70-month marriage with two toddler-age children end (even with a $1.42 million/month, $47,619/ day divorce settlement). In this divorce, everyone lost: Tiger, Elin, and their kids, as well as their families, golf fans, and (likely) the U.S. Treasury.

Whatever the outcome, we will never know the exact details unless Tiger has a guilt-driven epiphany and tells us how much he paid Elin.

Rest assured that the final settlement was signed, sealed, and delivered to only their attorneys; in addition, the likely *preapproved* September 2010 *People* magazine article, with 12 pages, and lots of large color pictures, was helpful to all concerned. Certainly the settlement agreement contained a comprehensive confidentially clause forever prohibiting Elin from making the rounds with Barbara Walters, Diane Sawyer, Oprah, or any other such public forums to mention, discuss, or brag about her settlement or to write a book on her life with Tiger.

Injured spouses and the general public usually forgive those who are truly penitent and sincerely remorseful. Most celebrities, public officials, and others we hold in high esteem—but who have crossed the line—have been compelled to go on public television with Barbara, Diane, or Oprah and apologize for their transgressions. Somehow these public confessions seem to work and members of the public have now come to expect them. President Clinton and Kobe Bryant redeemed themselves via their confessions. Then there are those who make partial admissions, while withholding other material facts (John Edwards' extended denial of his love child's paternity?). Former President Nixon did neither, but rehabilitated himself by becoming a respected senior statesman via his prolific writing. Granted, there was no need for Tiger to come forth and give us the details of his indiscretions; besides, several of his mistresses have already done much of it for him. If you ever find yourself in this situation, always tell the truth and nothing but the full truth, for it will eventually come out. You also do not want to lose total credibility or cause further pain to others.

Paying the piper sometimes requires keeping everyone happy. I once represented a 15-year married woman whose spouse had been involved in similar unacceptable husband behavior. Negotiations led to a new postnup that provided for a $456,789.10 (one-third of his net-worth) payout to my client if they divorced, and an annual $7,654.32 payment to her mother, from my client's unfaithful spouse. I had her husband agree, in addition, to bring his mother-in-law along with them on semi-annual ocean cruises. Later, his attorney made a counteroffer whereby his client would increase the mother-in-law's annual allowance to $9,876.54, without her accompanying our respective clients on their ocean cruises. My client's mother willingly accepted the counteroffer.

But wait again. Two months after the negotiations were finalized, my client contacted me again. This time she wanted me to invite her husband's attorney to accompany her mother (they had met at my office when signing the final settlement agreements) on a cruise to South America—all expenses paid, of course. He graciously accepted. They had a great time and are planning to go [Dutch] next year.

Collateral Reconciliations

As would be expected, collateral-factor marriage interruptions, over which neither spouse had any control or influence, present the least redeemable reconciliation prospects. These precipitous interruptions can cause or affect one or both spouses, to the degree where one could not cope with the resulting consequences mentioned in Chapter 1. Often there are no hopes or possible reconciliations in these troubled situations unless the affected spouse undergoes a major transformation.

Reconciliation Requirements

Now that we have considered all three major internal causes of marriage interruptions, let's take a closer look at other necessary requirement factors for successful reconciliations. Interest in reconciliation seems to blossom during holiday seasons, because we frequently recall pleasant, shared times with ex-spouses, family, and others who were once close. Those who are alone are even more susceptible to these pleasant memories. Sometimes reconciliation efforts can work; however, without competent couples's counseling and heaps of hard work from both estranged or ex-spouses, couples frequently fall back into the same familiar patterns and destructive practices.

Successful reconciliations are often based on change, cooperation, and compassion. Divorce and separation frequently stem from spousal selfishness, unrealistic desires to be married, and the need, always, to have it *one's own way*. Many spouses put themselves first, their children second, and their parents third, then golf, tennis, or fishing fourth, followed by traveling, and their marriages sometimes sixth or seventh.

These selfish spouses need to be retrained to realize their marriage, and not they, come first; both spouses are second, and then everyone else. Insensitive spouses must also be reprogrammed to acknowledge and accept that successful marriages require trading off and taking turns in getting things one's own way. Whether it is vacations, restaurants, wine choices, movies, new wallpaper selections, or even who's on top tonight, each should get her/his turn. Again, this "me first syndrome" (MFS) is not only selfish, immature, and unreasonable, it is unacceptable.

Divorced or divorcing couples contemplating reconciliation must have a good therapist to coach and guide them through the difficult reconciliation process. There are situations in life when professional assistance is required. Marital reconciliation is certainly one of them. Here are a few good suggestions from my psychology colleagues to consider:

- Couples seriously contemplating reconciliation should first meet jointly with their therapists to review past issues that caused them to divorce in the first place. Meeting together is more powerful and productive than doing so individually.

- Couples could list the desired/required changes they need to see in the other ex-spouse, as well as concessions and compromises they would be willing to make toward their reconciliation objectives.

- Couples must honestly and objectively review and discuss their lists to determine if common ground may exist on negotiable issues or whether it's hopeless and unachievable wishful thinking.

Of course, almost anything is possible, provided both individuals are willing to accommodate. There are certain things, however, which must be accepted as unchangeable and that even couples's therapy can't change. If you simply cannot accept your ex-spouse's uncorrectable weight, drinking, or other actions, and you'll also not budge on your demands, then there's no need to proceed further.

If, on the other hand, you find some behavior that can be modified or overcome, then you may have something worth pursuing. Often, successful attitudinal adjustments and behavioral modifications, based on compassion and compromise, come to those who are accommodating and loving.

Couples involved in the reconciliation process must realize that overcoming past problems requires a joint effort. The ex/estranged spouse requesting the change must be sympathetic, supportive, and supersensitive to the other spouse's effort and commitment. The ex/estranged spouse attempting the modification must be committed to the change, dedicated to the necessary behavior modification, and tenacious in their efforts to reach their goals.

Spouses from all walks of life marry, divorce, and remarry each other again. Is this phenomenon more common than we think? No one knows for sure how many divorced couples remarry, because neither the National Statistics nor the Census Bureau keeps track. The answers as to why divorced couples remarry each other again after divorcing may be as complicated as why they divorce in the first place. Many, no doubt, found solutions to their past problems (former lover moved to France; mother-in-law died; ex-spouse stopped smoking, or lost 35 pounds). Some needed time apart to grow up (I can't always have it my way?), and others needed to realize that the grass was not greener on the other side after all.

Often, remarrying a former spouse can be easier than taking on a new partner. In one sense you'll not be starting all over again. You do not have to acquire new towels, get new driver's licenses, or obtain other name-change required documents. What about marrying a spouse similarly named? Johnny Carson married three women named JoAnna/Joanne and one Alexis. While he may have saved on monogrammed towels, he paid dearly on spousal support. Johnny first married Jody "JoAnna" Morrill Wolcott in October 1949; they were 23-year-old college sweethearts. They split in 1963 (he kept calling her Joanne). Next, there was Joanne Copeland. Wedding date: August 1963; he was 37, she was 31. They divorced in 1972 (Johnny kept calling her JoAnna). Then Johnny married the much younger JoAnna Holland months later in September of 1972, and they divorced in 1983 (he kept calling her Joanne). Finally there was Alexis, who was walking along the beach holding an empty wine glass near Johnny's home at Malibu, California. He saw her on the beach and ran up to fill her glass. They married in June 1987 (he at the age of 61, she at 35). Finally, new towels! They remained married till Johnny's death in January of 2005 (he was 79).

Reconciliation and remarriage with a former spouse may have other collateral benefits. There's usually no need to reestablish roles because both are already familiar with their spouse's good, bad, and ugly aspects. Some spouses actually do change and have undergone major behavioral or attitudinal transformations, either on their own or as a part of an orchestrated reconciliation program. Financial parameters do not have to be relearned or reestablished, but, perhaps, adjusted to newer incomes or expenses. Spousal emotional ties do not have to be rebuilt. Then again, perhaps they should be replaced to avoid past repetitive problems.

Now, besides saving on towels, marrying a new spouse with the same name as the former spouse(s) protects both men and women from innocently or inadvertently calling out the wrong name during moments of excitement, joy, or great sex. It's also good when seeing lost and former friends whom you have not seen for a number of years. Chances are they will remember her/his name but not the face, for we all age with time.

Every now and then divorced couples do not formally reconcile, but stay in close touch and actively interact with one another. Such was the case with Dean Martin and Jeanne, his second wife of 24 years. Like Sinatra, Dean divorced three times. Sinatra at the age of 50 married Mia Farrow (age 21) in 1966. Dean at the age of 56 married Catherine Hawn (age 26) in 1973 (monkey see, monkey do). Frank's marriage to Mia lasted only two years; Dean's marriage to Catherine lasted three years. After Dean's third divorce, he and former second ex-wife Jeanne Martin remained close friends. Eventually, Dean and Jeanne reconciled their romantic relationship, though they never re-married. They would meet at the now closed Romeo & Juliet's French Restaurant in Beverly Hills and later at *DaVinci Ristorante* on Little Santa Monica, in Dean's reserved booth, for quiet weekly Wednesday dinners.

While the following does not bear directly on divorce issues, it demonstrates that often other concerned persons (children, parents, good friends, business partners, and others) will step in to help. Such was the case when Dean made a public reconciliation with Jerry Lewis on Lewis's Labor Day Muscular Dystrophy telethon in 1976. Sinatra shocked Lewis and the world by bringing Dean out on stage. As Martin and Lewis hugged and smiled, after not speaking to each other for over 10 years, the audience erupted in cheers and the phone banks lit up, resulting in the telethon's most profitable hour ever to date. See, another successful cerebral coffee break. I told you it works.

Keep in mind that the admonitions in the Introduction are applicable to reconciliations because you may end up in the same place: alone again.

> Finally, be forewarned: divorcing and returning to the single life is sometimes not as exciting, glamorous, or romantic as it is portrayed in movies, television, and stories from other singles. To some, the remaining groups of eligible, single men and women may leave much to be desired.

Although reconciliation is not always a viable option, the foregoing admonitions make it apparent that dateable people have their own problems. For these reasons, reconciliation may remain one possible alternative to be considered before fully closing the door on this option. Also, beware of stress-free, easygoing tender traps. While stress is a necessary component in our daily lives, it sometimes impacts us in harmful ways. Going on a cruise, vacation, or other stress-free activity with your ex before deciding to reconcile may not be a good idea; instead, get back into the boiler (invite your mother over for a week or two) with him/her and see how he/she reacts in this situation (you may not want to reconcile after all). After all, we spend most of our time in the stress-filled boiler, as distinct from the occasional restful and relaxing cruises and other low-stress romantic tender trap activities.

What to Look For

First, review the details prescribed in Chapter 2: *Departing with Dignity.* As mentioned therein, did your ex leave with class, dignity, and respect? Were you a Jackie Kennedy or a Cary Grant, leaving yourself eligible for a possible reconciliation? Was he or she mean or rude, thereby closing the reconciliation door forever? It's like leaving a job. Never ever burn your bridges when leaving; you may want to come back one day or need a reference for your next job.

Ex-spouses sometimes regain favor when they lose a successor spouse or new lover. These now abandoned former spouses come calling, seeking the comfort and counsel of their still trusted ex-spouses. Talking things over with a caring person helps them heal their open emotional wounds.

But beware, for emotionally unbalanced former spouses are vulnerable and usually not good reconciliation candidates while in transition. Give them at least eight months to recover before seeing them on a permanent basis. Sometimes, post-divorce reconciliation and remarriage with a former spouse can work. After all, former spouses come with previous approval, shared histories, and other welcomed factors. This chapter includes several celebrity divorced couples that remarried each other again after their first divorce. Sometimes it works; often it doesn't and they return to court for a second divorce (Elizabeth Taylor and Richard Burton, as well as Steve and Elaine Wynn, and many others).

Reconciliations based on sympathy, sadness, or support needs are specious justifications for getting back together with someone you may have once loved. Concerns about your children's welfare and support, and other such unilateral altruistic needs, may not be in your long-term best interests.

Most of the foregoing *pressing reasons* seem to be transitory and subject to correction with the passage of time or proactive action on your part. Children will eventually grow up, become self-sufficient, and leave the nest. Continuing education study can bring new employment opportunities and enhance your economic earnings. These realities can help you can overcome the pressures that may have pushed you earlier. Still, sometimes reconciliations can lead to lasting reunions.

When you review the available literature and selected case studies on successful post-divorce reconciliations, several common characteristics appear. Here is a brief list for your review:

- Successful reconciliations occur where the past break-up was devoid of the acrimonious high drama or lasting traumas associated with most divorces. There is little or no blood left on the carpet.

- Divorced couples who maintain high degrees of mutual respect and open communication are good candidates for possible reconciliation.

- Both former spouses are back on track after their divorce. These individuals have improved their personal profiles via enhanced personal growth and other advancements brought about by therapy and other successful self-improvement experiences.

- In various successful reconciliations, some men and only several women have been involved in other relationships. These experiences may provide welcomed improvement about missing skills.

- Post-divorce relationships may provide a valuable resource for a former spouse to compare the new person with the past spouse, to realize possibly, that the former spouse was really not that bad (and perhaps even better).

It has been said:

> Tis better to have loved and lost
> Than never to have loved at all.
> Alfred Lord Tennyson

> Then again, there's:
> It is better to have loved and lost
> Than never to have lost at all.
> Samuel Butler

Again, look at the people in the front of this book, and your family and friends. For most it has taken three, four, and sometimes as many as eight (Larry King) or nine (Zsa Zsa Gabor) marriages to get it right.

Standards and Alternatives

It seems as if there has been a recent lowering of spousal selection standards in first, second, and subsequent remarriages, as well as in reconciliations thereafter. While the inventories of single and divorced people continue to increase across America and abroad, these groups are compressed and quickly shrink when you add in the word *quality.* Problems of being single or divorced and getting older seems to be greater for women than men. Reconciliation for both sexes is also impacted throughout the world by divorced couples who opted out of remarriage, and chose instead to cohabitate with an ex-spouse without commitment, which can be easily ended by simply posting a *Thirty-Day Notice to Quit.* Cohabitation rates have increased enormously over the last generation; still, cohabitation longevity is far less stable.

Finally, perhaps the paramount reconciliation characteristic is a spouse's attitude. Most of what has been reviewed in this chapter could be wrapped into one word: ATTITUDE. "I now have a better attitude." Oh, how often we must have wished we could have heard these sweet, wonderful words from a former spouse. Sometimes attitudinal issues leave lasting, injured feelings, especially where one spouse is sincerely attempting to help in a difficult situation that is under the exclusive control of the other spouse (like unfortunate, battered Luke in Chapter 2).

Sometimes, time alone or with others helps bring attitudinal changes for separated and divorced spouses. Separated and divorcing individuals experience severe stresses in their breakups; for some, acceptance or realization of their shortcomings brought to their attention by others becomes the necessary "wake-up call." Oh! "It was because of me (as super-stubborn John in Chapter 1 and several of the other men and women referred to in this book)! Sadly, many post-divorce redeemed spouses later discover that they were the cause of their divorce and that their former spouse has moved on, has remarried, and is no longer available.

Reconciliation is even more difficult because of unknown relationship personality abnormalities perhaps not yet realized. Problematic personality types that warrant caution in attempted reconciliation are spouses who may have been co-dependent or passive-aggressive.

Co-Dependent Spouses

Psychologists define co-dependency as a fixed pattern of detrimental behavioral interactions within a dysfunctional relationship. Marriage can be a natural nest for codependency, because codependent behaviors can be explained away as the actions of a devoted and [over caring] loving spouse. Marriages with mutually dependent spouses, where one spouse is addicted (the dependent) to alcohol, drugs, or gambling, or other uncontrolled self-destructive behavior, are common. These mutually dependent marriages provide their partners with a life-long mission and a cause to go on, and on.

If you or your former spouse were an individual who exhibited excessive or often inappropriate caring (enabling, masquerading as being compassionate) for each other, you may be codependent. You may unconsciously have been one side of a marriage of mutually needy people. The dependent spouse typically characterizes such marriages. The codependent spouse exhibits behavior that controls, enables, and excuses the other spouse's abnormal actions. These over caring spouses unwittingly perpetuate the needy spouse's condition and weakness by becoming their enabler; they seek to rescue and take care of their troubled spouse. Sometimes, both spouses have the same degree of neediness; usually, however, their needs are different. Often these spouses erode their own self-esteem via negative or unappreciated compliment responses. They continuously judge themselves harshly, which lowers their self-esteem even further.

She says, "You really look great in those slacks." He says, "Oh, I have to lose five pounds." Another compliment: He says, "I really like your hair." Another discount: She says, "Oh, I have to get it cut." After repeated discounted compliments, the other spouse stops offering praise because it is not appreciated and it adds further negative tension to the couple's already festering unhappiness.

Whether you're the dependent or the codependent ex-spouse, your reconciliation situation could be more difficult because, as a dependent, you may no longer need someone to comfort and talk to you. As the codependent, you may no longer need someone to care for. These problems, if not recognized and repaired, will impede reconciliation efforts significantly.

Passive-Aggressive Personalities

Next, the passive-aggressive personality: this military term was coined to refer to personnel who appeared to comply aggressively with an order, yet undermined what needed to be done in a passive manner. They are often said to be their own worst enemy. In the process, these persons can become increasingly angry and hostile. Many resent responsibility and show it through their conduct rather than by openly expressing their feelings. They employ a host of behaviors to avoid doing what has been requested of them. They express their anger in covert and clandestine ways, usually by withholding things they know you want or need, including affection, approval, and sex. The moment you let a passive-aggressive person know you like something, you had best prepare to do without it.

Remember, a passive-aggressive spouse does not know how to say, "That hurts my feelings," or "That makes me angry." Like Michael *Controlleone*, the confident, calculating protagonist in Mario Puzo's novels, they handle their problems differently. Consider, too, that in addition to Michael *Controlleones* there are Michelle *Controlleones*, and both are confident, cold, and calculating when it comes to stabbing you in the back, while smiling at you the entire time. They come off as being such good people who would never do anything to hurt you. All the while, they are secretly punishing you in ways that make you doubt your sanity. If you have been in a former marriage with a Michael or Michelle *Controlleone* personality who seemed too good to be true, then it probably was. Past positive recollections may not be the same. Be careful if you're considering reconciling with one of the *Controlleones*.

Be careful you do not get trampled or blindsided by someone you feel you [really] know!

WHAT YOU NOW RECOGNIZE, UNDERSTAND, AND ACCEPT

1. As Pattie LaBelle should have said: "Perhaps you, too, can get a new attitude."

2. Reconciliations are few; successful reconciliations fewer yet.

3. External-factor marriage interruptions (with effective counseling) provide the best odds for reconciliation.

4. Post-divorce civility by your former spouse is a big plus.

5. Altruistic and economic reasons/needs are not good reasons to reconcile.

6. Couples must first write down what they need and expect, as well as what they will give up and forgive.

7. You should have a competent psychotherapist to coach and guide you.

8. Your estranged spouse may still be strange: be alert and cautious.

9. Money, sex problems, and lack of communication cause the majority of marriage interruptions.

10. Beware of MFS (me first syndrome) and passive-aggressive reconcilers.

CHAPTER SEVEN

Sisters & Brothers, We're Not Alone

Law firms are turning heads with new billboard blunt messages:

You may have already seen 20-foot-high billboard messages, as the one on the previous page, in Atlanta, Boston, and Chicago, as well as in West Virginia, Wisconsin, and Wyoming. Lawyers! Such signs have sparked negative reactions from local churches, marriage counselors, and divorce lawyers, as well as from plumbers, other lawyers, and the general public. Even the ladies on The View expressed their dissatisfaction.

Divorce and Remarriage

Divorce season is now a year-round event. Dating and married couples occasionally get into troublesome squabbles with legal repercussions. Charlie Sheen may be a recent example. Amazingly, he has been charged with several offenses, including possession of controlled substances, and parole violations, and he has even had various arrest warrants issued. Back in 1990, Charlie *accidentally* shot then-fiancée Kelly Preston (the current Mrs. John Travolta) in the arm. Charlie was not charged, but Kelly broke off the engagement immediately thereafter.

Next, Charlie used his *get out of a felony card* back in 1997 in Los Angeles, when he was allowed to enter a no-contest plea to reduced misdemeanor domestic battery charges, dealing with a heated incident with a then-girlfriend. In 2006 Charlie and his second wife, Denise Richards, went through an acrimonious divorce. The divorce included Denise's detailed 37-paragraph declaration (under penalty of perjury) regarding Charlie's alleged alcohol, drug, and gambling abuses, as well as other vices she reported witnessing during their 33-month marriage.

Teflon Charlie's latest marital criminal charges deal with one alleged felony and two misdemeanor domestic violence charges on Christmas Day 2009 in Aspen, Colorado. Allegedly, Charlie and his (third) wife, Brooke, may have both been under the influence when "heated words" were followed with what may have possibly been "threatening acts" (this marriage also did not last). It seems as if the resolution of this episode will likely include more creative lawyering: plea to a third-degree misdemeanor charge, with a suspended jail sentence, plus anger management classes, community service, probation, and possibly Charlie giving acting lessons and autographs to the local prosecutors and judges.

Sometimes a couple's stormy union is off, then on, then off again. Such was the case for actors Sean Penn and Robin Wright during their stormy marriage. They married first in 1996. Eleven years later (a success in itself), Sean allegedly initiated divorce proceedings in December 2007 but reconciled weeks later. On or about April of 2009, Sean filed for a legal separation but again withdrew his request after several days. Their third was a divorce filing in August 2009. This time it was Robin's call; their divorce was finalized in July 2010.

Marriage can be a bumpy road for all of us, yet marriages subjected to serial separations and successive divorce filings seem doomed, and then usually do not last because of the trauma that preceded their multiple filings. It's like repeatedly pulling a potted plant out of its pot to see if its roots are growing, then pushing it back into the pot, and expecting it to live. Sean and Robin, as well as many other married couples, have endured multiple separation/divorce filings. While it may be a good way of getting someone's attention, these practices are often not productive and sometimes even backfire. Here's the circular thinking this conduct often generates: my spouse is unhappy in our marriage; I'm unhappy in our marriage; thus, we are both unhappy. Since we are both unhappy, I should leave. Instead of leaving, couples experiencing these explosive episodes should seek professional Italian counseling: my mother or yours? Sure, it's always easier to be a Monday-morning quarterback, although, in the heat of marriage battle we are not as rational as we would be when calm. Departing spouses often take preemptive action, such as emptying joint savings accounts, taking available cash or the dog.

In March 2009, casino and resort developers Steve and Elaine Wynn, both 67 and married for 41 years with a five-year respite in the middle, announced that they were ending their 18-year second marriage. Elaine will remain on the Board of Directors of the vast Wynn Development holdings. Like many other divorcing couples, countless individual spouses can work and intelligently interact together but can no longer live together.

One month later, in April, Mel Gibson's wife, Robyn, filed for divorce after 28 years of marriage, seven children, and Mel's younger then-pregnant Russian girlfriend Oksana; thus, we see that even tenured marriages are not always lasting.

In October, Mel himself said, "I guess I'm Octo-Mel." Six months later in April 2010, Mel and Oksana had a heated separation and went their separate ways; soon after, they were embroiled in an even hotter custody battle with super-heated tape-recorded words flying in mid June.

In mid-September of 2008, New York Yankees star Alex Rodriguez, 33, and Cynthia Rodriguez, 35, reached a final divorce settlement and ended their five-and-a-half-year marriage. Cynthia had filed for divorce in July 2008, claiming that Alex was repeatedly unfaithful (at least he was consistent). There were allegations of a romance with pop star Madonna, which both repeatedly denied. The terms of Alex and Cynthia's settlement were not disclosed; however, both sides said it was fair. Alex was in the first year of a 10-year contract that pays him a total of $275 million. Needless to say, Cynthia can continue to shop at Bloomingdale's and Bergdorf Goodman's every day.

Dual-Income Marriages

In this age of dual spousal employment, problems associated with dual careers have impacted marriages as never before. These clashes include work-related stresses, accompanying quarrels, and further reductions in spending necessary quality spousal time together. While most of us work, the career-work concept is compounded for the driven, extra-motivated, and self-employed. This reality is particularly prevalent in the professions of law and medicine, as well as in the entertainment industry. These careers are well known for their long hours, lack of marital quality spousal time, and higher-than-average divorce rates. Like many others, I've been in this group of workaholics; since age 12, I've worked two jobs simultaneously.

Men used to be the high-income earners in traditional marriages. Recent changes in the economic horizon have created new problems for marriage partners in this once tranquil area. Dual-income marriages where the female spouse is the higher income earner present a multitude of problems. Today, 24 percent of working wives earn more than their employed husbands. This trend will resume as women continue to be graduated from college and professional schools in greater numbers than men (presently 54 percent for women and 45 percent for men).

Younger individuals are not as entrenched in traditional gender roles about money as are their older counterparts. Once again we see, especially for those in mid-life, the fragile male ego threatened as the *once-assumed provider status* is taken away. In some of these marriages, the female spouse attains sudden success during the marriage, while in others it has been in place long before the marriage. It's easy to accept that some male spouses may have difficulty adjusting to their wives' newfound success. There's less pity for husbands who come to the problem they complain about only later. Hey, they saw the writing on the checks. They knew what was ahead, so why should they complain now?

In mid-July 2008, Madonna denied she was getting divorced. By mid-October, news of her divorce resurfaced and this time it was not denied. Madonna, 50, will pay Guy Ritchie, 41, $76 million to bring an end to their property dispute. The divorce, claimed Ritchie, had nothing to do with dollars. Of course not; it was about pounds (£). Ritchie said, "I'm just a guy named Guy. She's *Madonna!*" Again, let's do the math: $76 million over an eight-year marriage yields $9,500,000/year. This equals $26,027.39/day, and comes to $1,084.47 each and every hour. Not bad. Bloody good, in fact! I'm certain that Madonna's clever lawyers packaged this settlement with tax-deductible items, like her payment of his attorney fees, to save her a few dollars and still sweeten the deal for the guy named Guy.

The acrimonious battle royale between former supermodel Christie Brinkley and architect husband Peter Cook (fourth divorce for each) was sensational but short-lived. Christie's divorce trial came to an abrupt end the second Thursday in July 2008. Lawyers for the couple reached an out-of-court settlement, in part because of embarrassing findings from the court-appointed psychiatrist, who chastised both for being inadequate parents and having other significant personal issues. The psychiatrist allegedly went on to say, "Peter was a narcissist who needed constant reassurance that he was an accomplished, handsome, and terrific guy."

What is a narcissist? How can you tell? Any individual more concerned about her/his own individual needs while consistently ignoring the needs of others qualifies as a real narcissist. Narcissistic character traits include excessive self-admiration, self-centeredness, and self-regard.

In addition, there is being self-congratulatory and just self! Sound familiar? If you were married to a narcissist, you may have unwittingly contributed to the problem because narcissists seem to gravitate to low self-esteem individuals, those who will always admire and adore them in the manner in which they need to be relentlessly revered, respected, and reassured.

Sound marriages include healthy communication between spouses who can respond and react favorably to their partner's emotional needs. Individuals married to narcissists often subordinate personal needs for fear of losing the narcissist. Now that we know a little more about the personality type, we can better understand the three-month post-divorce settlement comments made by Peter:

> I blame my ex-wife's lack of emotional
> support for my affair. I cheated
> because I was seeking a connection I
> could not find in my own marriage.
> My ex-wife and I were more like
> brother and sister. I just wanted a little
> acknowledgement, a little attention,
> a little thank you every now and then
> for my efforts, for the amount of time
> I took to care of us and my family, for
> the wealth I was building.

Taking your emotional needs outside the marriage is unacceptable and brings stress to everyone involved. It is a clear violation of trust and commitment. To a degree, however, I can empathize with Peter. His listed complaints, lack of acknowledgement, attention, and a little thank you now and then, are familiar rings on the emotional cell phones of men and women today. I've seen countless other attention-, affection-, and appreciation-deprived men and women receive these familiar *phone rings* (Betty, Ruth, and Ralph in Chapter 1). Petty jealousies, along with bruised male and female egos are common; they surface in marriages where one or both spouses are self-centered and caught up in their own worlds.

Still, even hassled husbands and wounded wives need acknowl-edgement, attention, and a little thank you now and then. This problem is easy to recognize, and so easy to fix, though offending spouses are often oblivious to this moral, yet simple, obligation. How much time does it take to tell someone that you appreciate them? What does it take to give a peck, kiss, smile, a quick "I love you," or other small token of affection? What does it cost to verbalize gratitude?

Fear of divorce is far greater than the fear of marriage, yet divorce rates are still rising worldwide. Nearly 54 percent of America's adult population of 260 million is married, including some who are separated but not yet divorced. Divorce rates are supposedly declining in America, but there's no accurate count because this rate applies only to states that track the number of divorces. California, Colorado, Georgia, and Hawaii, as well as Indiana, Louisiana and Minnesota, do not. In this age of austere budgets, shrinking tax revenues and federal bailouts, it's likely that more states will cease keeping data on divorce statistics.

During the 1950s, more than 90 percent of married couples stayed together for 10 years or more. By the 1990s this percentage had fallen to below 50 percent. In recent years (a.k.a. the Viagra years), older adults have been getting divorced after they turn 50, 60, and even 70 years old. Hugh Hefner, the 83-year-old founder of *Playboy* magazine, filed for divorce in September 2009, seeking to end his marriage to 47-year-old former playmate Kimberley Conrad, after a 12-year separation (they were married July of 1989 and separated in January 1998) funded with his $1 million per year support payments.

Everyone was caught by surprise when Al and Tipper Gore's 40-year (near) perfect marriage came to a "mutually mutual" separation in the first week of June 2010. Appearances are not always what they seem; given the Monica incident and the nationally televised convention-nomination extended kiss, it was the Clintons, not the Gores, who seemed headed for divorce court.

Today, couples in their 60s (Al is 62, Tipper is 60) can end a lifeless (second, third, or other) marriage, take time to find a new spouse, and still look forward to twenty-plus years of *new* marital bliss, because life at sixty today is not what it used to be.

Given the graying of America, the little blue pill, and green light for extended life expectancies, we are likely to see a higher level of divorcing boomers in senior-tenured marriages.

Of all issued licenses, a marriage license seems to be the only one without an expiration date. There are no requirements for continuing education, retesting or payment of additional fees for said license to remain in effect. One marriage license can last a lifetime, but many have purchased several. I have two, both on my wall next to my Enron stock certificates that are also worthless. (Darts anyone?)

Adultery is Pervasive

History has long recorded adultery among kings, queens, and others. Adults seem pre-programmed to partake in adultery; it may be in our DNA-AM (dating not abolished after marriage). Adultery permeates every layer and level of our society from presidents, senators, and governors, to athletes and ministers (Jim Bakker with Jessica Hahn, and Jimmy Swaggart and his pick-up escort in Indio, California), and many others.

Remember the Monica incident in the president's office, under the desk, in the White House? Former presidential candidates John Edwards and Gary Hart both did a little *workday shopping*. Governor Eliot Spitzer was forced to resign because he was seeking something that was already available at home. Then there was Senator John Ensign (R-Nevada), who acknowledged an affair with the wife of a staff member, and Senator David Vitter (R-Louisiana), who admitted recent visits to local prostitutes. All six of these powerful men would now acknowledge that the truth eventually comes out. Perhaps Lord Acton was right when he said, "Power tends to corrupt, and absolute power corrupts absolutely."

It's common knowledge that substitute sex is available in the halls of government and other work locations. This is especially true when on the road and away from home. Our national sports heroes have shed light on this dark practice. Consider the incident where married L.A. Lakers' star Kobe Bryant was charged with two personal fouls (sexual assault and sexual battery).

Fortunately for Kobe, the criminal case was dropped, and he quietly settled the civil case. This short segment from a press release followed on March 3, 2005:

> Terms of the out-of-court agreement were not
> released. A two-sentence statement by the sides
> said only that the civil case "has been resolved
> to the satisfaction of both parties." It said
> Bryant, his 20-year-old accuser and their lawyers
> have agreed that no further comments about
> the matter can or will be made.

Since married men and women have long been looking elsewhere for what is available at home, but perhaps no longer on the marriage menu, the question becomes: What was it? Just what did the former New York governor Eliot Spitzer receive that cost him $5,000 per hour? Again, it was not breakfast, not even breakfast in bed. South Carolina governor Mark Sanford traveled more than 5,000 miles over Father's Day of 2009 to visit his Argentinean mistress for five days. Mark had a new approach: he wanted to have both his wife Jenny and his soul mate (his mistress Maria Belen Shapur). He repeatedly asked Jenny for marital furloughs to visit his soul mate in Buenos Aires. Jenny repeatedly said "NO!" Next, Mark reportedly played the *closure card:* "I just wanted to go to say goodbye!" It seems as if Jenny agreed, and he went to *say goodbye* (five-days?).

To be fair, we've only had a few (known) female heads of state that stray. Perhaps Diana, Princess of Wales, was our closest figure who, via her own admissions, acknowledged her marital indiscretions. Of course, we did not fault her, for she was then married to Cheating Charles who had his own long-term *thing* going with the *lovely* Camilla Parker Bowles. After a long relationship, Prince Charles married Camilla (now the Duchess of Cornwall) in 2005.

But wait; there's been recent activity in Northern Ireland's Belfast political circles. In March, 2009, Mr. Robinson, the first minister, discovered that his *beloved* 59-year-old wife *Mrs. Robinson* had seduced 19-year-old *Ben Bradd*, the son of a recently deceased close friend.

Mrs. Robinson (an elected officeholder herself and a strong advocate of family values) disappeared after the disclosures were made public. She claimed mental illness and later resigned her office.

Society has inaccurately identified women as less sexual than men. Such is not true. Women have the same, and sometimes higher sexual needs than men. Women are multi-orgasmic because, unlike men, they do not experience a refractory period (after men ejaculate, fall asleep, and cannot be aroused). Commentators report that women reach their sexual peaks in their mid-to-late 30s, while men reach theirs in their early 20s. Men traditionally marry younger women, and this age difference contributes to decreased sexual frequency and satisfaction later in their marriages.

Sexual incompatibilities may fester to the point where satisfaction is sought elsewhere. For men, having an affair may bring a younger partner, sexual adventure and new excitement. For women, having an affair with a man who will give her love and attention, when the husband at home is distracted or is elsewhere, can fill a vast emptiness. Neither may want to leave their spouse, but both want to feel excitement and appreciation.

Contrary to statistical reports, women seem to engage in more marital transgressions than reported. Perhaps women are smarter in dealing with their rendezvous and in handling the aftereffects, as well as not bragging about their conquests (in the manner that most men do).

Hollywood Marriages

As we already know, most Hollywood marriages do not usually last long. Britney Spears' five-hour marriage to Jason Allen Alexander may have set the record for the shortest celebrity marriage ever. John and Amelia Rocchio of Rhode Island, on the other hand, reportedly were married for more than 83 years, a record for the longest-married couple in the world. As my colleagues in the Statistics Department would say, "That is really not that bad." Taken together, the Rocchios' long marriage and Britney's five-hour marriage would average 41.49 years. Obviously, such is not the case. The duration of successful marriages seems to be shrinking (first in California, then) throughout the United States. Shorter marriages are now becoming the norm worldwide.

The most serial-married person in the world was not Yul Brynner, who only played King Mongkut of Siam, the monarch in *The King and I*. The real King Mongkut had 9,000 wives and concubines (how did he remember their names? He called them all *honey!*). Yul Brynner, however, will be remembered for his *Magnificent Seven*, his four marriages, and three divorces. Next there was King Solomon of the Old Testament, who reportedly had 700 wives and 50 good Jewish lawyers. He made out well. King Henry VIII of England had six wives and was only divorced twice. Of the remaining four, one wife was widowed, one died, and the other two were executed (no lawyers, no division of property, and no alimony). Our own Larry King has had eight marriages, seven divorces, and seven wives (he remarried and divorced a former wife). He is still married to wife number seven (who is actually his eighth wife, if you are counting); thus, we see that even these four Kings could not escape DSS.

Women also participate in serial marriage. Liz Taylor and Lana Turner had eight marriages; Liz had seven divorces and Lana had eight (they both divorced and remarried a previous husband). Zsa Zsa Gabor attracted nine husbands and has had eight divorces. To all, she said: "I am a marvelous housekeeper. Every time I leave a man, I keep his house."

While there are no accurate statistics, it seems as if more than half of us have been married more than once, while at least a third of us are on our third marriage. Today, multiple marriages are common for men and women. Given today's extended life expectancies, multiple-marriages may be a growing trend. It is quite possible to have as many as six 10-year marriages or hookups (assuming a first marriage at age 20 and subsequent hookups/marriages of 10-year durations repeatedly thereafter, with brief respites in between).

This is nothing new. Pablo Picasso (1881-1973), the great Spanish artist, lived such a life with multiple companions. Picasso's wives and lovers included Fernande Olivier for seven years. He then hooked up with the much younger Eva Gouel, followed by yet another younger conquest, Gaby Lespinasse. In 1918, when Picasso was 37, he married the much younger Olga Khokhlova, a ballerina who introduced Picasso to formal dinner parties, French toast, and the social niceties of the Parisian Roaring Twenties.

In 1927, when Picasso was 46 and still married to Olga, he began an affair with 17-year-old Marie Therese Walter. In 1936, when Picasso was 54 years old, he met 29-year-old Dora Maar. She became Picasso's lover for almost eight years. By mid 1944, Picasso encountered Françoise Gilot. The two eventually became lovers. Next, Picasso married the much younger Jacqueline Roque in 1961, when he was almost 79; they stayed together until his death on April 8, 1973. Wow, that's eight.

Despite accepted cohabitation practices and liberal marital trends of voguish Europe, puritanical America remains far behind today. Witness the recent Eliot Spitzer prostitution scandal, which ultimately forced his resignation as governor of New York. This resignation never would have happened in Europe. *C'est la vie!*

Presidential Marriages

Former French President François Mitterrand died at the age of 79 in January of 1996, eight months after leaving office. At his funeral, his devoted mistress Anne Pingeot, their 20-year-old daughter Mazaine, and his dutiful wife, Danielle, sat next to one another, hand in hand, grieving together over the man they all obviously still loved. Can you imagine Hillary and Monica, or Jennifer and Paula, all sitting together at President Bill's funeral one day?

Although shocking when first reported, presidential extramarital activity in America is nothing new. Bill Clinton, John F. Kennedy and Franklin Roosevelt, as well as Warren Harding and Thomas Jefferson, are all said to have had documented extramarital affairs. Other presidents, going back to George Washington, have been mentioned as having "made presidential whoopee with other women." Thomas Jefferson was attracted to the much younger Sally Hemings, the daughter of a slave at the Jefferson estate at Monticello. Apparently, he fathered a child with her.

Warren G. Harding had long affairs with at least two different women (one a Democrat and the other a Republican?). One of them was Nan Britton, who claims to have given birth to his daughter. Nan was instrumental in having the word *illegitimate* removed from birth certificates of children born out of wedlock.

In 1913, Eleanor Roosevelt hired Lucy Mercer as her social secretary. Lucy was a tall and beautiful young woman with thick blond hair and become romantically involved with FDR when he was secretary of the Navy, sometime in 1915. Ostensibly, the affair ended but was resumed in 1944 (and continued into 1945). Lucy, not Eleanor, was with FDR at Warm Springs, Georgia, at the time of his death.

Eleanor had offered to divorce FDR, but she later agreed to stay, on the condition that FDR end his affair and that he never again share Eleanor's bed. Eleanor had her own separate White House bedroom and was said to have had intimate relations with several female lovers. Associated Press reporter Lorena Hickok quit her job as White House correspondent to live in the White House with Eleanor. The First Lady was said to have also shared her love with other women lovers, including Marlene Dietrich and the beautiful, globetrotting Mercedes de Acosta. Wow! No wonder FDR called it *The New Deal.* But wait, it only gets better, for now we really understand what FDR meant when he said *"The only thing we have to fear* (if the Republicans find out about Eleanor or Lucy) *is fear itself."*

But wait again. Bill Clinton and JFK before him seemed to have known no limits (Democrats). JFK is said to have had numerous affairs with White House workers, staff members, and visitors, as well as with reporters, movie stars, gangsters' girlfriends, an intern, and many others, and all of this with a bad back. Recently, Mimi Beardsley Alford, a retired New York former church administrator, has written her memoirs that include details about an 18-month affair (from June 1962 to November 1963) with President John F. Kennedy. She was a 19-year-old Republican intern in the White House at the time; he was a 45-year-old *active* president. The affair ended with the president's assassination on November 23, 1963.

Three short decades ago divorce in America was still deemed an unacceptable taboo, a badge of failure, and often a bar to social, economic, and political advancement. Ronald Reagan's second run for the presidency in 1980 gave us our first ever divorced president. The last two presidential elections both had divorced presidential candidates: Senators John Kerry in 2004 and John McCain in 2008.

Senator Kerry was *swift boated* about his military service; however, no one mentioned his divorce. Senator McCain brought up his divorce in response to one of Reverend Rick Warren's questions. Senator McCain was smart in being honest, open, and contrite about having left his wife Carol to marry Cindy, whom he had met the year before.

The last presidential primary elections were marked by divorce overtones. Rudy Giuliani's children rebuffed him because of his divorces. Still, Rudy enjoyed strong support among evangelicals as a presidential candidate, which surprised many. A little research revealed that the divorce rate among evangelicals is actually as high as 52 percent; in fact, the Bible Belt has the highest divorce rates compared to other large religious geographic areas in the United States. The 2004 presidential election had other interesting facts. Red states had a divorce rate 27 percent higher than blue states. Blue states had higher education and income levels than red states. Marriage rates have fallen nearly 30 percent since 1970, while the divorce rate has increased by 40 percent.

No-Fault Divorce Laws

The increase in divorce rates started in 1965, when modern and progressive Oklahoma surprised everyone (including itself) by passing the country's first ever no-fault divorce law. It took modern, progressive California an additional five long years to adopt its own no-fault divorce laws. This legislation was fostered by the cogent contributions and rational recommendations of Professor, and later Dean, Herma Hill Kay of the University of California, Berkeley Boalt Hall School of Law (one of my best former professors). Professor Kay's efforts culminated in her co-authoring California's no-fault divorce law that took effect on January 1, 1970. Several other states soon followed California's adoption of no-fault divorce laws.

California became the second no-fault divorce law system in the United States, making it easier for its citizens to exit their troubled and sometimes already dead marriages. Previously, obtaining a divorce required one spouse alleging and then proving that the other spouse had done something seriously wrong or had acted in a way that caused the breakdown of the marriage, often requiring testimony by children, parents, relatives, as well as in-laws, neighbors, the cable-repair person, gardeners, and others.

The new California no-fault standard has now been expanded to include not wearing the right perfume or aftershave lotion, squeezing the toothpaste tube in the middle (as opposed to carefully rolling-up the tube from the back), or even listening to country music. California, and several other states, requires a six-month period after the non-filing spouse is served with divorce papers, before a divorce can be granted (it's a cooling off period). Others states require longer periods. Just as in days past, Go West, young woman/man became the mantra for quickie divorce seekers because Nevada has the shortest final divorce waiting period, a mere six weeks wait for a final divorce decree. Nevada also has the highest divorce rate in the country, and may soon provide drive-in divorce service to complement its already existing drive-in marriage and drive-in funeral viewing facilities.

Massachusetts and Connecticut rank first and second, respectively, for having the lowest divorce rates in America. Connecticut and Massachusetts both require a 12-month residency and a three-month waiting period for the final decree.

Sociological Aspects of Divorce

The advent of no-fault divorce continued to bring change, as noted in a 2002 report prepared by the CDC's National Center for Health Statistics that shed new light on trends and patterns in marriage, divorce, separation, and cohabitation. This report, based on interviews with 11,000 women aged 15 to 45, focused on individual factors and community conditions associated with long-term marriages, divorce, and separation.

Significant report findings included:

- By age thirty, three-quarters of women in the U.S. have been married and about half have cohabited, at least once, outside of marriage.

- The probability of a first marriage ending in separation or divorce within five years is 20 percent, but the probability of a premarital cohabitation breaking up within five years is 49 percent.

- After ten years, the probability of a first marriage ending in divorce is 36 percent, compared with 63 percent for cohabitations.

Social commentators suggest there are increasing reasons for the rising tide of divorce, including increased life spans fostered by medical advancements and new generational values (like healthier lifestyles). Increasing economic independence among higher-educated women enables them to leave unfulfilled marriages. Divorce rates have been accelerating with the arrival of the no-fault divorce laws adopted in the United States in the early 70s and later throughout the world. No doubt the economic slump that began in 2006 is having an impact on divorce statistics. Divorce rates during this recessionary period are down by as much as 38 percent and were also down during the Depression era, when two could live as economically as one (as long as one did not eat).

Current academic findings indicate that remarried life in the U.S. is better understood than before, yet divorce rates among remarried spouses remain high. It has now been quantified that gender, age, and education, as well as employment and race differences, affect rates of remarriage. Compared with women, men remarry sooner and generally marry someone five to 11 years younger than women who choose to remarry.

The more education and resources a man has, the more likely he is to remarry (smart). Conversely, older educated women with financial resources are less likely to remarry (smarter). That said, women with high-status employment who divorce when they are older, tend to remarry sooner than women lacking such employment, due to employment-related expectations and responsibilities. Frequencies of remarriage and re-divorcing decrease as people age. In the 21st century and later, the numbers of later-life remarriages are expected to increase, as baby boomers will be living healthier and longer lives. In general, widowed men usually remarry sooner and younger than widowed women, who marry later (if at all) and older. Widowed individuals are still less likely to remarry than are divorced individuals. Again, age is a factor.

The above statistics are based solely on the heterosexual population. Unknown numbers of gay, lesbian, and bisexual couples have similar patterns of coupling, uncoupling, and re-coupling. There are no data, however, relating to coupling transitions for these groups, since they could not legally marry or divorce prior to 2006. Still, sexual orientation does not change the presence or consequence of DSS; ask Rosie O'Donnell, who has found a new partner and elected to end her marriage.

Same Sex Marriages

American divorce rates are expected to increase as gay and lesbian couples gain the privilege to marry and the right to divorce from coast to coast. First in Massachusetts, then California (albeit interrupted by the passage of Proposition 8, which seems to be unconstitutional); next, Connecticut, Iowa, Vermont, Maine (later repealed by voters in the November 2009 election) and New Hampshire and Washington DC followed. Soon other states (CA and NY) are likely to follow.

Change has been underway worldwide. The countries listed below all recognize same sex marriages:

The Netherlands, 2001	Norway, 2009
Belgium, 2003	Sweden, 2009
Canada, 2005	Argentina, 2010
Spain, 2005	Iceland, 2010
South Africa, 2006	Portugal, 2010

Divorce has become common, acceptable, and fashionable. *The New York Times* Sunday society pages, once traditionally reserved for engagement, wedding, and anniversary announcements, now contain descriptive divorce announcements. Today, couples not only announce their forthcoming divorce but some actually set out their entire property settlement agreements, even listing who gets what assets. Recently, one of my students commented that this public listing would be a smooth way to let others know that one would soon be available (again).

Listing one's assets could favorably enhance one's desirability. This could catch someone's eye! This new practice begs the question: why not have divorce receptions with flowers, photographers, and of course, a last dance by the now divorced couple? Oh my, but what to wear? This new practice could start a new trend. Macy's, Bloomingdale's, Home Depot, Amazon.com, and others may soon have a *divorce registry*. Why hasn't Hallmark thought about this before?

As divorce continues to become more socially accepted, we will continue to see accompanying societal changes. I recently heard of a divorced couple's children holding a *What Would Have Been 25th* wedding anniversary party for their divorced parents. Other divorced couples jointly host divorce parties celebrating their divorced years apart. Former friends who are also divorced are invited and even their lawyers attend (I've been to three). It's just wonderful because everyone already knows everyone else. Perhaps one day we will all observe a national divorce day and celebrate our divorces together. Hark, it could be held on June 6th as the real D-Day. What about all of us giving thanks on the second Monday in October? We could all be Canadians for the day.

Stories about spouses hooking up with the other spouse's boss, relative, their minister, or other individuals are familiar. It's common to hear that someone introduced by a spouse to another person later runs off with your spouse. It happens every day at work. After nearly four years, it is reported that Jennifer Aniston finally ended her silence about the breakup of her marriage to Mr. Smith (Brad Pitt). Jennifer's recent fall 2009 magazine articles now disclose that Mrs. Smith (Angelina Jolie) was not Jackie Kennedy, because Mrs. Smith revealed that she and Mr. Smith fell in love while at work. At work, at church, at Costco, or at Home Depot, it can happen anywhere.

Many who lose a spouse to another harbor ill thoughts and hard feelings toward the person who has broken up their marriage. We've even coined several names for these individuals, including home-wrecker, bitch, and many others. Some seem to equate this marital interruption with the loss of a chattel (an item of tangible movable property) rather than the loss of a person. We often hear: "He/she took my most precious possession."

But wait! What can you do "if someone takes your spouse?" Centuries ago, English common law recognized civil actions for alienation of affection. This was an intentional tort action brought by a deserted husband against the woman (and her husband if married) who allegedly was responsible for his marriage interruption. Most states today have abolished civil actions for alienation of affection. After all, if someone wants to leave, that person should be allowed to go. Only North Carolina (some 200 filings/year) and Mississippi still allow alienation of affection lawsuits; however, they have had some real whoppers! Democratic Party chairman Jamie Franks sued *the other man*, and Leisha Pickering, the estranged wife of former U.S. Rep. Chip Pickering, is suing Elizabeth Creekmore Byrd *(the other woman)* whose family owns Cellular South).

Jackie Kennedy- or Cary Grant-like behavior applies to the person who may have interrupted your marriage and may now have taken your spouse. Remember, you did not own your spouse, and you may have been part of the reason why he or she elected to leave. Perhaps your former spouse was either unhappy with you or is happier with the new companion; no one can steal a heart that doesn't want to be stolen. Harboring anger and hate toward someone else only hurts you, for it is the hater, not the hated, who really suffers in these situations.

There seems to be no magical pattern, sequence, or order to successful marriages. For many (Johnny Carson), first, second, or even third marriages are the short unions (with an average of 10 years), followed by a lasting final marriage of 18 years. For many others, first marriages are the longer lasting of subsequent shorter nuptials. Such was the case for Lido Iacocca.

Lido "Lee" was married three times. First he married Mary McCleary in 1956. Mary died in 1983 after a long struggle with diabetes. Next, Lee married Peggy Johnson in April of 1986 (he was then 62, she was 35), but in 1987 their nine-month marriage ended by Lee's initiated annulment. Peggy suffered a heart attack and died at the age of 49. Next, Lee married a third wife, Darrien Earle, in 1991 (Lee was then 67, she was 52). They were divorced three years later (after heated divorce filings in California and Michigan) in 1994. Lee successfully managed Chrysler, but was not as successful in his later marriages.

WHAT YOU NOW RECOGNIZE, UNDERSTAND, AND ACCEPT

1. Dual income marriages often come with their own problems.

2. Dual-income spouses frequently get divorced.

3. Nevada has the highest divorce rate; Massachusetts and Connecticut have the lowest.

4. Adultery is everywhere and in every segment of society.

5. Divorced men remarry sooner (and younger) than divorced women.

6. No-fault divorce is now allowed in almost every country throughout the world (except for Malta, The Vatican, and the Philippine Islands. See Appendix).

7. A few presidents, several senators, and many athletes mess around.

8. Single people pursue married persons and married persons pursue singles.

9. The odds for a long marriage are diminishing worldwide.

10. There seems to be no set pattern for a successful marriage.

CHAPTER EIGHT

Keeping Your Lawyer(s) and Yourself Honest

A local United Way office realized that the organization had never received a donation from the town's most successful lawyer. The person in charge of contributions calls him to persuade him to contribute.

"Our research shows that out of a yearly income of at least five hundred thousand dollars, you gave not a penny to charity. Wouldn't you like to give back to the community in some way?" The lawyer mulls this over for a moment and replies,

"First, did your research show that my mother is eighty-nine years old, dying after a long illness, and has medical bills that are several times her annual income?" Embarrassed, the United Way rep mumbles, "Um ... no." The lawyer interrupts,

"Or that my brother, a disabled veteran, is blind and confined to a wheelchair with only one arm?" The stricken United Way rep begins to stammer out an apology, but is interrupted again.

"I just had no idea ..." On a roll, the lawyer cuts him off once again,

"So if I don't give any money to them, why should I give any to you?"

Marriage is grand; an average divorce is about eighteen grand. In the year 2010 competent family law divorce lawyers were charging clients $400 to $600 per hour for their services. Complicated divorces, in addition, often require business appraisers and forensic CPAs, as well as real estate agents and other experts, who charge similarly expensive hourly fees or percentage-based commissions. As all litigants will attest, when it comes to divorce court, win or lose, you always lose. Settling early can stop the flow of emotions and hemorrhaging of dollars for legal fees and costs. I've seen many divorcing couples fight over used, generic household items while paying $525 an hour or more to each of their attorneys. Apprehensive, abandoned, and angry spouses do not realize or care that they can go to Bloomingdale's, Costco, or Home Depot and purchase brand new similar items for less than one-fifth of what they are often paying their attorneys for just that day's fees. Divorce seems to cause all logic, reason, and common sense to go out the window, because divorce is about winning, it's about ego, and "I'll show you!"

I've told several other lawyer friends that handling a divorce case can be far more stressful than handling a murder case. Much like a good Italian opera, divorce cases include anger, betrayal, and constipation, as well as envy, rejection, retaliation followed by vindictiveness, and other heated emotions. Shootings of spouses, lovers, and lawyers are not uncommon in the stressful world of divorce.

Still, all divorces involve only six issues.

- Child support
- Child custody
- Child visitation
- Spousal support
- Attorney fees and costs
- Division of community property

Here is a brief summary of the six issues listed divorce issues above. Naturally, each case and each state's laws are different. These issues must be negotiated between the parties or the court will determine the respective outcomes. They are:

1. CHILD SUPPORT: In general, most courts now use pre-determined gross income schedules, accompanied with three of your last pay stubs, to determine the amounts to be paid by the noncustodial spouse. You plug in the noncustodial parent's gross income from all sources, the number of children, into *DissoMaster* software and bingo: you get the net amount of child support due. The first half is usually paid on the first of each month, second half on the 15th. Income tax dependent-deductions for the supported child go to the paying parent.

These child support orders routinely remain in effect until the child reaches the age of majority (18 in most states) or further order of the court. Child support orders can be increased based on greater expenses or needs for the child, or on higher income of the supporting parent. Custodial parents, if employed, may also need to contribute.

Long ago, unpaid child support by "deadbeat dads" had become a national problem. On October 20, 1994, Congress [finally] passed the Full Faith and Credit for Child Support Orders Act (FFCCSOA, see details in Appendix 2). This legislation required all states to enforce the terms of any permanent or temporary order (including paternity orders) issued by a court or administrative authority of the issuing state, and it prohibits modification of other states' child support orders unless certain jurisdictional requirements are met. The act was long overdue, and finally curbed the problem of "state hopping" by deadbeat dads to avoid their support obligations.

2. CHILD CUSTODY ISSUES: As in the Britney Spears case, the court always does what's best for the children, granting custody to the more responsible and reliable parent. Joint custody has become popular and is encouraged. While mothers used to get custody of the children in 80 percent of cases, the trend seems to be changing.

Naturally, children are usually never split between feuding parents. In most states today, children over the age of 12 are generally allowed to make their own determination as to which parent they wish to live with, subject to the parent's approval and proof of available accommodations and supervision considerations.

3. CHILD VISITATION: This issue is also handled with predetermined court schedules, where the non-custodial parent is entitled to visitation as follows: every other weekend, from 7:00 p.m. Friday to 7:00 p.m. Sunday, plus one or more months during the summer. Fathers get Father's Day, their birthdays, and every other birthday of the child. Mothers get Mother's Day, their birthdays, and every other birthday of the child. Next, parents rotate holidays, as well as three-day weekends, even years for mothers and odd years for fathers. Parents are always free and encouraged to modify their visitation calendars to accommodate each other's often-busy schedules. The court can also order supervised visitation but will rarely deny total visitation by a parent.

If things get nasty and uncooperative between parents, courts merely drop the hammer on the uncooperative parent. The court can reinstate the standard predetermined court visitation schedule if necessary, with the offending party usually having to pay the attorney fees and court costs for the innocent parent, as well as her or his own fees and costs. As you may already know, children can greatly impact divorce. But wait, for medical science has now confirmed that having children is hereditary, i.e., if your parents did not have any children, you, too, will not have any children (if you're not laughing, read it again). Oh!

4. SPOUSAL SUPPORT: This issue can be preempted by a prenuptial agreement (see Chapter 10). As with child support, courts now use gross income schedules (also accompanied with three of your last pay stubs) with *DissoMaster* to determine the amount of spousal support. Support is usually paid bimonthly: first half is typically paid on the first of each month; second half on the fifteenth. In long-term marriages (over 10 years in most states), these orders usually remain in effect until the spouse remarries, cohabitates with either male or female partners, dies, or upon further order of the court. Shorter marriage support orders are usually on a 2:1-year basis, e.g., a six-year marriage will yield three years of support. Spousal support orders are subject to increases or decreases based on changes in circumstances. An increase in income for the paying spouse or an increase in the supported spouse's expenses may justify an increase in support. If the paying spouse remarries, her/his new spouse's income

can be included as an increase in her/his income, triggering a possible increase to the supported spouse. Wow—what a way to start a marriage! Income tax considerations are a vital aspect of these payments. Spousal support is generally taxable to the recipient spouse and usually deductible by the paying spouse; deductions can also be waived (because of income tax considerations, as Tiger Woods may have; see Chapter 6).

Spouses sometimes have the, "I don't need or want anything from him or her," or its corollary, "I wouldn't even take a dollar from her or him," mindset. Ladies and gentlemen, in this day and age of gender equality, this response can be a major mistake. Always take the dollar. As mentioned above, spouses in long-term marriages are entitled to support for extended periods. Even if you do not need, want, or use the dollar, take it. Here's why. By taking the dollar, the court retains jurisdiction over the spousal support issue and allows you to come back later if you become unemployed, injured, or disabled to get more from your ex. Yes, this one-dollar may someday turn into a major source of funds. It's like getting Social Security at 47, 54, and 62. You should never waive this right unless you agree to a lump-sum settlement. Who knows what the future holds? Bet you hadn't thought about getting divorced, either.

Spousal support can also be settled for a negotiated lump-sum amount totaling $25,000, $50,000, or other negotiated amount, paid in one payment or sometimes in a few installments. This support payment is subject to the same income tax consequences as mentioned above. There are good endings and sad stories for both sides of lump-sum support settlement selections. Wives often come out way ahead after receipt of a large lump-sum support settlement and remarriage. Sometimes ex-wives miss out when ex-hubby gets a big raise, wins the lottery, or marries a high-income new spouse, all after a lump-sum support payment. The ex-wife, in all three of these cases, may have been entitled to possible increased monthly support payments, but for the lump-sum settlement payment already paid. Yes, as many ex-husbands have said, "There is a God."

Some spousal support settlements are truly interesting and unique. In 1971, Howard Hughes divorced Jean Peters, his second wife. He agreed to pay her between $70,000 and $140,000 a year for 20 years (the actual amount to be determined by the local consumer price index).

Howard was a master of negotiating good deals; still, Jean was very well provided for (she also received a paid home in Beverly Hills). She waived all claims to Hughes's estate, and, surprisingly, Howard "did not insist on a confidentiality agreement from Jean." Or did he?

Peters later told *Newsweek* magazine:

> "My life with Howard Hughes was
> and shall remain a matter on which
> I shall have no comment whatsoever."

Confidentiality: Deal or no deal? What do you think? It seems as if Howard's 20-year payout settlement was not subject to a remarriage termination clause, because Jean immediately married Stanley Hough, a 20th Century Fox executive (he was outside, waiting in the car with the engine running to head for the closest judge to get married). Hey, why wait? If you can remarry and still get Howard's yearly stipend, go for it.

5. ATTORNEY FEES AND COSTS: Payments (usually her and his) are allocated to the higher-income-earning spouse. Given the expensive fees being charged today, it always is in the parties's best interests to settle early and save on legal fees and costs. Because husbands sometimes earn more than their wives, they are often ordered to pay for the soon-to-be ex-wife's legal fees and costs, as well as their own attorney fees and costs. Things are changing, however. High-income female parent/spouses may now be required to pay all of the fees for both sides in ongoing custody/visitation battles.

California's statutes listed below (Family Law Act §270-271.) on the payment of legal fees and costs have been helpful in establishing legislative guidelines for judges to follow. Here are the relevant sections of California law on the question of attorney fees, with modest commentary:

> CALIFORNIA FAMILY CODE SECTIONS 270-271
> 270. If a court orders a party to pay attorney's fees
> or costs under this code, the court shall first determine
> that the party has or is reasonably likely to have the
> ability to pay.

271. (a) Notwithstanding any other provision of this code, the court may base an award of attorney's fees and costs on the extent to which the conduct of each party or attorney furthers or frustrates the policy of the law to promote settlement of litigation and, where possible, to reduce the cost of litigation by encouraging cooperation between the parties and attorneys. An award of attorney's fees and costs pursuant to this section is in the nature of a sanction.

As noted, first the court determines ability to pay. The old saying, "You can't get blood out of a turnip," is recognized here. The court will note each party's levels of delay, frustration, and furtherance of settlement progress. If one of the parties frustrates and delays settlement progress, that party may be ordered to pay or contribute toward payment of the other party's fees and costs, as well as pay his or her own fees. Most legal fees related to divorce-property issues are tax-deductible. Check with your accountant and lawyer to be certain.

6. DIVISION OF COMMUNITY PROPERTY: First, the court determines if the parties had an enforceable prenup to address this issue. If there's a prenup, then the listed property is distributed accordingly. Interestingly, many lawyers will still challenge the validity of a prenup to force a more favorable compromised settlement, which will provide more for their clients and save the opposition money by avoiding a full trial on that issue. In divorce cases without a prenup, the court orders property to be valued at garage sale prices and allows the parties to divide their property so as to provide them with an equitable in-kind distribution: first she picks an item, and then he picks an item, and so on. Vested pensions and retirement benefits earned or accruing during the marriage are community property assets, and the other spouse has a property interest in said retirement benefits, which must be apportioned and divided at divorce.

A few years back, a psychology professor friend and his now ex-wife agreed to almost everything in their divorce, but for her piano and his pickup truck. He told me that they both had expert witnesses who would low-ball each other's desired item. After one hour of morning testimony, the judge became exasperated with both of them and awarded the piano to my friend and the pickup to his ex-wife. Immediately thereafter, he told me, they went out to the parking lot and traded for what they each wanted (reason finally prevailed, but *reason* can be expensive).

Sometimes sullen spouses and their aggressive attorneys become unreasonable and will not agree to anything. In these cases, the court orders all of the property sold, and the selling expenses deducted from the sale proceeds. Remaining marital debts are paid, and all other property is equalized between the parties. The remaining net balance, if any, is then divided between the parties.

There are cases where there are no assets, but only community debts to be divided between the divorcing spouses. The debt is usually apportioned between the spouses based on their earning capacities, if any, and this becomes a part of the final judgment. Both spouses usually remain liable to the respective creditors until their debts are paid in full.

The following division of property story is sad, but true. A middle-aged divorcing couple had no children, but had an eight-year-old toy French poodle named Lord Beaumont. Both husband and wife loved and treasured this dog, and both were emotionally attached to him. They both wanted Lord Beaumont. They spent thousands of dollars fighting over the dog at trial. The husband retained a dog psychologist; the wife retained two. The husband's psychologist introduced evidence that when the husband turned the corner three blocks away, Lord Beaumont would run to the front window and start frantically wagging his tail.

Not to be outdone, the wife's lawyers and canine psychologists introduced testimony from five interviewed witnesses who all testified as to the bond between the wife and Lord Beaumont (he slept on her side of the bed). As fate would have it, the judge awarded permanent physical custody of Lord Beaumont to the wife, with four-hour visitation periods to the husband on all even-days of every month. During his second visit to see Lord Beaumont, the still distraught husband pulled out a gun and shot and killed him on Bastille Day (July 14). Lord Beaumont was cremated. His remains were placed in an ornate French goblet urn and a formal funeral followed. Later (oh, it's not over yet), the still grief-stricken wife sued her distraught ex-husband for Lord Beaumont's wrongful death.

Now it really gets crazy, because the court dismissed the wife's wrongful death lawsuit. She immediately retained new counsel and new lawsuits were filed against her ex-husband that sought all of Lord Beaumont's ashes and $2,989 for a replacement toy French poodle. This case actually went to trial and a passionate jury (four of the twelve jurors and the trial judge were dog owners) awarded:

> Two/thirds of Lord Beaumont's
> remaining ashes to the wife;
> one/third of Lord Beaumont's
> remaining ashes to the husband.
> The wife also received $379 for
> a replacement dog, based on
> Lord Beaumont's pro-rated
> life-expectancy, and 50 percent
> ownership interest therein.

Each divorce case is unique onto itself; here's yet another. Recently, I heard of a divorce client named Gene who fired his former lawyer because he had become frustrated by his lawyer's outrageous bills, lack of progress, and apparent friendship with opposing counsel. Gene's divorce case had dragged on for two years without any settlement progress. He elected to go it alone, *in pro per* (representing himself), with the helpful guidance of his able business *consigliere* (legal advisor) in the background. Gene was a quick study and soon discovered that his proven business skills could be used in the divorce arena, along with his business lawyer's guidance. Gene soon realized that he could bifurcate the case (terminate the marriage immediately), leaving the property settlement until later. This was a good move because it drained much of the emotion on both sides.

Within days, the marriage was legally terminated. Gene discovered that favorable, generous, front-loaded settlement offers were better in the long run; spend more on your ex or on attorneys, and it's still going to cost you.

Troubled Clients

I once had a female divorce client come to see me about taking over her case. She was disappointed with her apathetic attorney and was looking for a more aggressive and competent (fourth) lawyer. I politely asked this woman what she wanted. Without stopping to gather her thoughts or catch, she told me that:

> She wanted me to make her husband (who was involved with a younger woman) miserable. She wanted me to make her husband suffer. She wanted everything, everything. She wanted both houses, both cars, all of their stocks, bonds, and mutual funds. She wanted all of it and she was ready, willing, and able to pay for it NOW!

I immediately realized I did not want to take her case (her three previous lawyers were not a problem; she was). I did not quote her an extremely high retainer fee, hoping she would go away, because of a past experience that once backfired. I once had a client referred to me by our mutual CPA. After reviewing his case, I did not want to take it but could not tell the client because of the referral. This new client had an extremely complicated divorce case with complex real estate issues that required immediate attention. I told the prospective client that I would need a check for $45,000 to start the case. The client reflexively wrote me a check for $50,000 and told me to start immediately. Remembering this incident, I was certain that if I had asked the disparaged woman before me for a $100,000 retainer, she would have given me her check to start forthwith. I was glad I passed on this one.

Today's expensive and clever divorce lawyers and angry, vindictive, and hurt clients make for bad combinations. It's like being in a fast car with two accelerators and no brakes at all.

Divorce clients usually want much more than just a scorched-earth ending. Struggling with abandonment and rejection, they seek far more than justice. Often divorce clients want and insist on a couple pounds of flesh, an arm and a leg, and, of course, attorney fees. Modern divorce litigation has become a new battleground, with weapons of mass discovery, false accusations, along with demands for public open trials and other such tactics, which can collectively be characterized as *aggressive lawyering* as confirmed below.

In our heated moments of rejection and retaliation, we all sometimes need a guardian angel to save us from ourselves. Yet our commercialized legal system sends us to *lawyers*, to help guide us through the forest of recovery. Most would agree that anger, hate, and vindictiveness only beget more anger, hate, and vindictiveness, all of which some lawyers sometimes seem to appreciate. It is easy to see why the legal profession is always being accused of lacking compassion for those they represent. It's like the old tale of dentists giving candy to their patients.

The recent posting of a six-minute video on YouTube by British stage actress Tricia Walsh-Smith has had quite a viewing. As stated by many, "This woman doesn't get mad, she gets even." In her video she aired her husband's personal dirty laundry. She claimed he was trying to evict her from their apartment. These super-hostile video tactics were a first in our modern divorce wars. She finally accepted $750,000 from her 35-year-older husband as a full settlement. This new high-technology-driven approach to uncompromising divorce litigation is said to be fair, because all is fair in love and war, and divorce is war.

> Why are Divorces so Expensive?
> It's Because they're Worth it!

Recently, spouses and their assertive lawyers have increased the use of false allegations against the other spouse by including entirely new accusations of criminal and civil misdeeds to force more favorable settlements. Some of the allegations are beyond the pale.

These false and inflammatory allegations now include:

- Pet abuse
- Drug abuse
- Income tax evasion
- Child abuse/molestation
- Pornography dependency
- Smoking illegal controlled substances
- Being a Democrat/Republican and having associated with terrorists
- Anything and everything else which would be sure to cause embarrassment or additional expense to the other side

These items are now listed in divorce actions and prioritized for their poker chip settlement worth in negotiating more favorable payouts, via their intrinsic value of shame and embarrassment upon the accused. Several states prohibit the use, or threats of use, of criminal actions to force civil settlements.

> South Carolina Rule 4.5, Rule 407, states:
> "[a] lawyer shall not present, participate in presenting or threaten to present criminal charges solely to obtain an advantage in a civil matter."

> California law, as stated in THE STATE BAR OF CALIFORNIA STANDING COMMITTEE ON PROFESSIONAL RESPONSIBILITY AND CONDUCT FORMAL OPINION NO. 1984-81 goes even further:

> Rule 7-104 contains two essential components: First, the rule prohibits threatening to file criminal, administrative, or disciplinary charges to obtain an advantage in a civil action. Second, the rule also prohibits an attorney from presenting criminal, administrative, or disciplinary charges solely to obtain an advantage in a civil matter.

These rules and regulations prohibiting aggressive tactics help. Despite the listed laws, lawyers should bear the ultimate responsibility to draw the line on some of these antics. The cardinal rule in business—that the customer/client is always right—should not be applicable in divorce cases, principally where the client is out of control, retaliatory, and vindictive, and the lawyer has bought a bigger boat.

Almost everyone remembers the acrimonious divorce battle between Burt Reynolds and Loni Anderson. This heated divorce became a highly publicized bitter feud with allegations, counter-allegations, and more. Books, television commentary, and magazine articles followed, with even more books and other public airings. Good heavens, it was as bad as the 2009 divorce saga of *John-and-Kate less Eight!*

Witness the salvo of allegations against Bill Murray brought by his estranged wife in June 2008. She accused Bill of being "a marijuana user, a Republican, an alcohol and drug addict, as well as a physical abuser, a sexual addict guilty of recurrent desertion and frequently traveling overseas where he would engage in public and private sexual liaisons." Wow!

Robin Williams' second wife, Marsha Garces, on the other hand, exhibited divorce diplomacy in filing her divorce one month after Mrs. Murray's action. Marsha's divorce petition was solely on the grounds of irreconcilable differences. They had been married for 19 years. Robin met Marsha while she was working as a nanny for his son Zachary.

Today's insistent clients and creative lawyers engage in serving the other side with salvos of burdensome and oppressive legal discovery demands, sending out extensive Interrogatories, voluminous Requests for Admissions, and oppressive Notice(s) to Produce bankers's boxes of documents, emails, and text messages. While aggressive discovery is occasionally justified, the receiving party must either file a Motion for an immediate Protective Order or fire up the copy machine. Sometimes, sending out extensive discovery can be deemed good lawyering. Busy opponents would frequently rather settle at a premium than spend hours copying voluminous documents that may disclose privileged business communications or embarrassing information, all resulting in paying more in legal fees and added copy costs.

Spouses and others frequently discuss and disclose confidential personal information during pillow talk conversations with their partners. Perhaps spouses should be required to provide Miranda-type warnings to each other to ensure that these admissions and utterances can later be used in divorce court.

Possibly:

> You have the right to remain silent.
> Anything you say before, during, and after
> sex can and will be used against you later
> in divorce court. You have the right to
> have a lawyer present during foreplay, sex,
> after sex, and even smoking thereafter. If
> you cannot afford a lawyer, one will be
> appointed for you. Legal fees and costs
> will be deducted from your share of the
> property settlement proceeds, if any.

Bringing a lawyer to your hotel room or other meeting place and paying him or her to go back to the office, can be expensive. Why not just go to the lawyer's office and have sex there? Besides, people have been going to lawyers' offices for years to get screwed. Depending on your attorney, this arrangement could get interesting. You may not even be charged. If you really want to get creative, have two lawyers present, one for each person. No need to worry about the lawyers getting into bed with each other, for one lawyer would never screw another lawyer. It's called professional courtesy.

Given the increasing use of pillow talk admissions in divorce and other couple-splitting litigation, hotels may soon start to upgrade their services to accommodate guests's legal needs. Hotels may start offering in-room legal representation as a standard item. Just like the mini guest bar, you may soon have a mini lawyer already in your room. Alternatively, you could call the concierge to send up fresh strawberries, chilled champagne, and an attorney who can open and pour champagne to your room.

The advent of avid social networking may eliminate the need for hiring private investigators; these popular Internet sites now provide a cornucopia of free on line evidence to ex-spouses asking for many of the six-items of divorce issues listed a few pages back. Be careful what you post and be sure to discuss your existing posting with your lawyer, because the other side has already reviewed them.

Divorce lawyers can usually be hired in one of three ways:

- Flat fee
- Hourly rate fee
- Prepaid legal services programs

FLAT FEE: Payment of a one-time fee. This arrangement is becoming more popular. Under a flat-fee arrangement, the lawyer and the client agree to a lump-sum payment (usually paid up front) for representation in all trial-level matters in the entire case, excluding court costs. This arrangement includes all interview meetings, ten phone calls, and court appearances, together with an agreed number of Order to Show Cause hearings, the (initial) trial, and coffee. The client is protected, knowing that no additional monthly billings for legal fees will be sent and also gives the lawyer a great incentive to work smart, get the case finished and earn perhaps as much as $1,000 per hour, versus earning $100 per hour for taking longer.

HOURLY FEE: Like others who sell their services by the hour, lawyers do so as well; most divorces are handled on this basis. Divorce lawyers's work is often prepaid and charged against a paid retainer. When funds run low, attorneys will ask the client for a second advance.

Lawyers just love hourly rates, which usually include the meter running while driving to and from the courthouse and stopping at Starbucks along the way. Attorneys like two or more appearances at the same courthouse on the same day, for which they usually charge each client for an entire round trip, even though both appearances are completed in one round trip.

Some lawyers actually charge if they dream about their cases. That said, many of us lawyers mentally review our cases on a non-stop basis.

PREPAID LEGAL SERVICES: Just like the Auto Club, you can pay for a pre-determined menu of auto/legal services, and just like the Auto Club, some plans also have silver, gold, and platinum programs. Pre-paid legal programs continue to gain popularity, albeit without much divorce coverage yet. Perhaps one day prepaid legal plans will cover such divorce legal services, as hotel pre- and post-lovemaking counseling as mentioned above. You could even get a gold or platinum colored sticker to paste on your forehead or under clothing that reads: *Lovemaking legal coverage in effect!* This could be inviting to others; it could open *new doors* for you!

Sometimes divorce cases run amuck. The three-year battle between New York Giants' Michael Strahan and Jean, his wife of less than six years is a perfect example. The state appellate court reviewed the trial court's decision in April 2008, which awarded his wife the following:

1. The house (22,000 square feet)

2. $15.3 million cash settlement

3. $18,000 per month child support

4. $311,000 back child support

5. 91% of the kids' private school tuition

This division was well over half of Michael's estimated net worth of $22 million. Michael is paid $4 million a year from the Giants. He left his wife and two-year-old twin daughters for his mistress, Cupcake. The Strahans later settled the division of assets. The court sealed the agreement and their lawyers refused to divulge the details, but both were happy with the outcome. As they say in Disneyland, there's nothing better than two happy divorce lawyers.

Sometimes we lawyers really have an opportunity to help. At my lawyer's office one day during my first divorce, I met a woman named Wilma in the receptionist area where I had seen her before.

We gradually started talking, and she told me how her upset husband, William, had unexpectedly told her to go find a lawyer and start their divorce because he wanted out of their 12-year marriage.

The next time I saw Wilma, she told me how she still loved William and felt they could save their marriage. She stated, "William seemed more concerned with his bowling and consumed with his new bowling ball than saving our marriage. He refused to go to counseling because he did not want to air our dirty laundry before others."

I sympathized with her as I listened attentively. Then I was suddenly called to see Melissa, our mutual divorce lawyer. I wished Wilma well as I left. As I entered Melissa's office, she told me that she had noticed Wilma talking to me and asked if I had any ideas on how to convince William to go to counseling.

My scheduled meeting with Melissa was to discuss the division of certain remaining community property items, including a modern 16-piece flatware set. I wanted the entire set because I frequently entertained large numbers of guests; Apollina wanted to divide the set because they belonged to us. All of a sudden, I had a great idea: "Divide the bowling ball!"

Just as the entire flatware set was important to me, it seemed William's new bowling ball was extremely important to him. I suggested to Melissa that Wilma bring the bowling ball to her office and hold it hostage to entice William to go to counseling. "Wow," Melissa said, "I'm so glad you're a lawyer. That's really a great idea!"

We finished our division of property discussion, and I left through the side door. The following week I received an urgent fax from Melissa. Here is what her fax said:

> After you left, I called Wilma to my office. I told her that I wanted her to bring William's new bowling ball to the office. Wilma responded that she could not do that because William's new bowling ball was his most precious possession. I went on to explain that under the law, Wilma had a 50 percent ownership interest in the bowling ball. After further discussion, Wilma finally agreed to bring the new bowling ball to my office the next day.

Four hours after the bowling ball had been dropped off, William called; here is a word-for-word transcript of our discussion:

William: "Lady lawyer, where's my bowling ball?"

Melissa: "It is here in my office."

William: "I am coming over to get it right now!"

Melissa: "Since it's half yours and half your wife's, I can have it cut in half, and you can pick up your half."

William: "No! You can't do that madam, I just had it balanced!"

Melissa: "You understand that it's half hers and you are the one who wants the divorce."

William: "Lady lawyer, what do I have to do to get my bowling ball back?"

Melissa: "Go to counseling with her."

William: "Well (long-pause), okay."

Five days later they started marriage counseling; three days after that, William received his bowling ball. Two weeks thereafter, Wilma was able to drop their divorce case.

Alternative Divorce Dispute Resolution (ADDR)

Divorce cases seem to take forever. Why do they take so long? It's because the Sixth Amendment guarantees a speedy trial to all criminals. Yes, arsonists, burglars, and drug dealers, as well as murderers, rapists, and robbers all get to go to trial first. All civil litigants (divorcing citizens) must yield to criminal trials before their day in civil court. Because of these mandated criminal priorities, we have congested civil court calendars. Alternative Dispute Resolution (ADR) has become a popular solution. To understand ADDR fully we must first comprehend ADR. The two most common forms of ADR are *arbitration* and *mediation*. While both have the same objective (to settle disputes), they differ in their fundamental process: Mediation is a procedure where the disputing parties submit their case to a mediator who will listen to both sides, ask questions, and offer settlement alternatives to the parties. The parties are free to accept, reject, or even make counter proposals. The salient characteristic here is that the mediator's recommendations are not binding on the parties.

Arbitration, on the other hand, requires that the parties be bound by the arbitrator's award, as the final judgment on the matter. Mediation and arbitration have become popular alternatives to civil litigation in recent years. These viable substitutes have worked their way into family law courts as ADDR. Courts have long been ordering divorcing parents to counseling evaluation for custody and visitation privileges and on to mediators for resolution recommendations for settlement. Courts have also been ordering entire divorce cases to mediation or binding judicial arbitration, where a retired judge or experienced divorce attorney serves as the mediator/arbitrator. Repeated successes with this process have resulted in an entire cottage industry of arbitration and mediation service companies. Some arbitration and mediation services specialize in certain cases (real estate, personal injury, or labor disputes), while others take any and all cases.

There are five Es to best describe ADR and ADDR:

- It's EXPEDIENT: You have your case heard reasonably soon. No waiting for criminal trials or other packed dockets.

- It's ECONOMICAL: No continuances or other usual court delays.

- It has EXPERTISE: Retired judges and experienced lawyers sit as arbitrators.

- It's EASY. No formal rules of evidence, no juries and fewer breaks.

- It's EFFICIENT. Once you agree that the results will
  be binding, you're on your way to a prompt and
  inexpensive resolution.

ADDR has taken on a warm and fuzzy approach. ADDR mediators are professionally trained to create atmospheres free of arguments, blame, or intimidation. The mediator's goal is to facilitate communication and cooperation between the parties in a non-adversarial setting conducive to settling remaining divorce issues. Lawyers usually do not attend the mediation sessions, but usually review proposed settlements for accuracy and content.

ADR and ADDR save taxpayers money by expediting civil disputes and family law adjudications, and by providing good constitutional protection for our common criminals. There are also other innovative dispute resolution methods for resolving divorce disputes. Some lawyers offer collaborative divorce (effective, team-guided divisions and distribution) resolution, while others recommend just splitting the assets and liabilities. One spouse takes all the assets; the other is given the liabilities. Remember, too, that marriage is supposed to be a give-and-take institution. Unfortunately, in most marriages today, one spouse often does all the giving, while the other usually does all the taking.

Most state bar associations have enacted consumer protection legislation to protect clients from unscrupulous and dishonest lawyers (the only profession where 90 percent give the remaining 10 percent a bad name). Most all states now require lawyers to provide monthly itemized billing statements to their clients. Most lawyers are now [finally] willing to represent aggrieved clients against their brethren in fee disputes and in legal malpractice cases. Needless to mention, judges, juries, Jay Leno, and David Letterman have all been supportive in cases brought by damaged clients against their overreaching and sometimes overzealous divorce lawyers.

How do you find and retain a good divorce lawyer? To start with, look for lawyers close to the courthouse where your case will be heard (no need paying for excess lawyer travel time). Most lawyers do not charge for an initial consultation (some do); always ask when making an appointment. Several states now have lawyers who are Certified Family Law Specialists.

You can always go on line at your state's website and check a lawyer's college and legal education, years of practice, and discipline record; ask her/him the same questions to see if you get consistent answers.

Ten Good Questions to Ask a Lawyer

- Where did you go to college and law school?
- How many cases similar to mine have you handled?
- How many divorce cases have you actually tried?
- What is your plan for dealing with my case?
- Are you comfortable with settling cases without a trial?
- Have you ever been disciplined by the state bar?
- What is your hourly fee and payment schedule?
- Can you provide me with five recent client references?
- May I attend one of your upcoming trials (they're open to the public and anyone can attend)?
- Can you validate my parking?

Because people go to lawyers when in criminal trouble or civil need, we lawyers have long been subjected to sometimes-unfair criticisms, jokes, and even outright ridicule. The famous line in Shakespeare's *Henry VI, Act IV, Scene 2*—"The first thing we do, let's kill all the lawyers"—is still misunderstood today. While frequently quoted, most fail to appreciate the genius of the quote. The scope of the quote is to show that the surest way to chaos and tyranny, even back then, was to remove the guardians of independent thinking, justice, and civility in society.

Then there's the other side. A male colleague here at the university divorced and several years later a local lawyer started dating my colleague's ex-wife. Two years later, the local lawyer married the professor's ex-wife. Several months thereafter, all three serendipitously ended up on the same cruise ship. On the men's second meeting, the ex-husband professor leaned over and asked the new-husband-lawyer, "So how do you like having a used wife?" The new-husband-lawyer responded with: "It's really not bad, once you get past the used part." Typical men. While women may think about asking similar questions, most would not ask such a question (unless of course, they were left for a younger woman. Fair is fair.).

Current statistics reveal 67.3 percent of divorces (compared to 31.6 percent filed by men) are initiated by women. Higher women-initiated divorce rates are found in Beverly Hills and Newport Beach, California, and New York City. Needless to mention, all metropolitan areas have high concentrations of divorce lawyers.

Being a lawyer is highly stressful. We usually pay a high price for this stress. Early deaths are common for lawyers. At one time I seriously considered leaving the university to devote even more time to my law practice. Once again I recalled my father's wise words, "You don't want to be the wealthiest lawyer in the graveyard." There are other difficulties, as well. Once while talking with an elderly Italian woman I told her I was an avocado. She looked at me with spontaneous laughter and said, "I think you meant an *"avvocato."*

Like most other professional associations, the attorney-client relationship requires effective communication, reasonable fees, and satisfactory results. Yet, the three most common client complaints about divorce lawyers are: a lack of communication (especially not returning phone calls), overcharges, and poor results. Meaningful communication between lawyer and client is essential, and all lawyers have a professional obligation to keep their clients informed about their cases. However, don't expect your divorce lawyer to communicate with you frequently since she/he is also working on other clients' cases at the same time. Limiting phone calls, in order to minimize service charges when working on an hourly rate, actually benefits the client.

It is also not uncommon for your lawyer to have a closely supervised paralegal, secretary, or other legal assistant assigned to working and communicating with individual clients. Thus, clients should contact these assistants for routine questions and assigned task.

As mentioned in Chapter 8, before formally hiring a lawyer, be sure that you completely understand the hourly-rate charges (travel, phone call minimums etc.); some lawyers may include other costs (such as postage and copies) on your bills. Lawyers are held to strict ethical standards; most states require them to provide their clients with monthly-itemized statements of their fees and costs. Still, fee disputes are common and clients have available alternatives to help resolve them, as mentioned in the referenced chapter.

Each and every divorce case has its own individual fixed facts, unique circumstances, and obvious limitations. Lawyers are not miracle-workers and they cannot spin straw into gold! Legal issues are resolved by established laws and adopted legal precedents. Favorable results require clear client communications and reasonable expectations. Given the foregoing, your lawyer can then assess the strengths and weaknesses of your case and evaluate the likelihood of an outcome that meets your expectations. Your lawyer may also provide acceptable alternatives for your needs.

Keep in mind that it is your case. If you are not content with your lawyer's handling of your divorce, she/he may not be aware of your discontent. Set up a meeting with your lawyer and discuss your dissatisfactions ASAP. Tell your lawyer exactly what is bothering you and give her or him an opportunity to remedy the problem. If you don't understand what your attorney is doing, ask for an explanation. Do not be afraid to ask "Why or how come?" If the problem happens to be the result of a misunderstanding, perhaps the lawyer-client relationship can be saved.

Finally, remember that you have an absolute right to seek the services of another lawyer; however, you will still need to pay your first attorney the fees for her or his legal work. You will also have to pay the new attorney for her or his time to review your case and if accepted for the time needed to get up to speed. If your attorney abandoned, neglected, or mishandled your case, that attorney may lose the right to compensation and may be possibly liable for your added expenses and other damages.

WHAT YOU NOW RECOGNIZE, UNDERSTAND, AND ACCEPT

1. Competent divorce lawyer fees average $400 to $600 per hour.

2. Divorces are expensive because they're worth it!

3. There are only six issues in all divorce cases: Child support, custody, and visitation, Supposal support, division of property, and, of course, attorney fees.

4. All is fair in love and war, and divorce is war.

5. Miranda-like warnings may be required; be careful what you say.

6. Go to your lawyer's office to have sex there.

7. The best time to find a good lawyer is before you file or are served.

8. You now know 10 good questions to ask lawyers about experience, strategies, costs, and fees (add others to the list as you think of them).

9. Lawyers are expensive. Counseling may be a better substitute.

10. Be sure your dog sleeps on your side of the bed.

CHAPTER NINE

Marital Financial Patterns and Divorce Ordeals

A man who lived in a city luxury high-rise condominium thought it was raining and put his hand out the window to check. As he did, a glass eye fell into his hand.

"Is this yours?" he asked the woman leaning over two floors above him.

She said, "Yes, could you bring it up?" On arrival she was profuse in her thanks and offered the man a drink, then dinner, then dancing. As the evening was drawing to a close the lady said, "I've had a marvelous evening. Would you like to stay the night?"

The man hesitated then said, "Do you act like this with every man you meet?"

"No," she replied, "only with those who catch my eye."

Even though the woman upstairs *had an eye out for her* neighbor, there was no money *mentioned in catching someone's eye*. Money, nevertheless is frequently one of the significant attractions that catch one's eye in relationships. The marriage cycle begins with meeting, dating, and slowly getting to know and appreciate a new, special person. We naturally gravitate toward those we find interesting, while effortlessly eliminating those determined to be not as promising. Soon we find ourselves going out of our way to impress this now favored individual. In the beginning, we look at this new exciting person to be the answer to our prayers. Finally, a man/woman whom I can imagine being with for the rest of my life. She/he seems perfect. Long lunches and dreamy dinners soon follow, with accompanying acts of thoughtfulness and fondness.

This surprised union leads to spending more time together, and, as the union blossoms via mutual exclusivity, further expressions of attention and affection are experienced. In due course, we feel a cohesive bonding and a powerful sense of mutual fulfillment with this now treasured partner. Next, rushed proposals and acceptances frequently follow, for we have received what we wished for. As George Bernard Shaw said, however, *"There are two great disappointments in life: Not getting what you want—and getting it."* These preliminary experiences can lead to magnificent weddings followed with delightful honeymoons. All too frequently, however, unexpected separations and unwanted divorces follow.

Financial Futures

Financial patterns start subconsciously during the dating days, expand through the engagement period, and reach full maturity in marriage. Later, they are reviewed in court to determine spousal support payments to be paid when the marriage has ended. All divorcing individuals wished they could've foreseen what was to come.

The dating starts with a scheduled afternoon event, function, or location. Let's assume that he is to pick her up at 2:00 in the afternoon. He arrives at 2:15, and she is not ready. Delayed by her hair, belt, shoes, or other uncompleted items that still need attention, she invites him in. He waits while she wraps up whatever it was that detained her.

There's an alternative scenario. It's 2:40, and she has been ready to go for the last half-hour. No calls from him, and now she waits and waits. Finally, at 3:10 he arrives with a list of reasons as to why he is late: traffic, incomplete directions, rain, and other justifications for his rude tardiness. Although nothing is said about the person who will be in charge, the parties are already subconsciously setting the ground rules for who will lead and who will follow. Yes, folks, it's about power: who will have it and who will yield. The stronger person in the relationship often leads and usually determines financial parameters; the parties usually do not even realize what is going on. This decision may never be reached if one of the parties is offended by the other's lateness. No second date will be asked for or accepted.

Parameters of power and financial concern will continue to evolve as the relationship grows. It is not uncommon for couples out on a date to visit a store or retail establishment. The following example will help explain what can happen. While passing through, the woman/man may say to their companion, "Could we [you] get one of these for us [me]?" It may be a small item or something of modest value. The answer is all-important, because it will set the stage for what can be expected in the future.

If the date says, "Why don't you get it?" or "I did not bring my wallet/ billfold," it's clear that this person is just not in a buying mood to purchase whatever was requested. The man/woman may feel uncomfortable already buying something for someone he/she hardly knows. He or she can also respond with, "Sure, why not," signaling that he/she may be a willing buyer, and perhaps a good follower. Sometimes this may be a subconscious test to determine if this person can possibly be *pushed* (and for how far and how long).

Men and women sometimes purchase a small memento or item for the persons they date (I would always bring a single long-stemmed rose when meeting someone for the first time). Women frequently express their appreciation by inviting the man in for coffee, a drink, or, if he is lucky, a goodnight kiss or two, and perhaps even three. Men will convey tokens of approval and affection for a woman with candy, flowers, or a shovel. These modest gestures are usually tacit expressions of approval or appreciation. If the woman/man is really lucky, it can actually be both.

Although the foregoing are not economic overtures, they are still symbolic approvals and clear manifestations of attraction. Sometimes women take the initiative to get to know a man they find appealing. In this day and age of impartiality, it is not uncommon for women to invite a man to dinner, theater, or even travel. Another side of the male involvement becomes clear; yes, men like to receive and appreciate simple thoughts and modest gifts.

Next we come to lunch, dinner, or drinks. Individuals used to send messages via their conduct when the bill was presented. In the past, offers to split the bill were usually characterized as strong manifestos that there may be no second date, or even, *I do not owe you any goodnight kisses.* Many post-divorced dating individuals now go Dutch (both paying for their own). We are living in changing times, and more and more women are offering to split bills or trade off in paying. I once dated a woman who insisted on paying when we were in her neighborhood. I would pay when we were in mine. Whatever the practice, *give and take* is manifested in other areas as the relationship blossoms and financial patterns continue to evolve.

Men frequently push the envelope to see what they can do, taking liberties to hold hands, sneak a kiss, or remove outer and under clothing while being amorous. As the dating process is played out, definite lines of power, authority, and limits are set. The relationship may even grow to the point where one completes the other. He or she completes her or his wardrobe, car, and other items that she or he may need and he or she may be willing to purchase or pay for her or him.

Given the unique and remarkable combinations mentioned above, if the subject couple goes on to marry, the fundamental lines and financial patterns will have already been established. Whether they split bills, she pays, or he pays, this arrangement may last until D-Day (divorce day).

Disclosures and More

Sometimes we walk right into it. Years ago, as my law practice continued to grow I realized I needed to be closer to the university. I had to get to and from my law office and back to and from my scheduled classes.

I soon found and moved into new offices on the 15th floor of an 18-story building much closer to school and with excellent freeway access.

We had a young woman named Jane as the floor receptionist. It was easy to understand why she was hired; it was always a pleasure to be greeted by her. Jane was extremely friendly, attractive, and always properly attired. Her hair, make-up, and manners were perfect. Soon James, one of the floor lawyers, took a liking to Jane and they started dating. It did not take long for this romance to blossom into an engagement, followed by a wonderful winter wedding after a brief courtship. The wedding was held at the intimate East Chapel at the grand Bellagio Resort Hotel in Las Vegas. Eighteen guests witnessed the loving ceremony and elegant reception outside at the *Terrazza Di Sogno* overlooking the Bellagio's romantic *Lago Di Como*. Dinner was later served in a private room at *Circo's* overlooking the lake. I've attended three weddings at the Bellagio; Lady Luck must have shined on those couples, for all three are still happily married.

Upon the lovebirds' return from their Australian honeymoon, all was not well. During the honeymoon, the new Mrs. Jane James Lawyer disclosed that she was deep in debt to the tune of $49,876.54. The bills for all those beautiful outfits, shoes, hairdos, and accessories apparently had not been paid.

I was asked to step in to mediate the dispute without finding fault and work to keep them together. Even though they admonished me not to find fault, I will share it with you. They were both at fault: Jane for not telling James, and James for not asking Jane. These two individuals had four marriages between them. This major debt was material information. He had an absolute right to know, and she had an absolute obligation to disclose her large debt. This union, it should be noted, was a 93-day relationship. It takes time to get to know others, their faults, warts, and outstanding bills.

Disillusionment is a common experience for many newlyweds. Many new spouses do not ask the necessary questions, while others do not disclose what is obviously important. Some may say, "Oh, I'll tell them later, after he or she falls in love with me. He or she will appreciate my other excellent qualities and be more compliant then."

> MATERIAL INFORMATION: any
> information that would cause a willing
> buyer or a willing seller to change one's
> decision to either purchase or sell.

This *marriage* was not a blind date, a weekend adventure, or a one-night stand. This commitment was till *debt do us part*. Although this situation did not have a seller or a buyer, it did have someone asking and someone accepting marriage, with added benefits and serious responsibilities. As a result, this deficit was material information. It was not only the amount of the indebtedness involved, it was also the lack of trust that permeated withholding of this vital information. James may have changed his mind about proposing had he known Jane's true financial situation. Jane may not have accepted if James had asked about her (stressed) financial circumstances. A week later, we met in my office and slowly started reviewing their concerns and looking for viable alternatives to resolve the problem and keep them together.

James was shocked that Jane had maxed out her credit cards and was just able to make the minimum payments. Jane was surprised that James was not more forgiving of her mistakes and that he could not accept what had already happened. As they sat across from my desk, it seemed obvious that they were still in love, yet both were in a state of mutual disappointment over the situation. I could tell by the shame and sadness in Jane's eyes and her sincere sorrow that she deeply regretted what had happened. I felt that she was willing to make an honest effort to fix things between them. James was attentive and holding her hand as we talked. I told them if they truly wanted to save their marriage, both would have to make a commitment to follow through on their promises and work to get Jane out of her financial predicament. I also told James that Jane was well aware of the problem and that there was no need for him to rehash or reprimand her for what had already happened.

After further discussion, it was agreed that:

- Jane would continue working.
- Jane would use all her earnings to pay down her debt.

- Jane would make no additional credit card purchases.

- James would make quarterly 10 percent pay downs to help.

- James would totally forgive Jane and not bring this up ever again.

It took them almost two years, but they did it. The experience brought them closer together, and they are still happily married today. Frequently, a loss or other unforeseen hardship brings couples together and binds them closer than before a shared ordeal. Fault or criticism is not applicable here; understanding, forgiveness and compassion are.

The book of divorce financial ordeals has many stories and several chapters. Divorce always brings added and unwanted financial burdens for all involved. Spouses quickly discover that their pre-divorce-filing lifestyles may have vanished before them. As one spouse usually moves out, this exit creates an immediate duplication in living expenses. Each spouse at different locations now pays rent/house payments, food, utilities, and transportation, as well as all other formerly shared expenses.

Many wives and several husbands have charged into their lawyers' offices with preconceived ideas that they would be maintained in exactly the same manner as before. Sometimes they are. Usually they are not. If you were married to a high-income-earning person or someone with accumulated wealth, assets, and an ample and continuous income stream, then you may be entitled to be maintained in the manner to which you have become accustomed. Sometimes the parties have already addressed support and severance payments in prenuptial agreements (see Chapter 10).

In filing or responding to divorce actions, both parties are compelled to complete comprehensive *Income and Expense Declaration* and *Preliminary Declaration of Asset Disclosure* under penalty of perjury. These declarations must be accompanied with paycheck stubs for three months and other records of income (interest, dividends, rents, stock sales). All assets must be disclosed. Divorcing spouses each have subpoena power and their attorneys can get to the other spouse's tax returns and all other financial records. Still, divorcing couples often have divergent totals on their respective net worth, as in the following:

Divorce Papers Reveal Hulk Hogan's Net Worth
Associated Press, September 5, 2008

Thousands of dollars spent on clothing,
grooming and vacations are among the average
monthly expenses for Hulk Hogan's wife,
according to financial affidavits filed in the
couple's impending divorce case near Tampa.

Linda Bollea's monthly expenses include
$7,258 on clothing; $1,318 on grooming and
$6,100 on vacations, the documents state.
Hogan, whose real name is Terry Bollea, spends
$102 on clothing by comparison, and more
than $38,000 on legal and accounting fees.
The couple disagrees over Hogan's net worth.
Hogan claims it is $32 million, while his wife,
Linda, claims it is $26.7 million.

This report is really strange. It's usually the other way around. Husbands always claim less while wives constantly claim their husbands have more. Spending $456,000 a year (1.53 percent of the estate) on accountants and lawyers is not really that bad. Besides, asset management fees are usually income tax deductible items. But wait, for this was no ordinary divorce. Allegedly, back in 2007, the Hulk had an affair with his daughter Brooke's former best friend, Christiane Plante. This incident, it is said, was responsible for Linda Hogan, his wife of 24 years, filing for divorce in November of 2008. Linda (48 at the time) then began dating 19-year-old Charlie Hill, a student at the same high school attended by her two children. Once again we have one of these loving situations where everyone already knows everyone else.

These *unique circumstances* led to a complicated 20-month divorce battle. Their divorce quickly became a tabloid circus with accusations, counter-accusations, heated public exchanges, and juvenile name-calling, as they chose their mean-spirited weapons for additional attacks. Why did you think your divorce was complicated?

Soon it had become worse than the Hulkster's ring-battles with Rocky Balboa. They finally settled their divorce in the 20th round/month. It seemed as if they were almost ready to get back together. They ended their divorce-day with departing kisses, tears, and mutual best wishes. As expected, terms of the settlement were not disclosed. Later, the Hulk started dating the much younger Jennifer McDaniel, who closely resembles his daughter, Brooke. The Hulkster and Linda both ended up with much younger partners, after divorcing and dividing their assets.

Pre-Divorce Preparation

Divorce is a problematic, prolonged, and pressurized process that requires careful consideration and thoughtful timing. Before you jump in, read as many books (at work or in private, unless you wish to send a message to your spouse) about the subject as possible and consult with legal and financial professionals. Go to as many out-of-town (you don't want any locals to see you) pre-divorce planning workshops and lectures when or wherever you can. Dress for the occasion: you might catch someone's eye while there.

Think about the timing of your separation. Is your spouse due a bonus or other windfall in the near future? Do not separate until after the windfall arrives, in order that it may remain community property, and when you're entitled to your half. Income earned after separation is deemed to be separate property. Johnny Carson's third divorce was all about the date of separation. He claimed it was in February and JoAnna claimed it was in November. Back then, Johnny was earning a mere $7 million per year. Let's do the math. $7 million/year equals $583,333/month. The disputed nine months's income totaled $5,294,999 to be characterized as separate property (all Johnny's), or as community property: half ($2,624,999) to each.

After extensive discovery, research, motions, and argument, the lawyers finally agreed to prorate and divide the disputed amount between their clients. Johnny received two-thirds: $3,529,646, which was $1,765,353 less than the entire sum. JoAnna received one-third: $1,764,823. The lawyers, of course, each picked up additional fees. Johnny later mentioned one evening on his show: "You can buy a lot of Tender Vittles [cat food] with $1,764,823."

In my first divorce, my former wife's lawyer wanted to include my occasional summer school earnings as part of my income for support purposes. I suggested that we flip for it. We did. I lost. The difference was me having to pay her an additional $427 per month. The combined fees (which I ended up paying) would have been 12 times this amount had I elected to litigate my added summer school income. Besides, I felt I owed it to her. It was better that it went to her than to our already overpaid attorneys. Lawyers (and I'm one of them)!

Think about Social Security. If you have been married eight years, you might want to stick it out for two years more, so that you can collect on your ex's earnings record. Check with your lawyer before filing. Remember, you put up with a lot; a little longer will provide you with years of earned Social Security benefits for life. Besides, you've earned it. Finally, don't just pack your bags and drive away in a car that needs four new tires. Before you separate, buy new clothes for yourself and tires for the car a few months before your planned exit.

I am reminded of the following story:

> One day a priest was entering a cemetery on his way to a burial service. He noted a man by a gravesite crying in extreme sadness and remorse. The priest passed and went on to his assigned burial. Almost two hours later, the man he had passed before was still there at the gravesite crying. The priest decided to stop and comfort the man. As he approached he heard the man passionately say: "Why did you have to go, why did you leave?"
>
> The priest embraced the man and said: "My son, your wife is in a much better place now!" The man turned to the priest and said, "Oh no, it was not my wife, it was her ex-husband. He was supporting both of us and now he's gone; now one of us will have to go to work!"

Divisions and Distributions

Hiding assets and concealing the dollars from the other spouse used to be the norm for divorcing couples. While it still occurs, this *game* has certainly become far more difficult and expensive to try today. The parties and their skilled lawyers will one day sit and go over each and every line item entry on the comprehensive pages of the *Income and Expense Declaration* and *Preliminary Declaration of Asset Disclosure* forms to ascertain the accuracy and completeness of these listings. Two lawyers at $400 to $600 per hour and an expensive deposition transcript all support the conclusion to reach an early settlement on this point and all other issues.

Remember: both lawyers' meters are running when working on your case. Issues of support are further complicated via business ownership, cash receipts, and secret cash funds, as well as other accumulations of income-producing assets, known or unknown to the other spouse. Men and women will regularly reduce their workloads and even retire in contemplation of divorce. Faked sickness and ill health are also seen here.

The objective is to lower their income and end up with lower support orders, which do not retire and may last long after the divorce is final. Men and women sometimes rush to the malls to stock up on clothing, golf clubs, and shoes, as well as *Le Mer* makeup and other expensive personal items so the other spouse can later help foot the bill as an ordinary expense obligation and not as a departing separation shopping spree.

Divorcing women and men have been known to have expensive prepaid elective cosmetic surgery prior to their already planned exit, charging the expense on their spouse's American Express card, often without her or him viewing the completed results. This has become such a pervasive practice that most states now require the exiting altered spouse to reimburse the paying spouse from their share of divided assets.

These departing bodywork improvements and pre-exit expenses are now characterized as *Reimbursable Expenses in Contemplation of Separation.* In view of that, ladies and gentlemen, get your expensive bodywork done early, stay for a while, and then leave without reimbursement. You may use the improvements to find someone new.

FCPAs

Most appreciate the wonderment of the popular TV series *CSI: Crime Scene Investigation*. Modern medical forensics has elevated criminal investigation to a science. Forensics is now used in divorce court with DSI (divorce science investigation) via the advent of forensic accountants. A forensic certified public accountant (FCPA) is almost a cross between a CPA and an attorney. Modern-day FCPAs utilize accounting and auditing skills, and apply sophisticated investigative and forensic skills to uncover what actually took place in complex financial settings or manipulated financial transactions.

FCPAs have the accounting, auditing, and investigative knowledge to search for and discover what may have been hidden. They are also experienced in uncovering sheltered business assets and laundered cash transactions. Their specialized expertise provides them with the necessary skills to unravel complex fraudulent conveyances and other sophisticated spousal antagonistic transfers used to conceal assets, cash, and property from the other spouse. FCPAs are effective in presenting evidence in court. They are also proficient and accomplished in withstanding aggressive cross-examination by competent opposing counsel.

Apollina's attorney wanted her to retain (and for me to pay) an FCPA to review my business assets, earnings, and expenses. I countered with the following. You hire and pay for the FCPA. If the FCPA finds or discovers any concealed assets, cash, recyclable aluminum cans, redeemable soda bottles, or anything else which would be deemed a community property asset, then I will pay for all of the FCPA's fees, plus treble (three times) the amount of the discovered asset's value. Fortunately, Apollina knew me to be a person of good character. She was always kept in the loop on my earnings, expenses, and other financial matters, and trusted me.

Beware, for you, too, may need an FCPA to guide you through the maze of your divorce, particularly if your spouse had a business before, during, or even after your marriage (where did all of that start-up money come from?). If you were a spouse who was not kept informed of your spouse's financial transactions, and he/she kept the business books (from you), perhaps you should discuss getting an FCPA with your attorney. When you have a complex medical problem, you go to a specialist.

As mentioned above, don't just leave. Of course, sometimes you have to. Past studies show that in the first year after divorces, women's standard of living dropped by almost 30 percent, while a man's increased by as much as 20 percent (the other 10 percent goes to the lawyers). This is reflected in support payments paid and received. But wait! Things have changed. Based on today's higher earnings for women, it's now frequently equal or the other way around.

Be forewarned that many spousal business owners going through a divorce have long prepared for this coming event. For some reason, without justification or legal authority, many business-working spouses feel that a community business is *their* business. Yes, they were the ones going in at 6:00 a.m. six days a week to open the doors. They put in the nine- to 12-hour days. They gave the orders, made payroll, and took the slings and arrows from customers and employees, as well as from suppliers and others. For these reasons and less they often conclude that it is their business!

Many business-owners forget that at the end of their demanding workdays, they came home to a good hot meal, a clean home, and a comfortable bed with a loving, warm spouse (really?). Because of this and other factors, legislators and courts long ago adopted the principles codified in *Code Napoleon*, where husband and wife were each recognized as one. This legislation was in direct opposition to what men called The Good Old Days of the *English Common Law*, where husband and wife were considered one and the husband was the one. *Code Napoleon* was the basis of community property in America via (Louisiana, Colorado, Idaho, Nevada, and Washington) the Louisiana Purchase in 1803. Texas, California, Arizona, and New Mexico followed.

Code Napoleon's wife-friendly concepts of freedom, liberty, and equality were not included in our *Constitution* or in the *Declaration of Independence* for women. Remember, ladies, the *Declaration of Independence* states, "... all men are created equal ... ." Actually, most women know that all men are not created equal. Some are truly blessed, while others are actually shortchanged.

Trophy Spouses

Blessed are those who seek trophy spouses, for most shall become engaged and married. Many will divorce, and several ex-husbands and some ex-wives will pay trophy support settlements. The trophy spouse idea is well-embedded in our culture. Historically, people have married for political, economic, and social motivations. Romantic love was seldom the sole or salient motivation. The enduring words of Henry Kissinger are certainly applicable here: "Power and money can each be great attractions. Combined they are one of most alluring of all aphrodisiacs known to mankind."

Today, even (cougar) women seek and find young trophy husbands, just as men seek and find younger, attractive trophy wives. To some, the term trophy spouse connotes an advantageous achievement, for nothing seems to say it better than having a younger, fresher, attractive spouse on your arm, yet, to others it's a colloquial synonym for *stupidity*. One could be looked at as a "sex-object," while the other may be seen as a "success-object." The trophy spouse is rarely the first. Usually, it's a younger and exceptionally more attractive person who suddenly finds an affluent older person seeking a spouse to whom he/she would otherwise not be suited. Younger, attractive trophy spouses come with their own fractures and flaws. Often, they may lack the maturity, sophistication, and experience the older partner has gained along the way. Even the characters in the film *Pretty Woman* had their incompatibilities, including her not knowing which fork to select for salad.

Still, her or his pleasing "trophy appearance," social demeanor, and attractiveness can reflect well upon the older spouse and can actually be mutually beneficial, even if she or he initially lacks sophistication. After all, look what Henry Higgins did for Eliza Doolittle and what she did for him (he grew accustomed to her face). Some trophy spouses find lasting happiness, while others become (recycled) trophy catches themselves.

There are many listed front-page celebrity husbands who married, divorced, and re-married trophy spouses; there are far fewer celebrity wives who married and divorced trophy husbands. Once again, it seems as if the women were more careful in these situations. There are many recognized benefits and regretful burdens to having a trophy spouse.

Benefits and Burdens of
a Much Younger Spouse:

BENEFITS FOR WOMEN:
- Someone to watch over and take care of you
- Someone to keep you active and thinking
- Someone to wash your back in the shower
- Someone to look at and keep you young
- Someone to help you experience life
- Someone who still can

BURDENS FOR WOMEN:
- Everyone thinks he's your nephew or son
- He wants you to join a gym and exercise
- He's always looking at younger women
- You can't go anywhere without him
- All of your female friends like him
- He wants to go again; you're tired

BENEFITS FOR MEN:
- Someone to show your friends you still have it
- Someone to look at and keep you feeling young
- Someone to spend your Social Security benefits
- Someone to drive you to and from the doctors
- Someone to tell you what others are saying
- Someone you still enjoy seeing naked

BURDENS FOR MEN:
- Everyone thinks she's your niece or daughter
- She wants to do it again; this is hard work
- Now you're in the bathroom crying
- She's still ready to go; you can't go
- She has to see you naked
- What did she say?

Many trophy (and non-trophy) spouses feel as if their high-profile super-spouses get all the attention and respect. Frequently trophy and low-profile spouses feel as though they were nobodies. These neglected spouses further complain that their super-spouses are unenlightened because they frequently are wrapped up in their own careers, avocations, or themselves. Trophy spouses often feel as if their super-spouses were not honest with them, causing a further loss of affection, trust, and respect. When infractions do occur, trophy spouses are usually bought off, via Tiffany or Bloomingdale gifts, to close their open wounds and hold off the onset of further resentment and indifference. Trophy (and other) spouses often feel as if their super-spouses suffer from a lack of *arhat*, the Buddhist word for one who has attained enlightenment and the acronym for attention, respect, honesty, affection, and trust.

Unfortunately, *arhat* cannot be purchased at Tiffany's, Henri Bendel's or at any such luxury stores; it's only found in the left ventricle of the heart as it exits with fresh oxygenated blood that is pumped to the brain for distribution on to its intended recipients. Male and female trophy spouses are always fitted with *Trump Armor* (a prenuptial agreement); it's like a financial chastity belt to prevent financial ravishment. With or without it, spouses encounter their own hazards in sailing stormy seas with a trophy spouse, as we have learned from Roseanne Barr, Jessica Simpson, Ivana Trump, and Madonna, as well as from George David, Ron Perelman, Sumner Redstone, Paul McCartney, and many others who have paid large sums as they travel the expensive toll roads of marriage, divorce, and remarriage.

Ronald Perelman, like Warren Buffett and Donald Trump, earned his business degree at Wharton School of Business at the University of Pennsylvania. After three interrupted marriages and as many messy divorces, Ron Perelman allegedly let it be known that he was looking for a young, *attractive Hollywood actress trophy wife*. Later, while at a *Vanity Fair* Oscar after-party in 1999, he met Ellen Barkin. Ellen immediately liked Perelman's charm, generosity, and impulsiveness. He sent her a gold Cartier watch on her birthday after knowing her only 12 days; his marriage proposal followed just two weeks after (that's less than a month).

Ellen later admitted that she was wowed by Perelman's money and life of extreme luxury. He maintained huge homes in New York, Florida, and the Hamptons, constantly jetting between them. Ellen said she was spellbound by the art hanging on his walls. "Are you joking me?" she once recalled saying to him. "I can sit for hours in *our* library or in *our* living room and stare at the Picassos alone.

After viewing the library artwork, the couple soon moved on to more important matters: the forthcoming Perelman-Barkin prenup. In the months leading to the wedding, Ellen told a friend that she and her lawyers had raised concerns about certain clauses of the agreement. Reportedly, this same close friend later supposedly commented, "I would never use the word naïve with Ellen Barkin in the same sentence." Ellen signed the prenup agreement the day before the wedding.

Divorces are deeply personal and emotional affairs; as spouses fight, anger escalates. Ron and Ellen's divorce inevitably became a matter of great interest, public discussion, and community fanfare. Allegations of legendary tempers and Perelman's control issues and financial considerations are said to have possibly caused him to file. It was alleged that, if Perelman didn't seek a divorce soon, a sunset clause in their prenuptial agreement provided for a likely significant increase in alimony benefits for Ellen, if they should later divorce. Perelman purportedly hired armed guards to watch Ellen as she moved out of their townhouse (what, me controlling?). He claimed that she received $60 million. She claimed "not a penny more" than $20 million. As was once said, "Be careful what you wish for." This story demonstrates that marrying for money has its inherent pitfalls; nevertheless, the day may eventually come when you just have to get out. Let's do the math: $20 million over a 66-month marriage yields $303,030/month; that's $10,101/day and $420/hour. Not bad. Not bad at all!

Remember, money matters are a cause of stress for singles and even the happiest of married couples. Many married couples experience money-related problems (the number one cause of divorce). For that reason, unless you take action, these financial problems could intensify. The parties who filed have the advantage, because they are driving the Mack truck that is about to hit you. They may have already prepared for their final marital exit without you.

Driving that Mack truck, however, takes your attention off other matters; filers must also be attentive to ensure that nothing is ignored.

The Appendix contains an excellent checklist of items which must be addressed prior to filing or immediately after being served with divorce papers; the following financial management suggestions must also be implemented. They include medical insurance coverage, revised budgets, and your credit, as well as important marital documents and financial records, business records, and videotaping what is there. If you have any of these issues present in your divorce, check the Appendix.

Sometimes, even $7,600 per day is not enough. That is what Marie Douglas-David, 36, claims. She reported no income and said she needed her husband, George David, 67, to pay her more than $53,000 a week to cover her *necessary* expenses. George stepped down last year as chief executive at Hartford-based United Technologies (sound familiar?); however, he is still chairman of the board and had an estimated net worth of $329 million. He may need it to pay Marie.

They married in 2002. David was twice as old as his second wife, Marie. They apparently lost their marital bliss 20 months later. The two supposedly accused each other of extramarital affairs and a host of other marital infractions. After several separations and reconciliations, they signed a postnup sometime in 2007 that would give Marie $43 million should they divorce. By fall 2009, Marie wanted their postnup voided and was asking for $100 million, and $130,000 in annual alimony. Keep in mind: he or she who seeks a young attractive trophy spouse pays trophy support. Consider what you wish for.

Testamentary Ordeals

Testamentary: relating to a will, trust, and the laws pertaining to its administration (probate), designed to take effect at the death of its owner/ author. Divorce financial ordeals are sometimes superseded by death-caused financial nightmares, which are also stressful and expensive for the surviving combatants. Fortunately, the decedent will be spared the pain, but not the costs of the ordeal. Both divorce and death financial ordeals can usually be avoided with advance legal planning to be discussed in the following chapter.

Here are a few examples of what family survivors can be left with when there's no testamentary planning. Women in the life of our beloved Italian tenor Luciano Pavarotti battled over his $492 million fortune; five ladies and one child slugging it out to claim the money. Adua Veroni, Pavarotti's first wife of 34 years (they divorced in 2000), and their three adult daughters were on one side. His second wife, Nicoletta Mantovani, (his former administrative assistant who was half his age) and their young daughter, Alice, were on the other side. Apparently, the parties came to an amicable resolution of the estate proceeds in mid-2009. Needless to mention, there was more than enough to go around for all, and they all loved *Nussen Dorma* Pavarotti's signature aria.

A similar long and bitter battle ensued among the wives and children of the late Bob Marley, who died without a will. Jerry Garcia's survivors experienced a similar battle because he also died [intestate] without having a will. Most of us will date, dine, remarry, and possibly divorce again; nevertheless, one day we all die. Be sure that you finish your divorce and that you make out a new will to provide for the distribution of your property. If you do not, you, too, may leave a royal battle for your heirs and ex-spouse(s) to fight over; however, like Jerry Garcia, Bob Marley and Pavarotti, you may have the last laugh!

Your final possible divorce financial ordeal may, surprisingly, be with your own attorney. You must remain vigilant to ensure that your own attorney does not take you to the cleaners, which can be a major problem. I've actually seen other divorce clients hire their own independent counsel to monitor and look over the already-hired divorce lawyer's work progress, accomplishments, and billings. But wait! Who's looking over the new lawyer's billings? "Who shall guard the guards?" Perhaps you need a third, then a fourth lawyer. Perchance that's why there are so many lawyers out there.

Be sure that no lawyer takes advantage of you in your divorce; however, be certain that you have a lawyer. Most surgeons would never attempt to remove their own appendix, even if they may have removed hundreds themselves. For that reason, you should never attempt to be your own lawyer, particularly when your ex has one or two of her or his own.

WHAT YOU NOW RECOGNIZE, UNDERSTAND, AND ACCEPT

1. Financial pathways start during the dating phase and are set in the marriage.

2. Men and women abhor being criticized and given orders on what to do.

3. Ask questions about all financial matters (debts, obligations, and expenses) prior to any engagement, and again before marriage.

4. Spousal support is based on the ability to pay and the needs of the spouse.

5. Support payments have tax consequences: deductible and income.

6. Divorce is a complicated, expensive, and prolonged process.

7. All men and women are NOT created equal.

8. Expenses in contemplation of separation must be repaid.

9. Lump-sum support settlements have benefits and burdens.

10. Revise your budgets, make out a new will, and make copies of everything.

CHAPTER TEN

Pre- and Postnuptial Agreements

Oftentimes, important things must be repeated:

"I would never marry without a solid bulletproof Prenuptial Agreement," said Donald Trump, before his first marriage.

"I would never remarry without two solid bulletproof and ironclad Prenuptial Agreements," Donald Trump repeated after his first divorce.

"I would never remarry, without three solid bulletproof, ironclad and Kevlar-lined Prenuptial Agreements," Donald Trump may have concluded after his second divorce.

An Overview of Prenuptial Agreements:
a.k.a. *"Trump Armor!"*

Prenuptial agreements (prenups) have been popularized by the rich and famous, most notably by The Donald, Britney Spears, and many of the listed persons in the front pages of this book. Prenups are increasingly being used by middle-class and upwardly-bound individuals.

A prenuptial agreement (prenup) is a written contract between two people contemplating marriage and entered into before marriage. Strangely, most are signed days before the wedding. Typically, a prenup lists all assets owned and all debts owed by each person, and specifies what each person's property rights will be before, during, and after marriage, be it ended by separation, annulment, or divorce. Prenups are also currently being used to protect the assets of prosperous widows/widowers. Speaking of affluent widowers, Warren Buffett remarried in 2006; surely, he had *Trump Armor.*

Former presidential candidates John McCain and John Kerry married well. Both of their wives had big bucks: Budweiser or Heinz ketchup anyone? Senator McCain and his second wife, Cindy, have kept their finances separate and apart throughout their 31-year (1980) marriage. Senator Kerry's second wife, Teresa, also kept her property separate and apart throughout their 16-year (1995) marriage. Prenups eliminate the most feared words that Maria Teresa Thierstein Simões-Ferreira Heinz Kerry, Cindy McCain, and all other similarly situated wealthy spouses could ever hear from their spouses: "I'm going to take you for half of everything you're worth!"

Previously, these agreements were considered to increase divorce filings. It was later discovered that prenups actually helped keep marriages together. Prenups (and no fault divorce) are now recognized in all 50 states. Contrary to popular opinion, prenups are not just for the rich and famous anymore. Family law attorneys report that they are preparing ten times as many of these agreements today than just ten years ago, particularly among couples who earn $80,000 and more. I've prepared many (engineers are by far the most difficult clients).

Couples with or without children, well-off or not, may simply want to clarify and memorialize their financial rights and responsibilities before, during, and after marriage. The principal reason for the growing popularity of prenups seems to be based on several sociological realities: men and women over age 30 account for 47 percent and 39 percent, respectively, of newlyweds, and most have substantial assets in tow. In 45 percent of this decade's marriages, moreover one or both partners have been married before (sound familiar?). Prenups can also be used for ancillary purposes; several examples are provided in this chapter.

Couples contemplating marriage may wish to avoid potential arguments if they later become physically or mentally disabled while still married, separated, or divorcing. Prenups can provide marital harmony and extended security by specifying specific intentions and expectations regarding divorce severance payouts, mutual waivers of further support, and other mutual rights and expected benefits. They can also be used to protect spouses from each other's premarital and post marital debts and obligations. Dual-income career couples may include their predetermined criteria under which they will relocate or even retire (and even who gets the dog, if they divorce).

Without a comprehensive prenup, applicable state property divorce laws may determine how your separate and marital assets will be divided and distributed at divorce. You may also need a coordinated will, living trust, or other testamentary instruments to protect yourself, your children and other loved ones fully in the event of death during marriage.

Reasonable Prenups

As prenups become even more common, courts scrutinize them with greater attention because these agreements almost always involve a waiver of legal rights and financial benefits, usually by a less affluent and much younger spouse. Still, sometimes the less prosperous younger spouse does very well. Jack Welch, the former CEO of General Electric, and his second wife, Jane Welch, had been married for 13 years; he was 17 years older than she. They reportedly had a unique (wife-friendly) sunset clause in their prenup.

This clause nullified the prenup after 10 years of marriage. As fate would have it, Jack fell in love with Suzy Wetlaufer, then editor of

Harvard Business Review, after the sun had set. They met when Suzy, 22 years his junior, was preparing an article about Jack's leadership skills for the magazine. Jack and Jane divorced, and Jane rode off into the sunset with $150 million. Jack still did well, because there was plenty to go around. He later married Suzy (sunset clause here?) and the two co-authored his next business book, titled *Winning* (it was not about his divorce). Why would anyone include a sunset clause in his or her prenup? Hey, what would you expect? Jane was a lawyer. Why have the sunset clause take effect after 10 years? The most difficult years of marriage are not the seventh, 10th, not even the 11th year. Everyone knows that the most difficult year of marriage is *the one you're in.*

Katie Holmes, also a smart lady, received excellent legal advice. What can you say? Her father, Marty, is an *avvocato specializzato en divorzi* (attorney specializing in divorces). Her prenup with Tom Cruise allegedly contained a clause stating that for each year the couple stays married, Katie collects $3 million from Tom if they divorce during the first ten years of marriage. Still, that's not bad. Again, let's do the math: $3 million per year equals $8,333/day, which equals $347/hour, plus room and board for each and every year they remain married, up to ten years ($30 million). If they divorce after 11 years of marriage, then the sun sets there, too (their prenup self-destructs—becomes null and void), and Katie receives half of Tom's entire fortune. Not good for Tom. He may indeed end up being *The Last Samurai!* One would think that 10- or 11-year marriages would be beyond the gates and fences of divorce. Obviously, such is not the case. In this day and age, it is not uncommon to see 30-, 40- or even 50-year marriages going into the tank.

Here is an interesting prenup agreement with a "keep it clean" clause. The Nicole Kidman-Keith Urban marriage was preceded by a prenup with a *no drugs* clause. If they divorce, their prenup allegedly nets Keith some $600,000 for each and every year that he is with Nicole and avoids illegal drugs (Keith was a former cocaine addict). If he uses illegal drugs and they get divorced, he will not receive a cent of Nicole's fortune, estimated at $150 million. Nicole was no dummy. No sunset clause here. See, the sun does not set in Australia; in addition, $600,000/ year is really not that much (compared to what Katie would get).

Don't believe me? Let's do the math: $600,000 a year equals $1,643/ day, every day; divided by 24 hours equals $68.49/hour, every hour. As noted, money can be a great incentive to influence behavior. Nicole (and perhaps Keith as well) may have considered their prenup as a legitimate vehicle to help Keith stick to his sobriety and stay on the straight and narrow. While this may reflect a lack of trust to some, it is a viable alternative for rational adults to protect themselves from acknowledged troublesome behavior. Prenups can be used to prohibit multiple contingencies with one document; why stop here? You can restrict cheesecake, sports, and even snoring (separate bedrooms).

Your prenup could also have a travel agenda that could include/exclude agreed destinations. Jessica Simpson said she knew her marriage to Nick Lachey was over when he refused to join her on a trip to Africa. Months later, Wayne Sakamoto refused to join his wife on a trip to Africa. Gee, this restriction could be a new precedent-setting reason for marriage interruptions. As Wayne said, "Why go to Africa when you can see the same animals free (third Thursday of every month) at the local zoo? Remember, safari is the acronym for:"

> Same
>
> Animals
>
> Free
>
> And
>
> Right
>
> Inside.

Jennifer Lopez added a *no cheating* clause to the prenup she and her (then) fiancé Ben Affleck were to sign before they suddenly cancelled their scheduled wedding. *Bennifer* was not the only couple to have an 11th-hour review over the terms of their agreement, followed by a 12th-hour wedding cancellation. Better now than later! Besides, a 50 percent return on deposits for their cancelled wedding reception is better than paying alimony, lawyers, and accountants.

Charlie Sheen and Denise Richards were so paranoid about (his) cheating that they signed a prenup that awarded a spouse $4 million per cheating/event (same person, same place?).

Their marriage (her first, his second) lasted only 33 months and was followed by bitter custody battles over their twin daughters. This "anti-cheating" clause might have been helpful to Elin Woods ($4 million x 13 mistresses times the number of encounters, which were rumored to have been over 100, would have added up to a significant amount of money).

Jane Fonda and Ted "CNN" Turner (now divorced) also had last minute prenuptial disagreements. Allegedly, Ted insisted that Jane give up her acting and other activities to be *a dutiful corporate wife* and champion his causes, charities, and other goals. Ted, like Jane, had already been twice divorced. Ted had vast accomplishments in media and philanthropy that filled his book, *Call Me Ted.* In this biography he wrote about his impulsive and exciting courtship with Jane. He proposed marriage, and she accepted (third-marriage for both). They signed prenups and were married in 1991. Nine years later, she walked out. After she left, Ted tells us, "Our closets faced each other. When I saw Jane's empty space, I sat down on the floor between them and cried."

Several of the listed persons in this book's beginning and many other well-to-do individuals struggled with their prenuptial negotiations. Michael Douglas and Catherine Zeta-Jones reportedly disagreed over details before signing on the dotted line. Brooke Shields and Andre Agassi took two years after announcing their engagement to finalize their prenup. They married in 1997 and divorced in 1999. In 2001, Brooke married Chris Henchy, and Andre later married Steffi Graf. Here again, everybody signed new prenups and everyone already knew everyone else.

Britney Spears and her husband K-Fed, now divorced, were said to be still arguing and haggling over their prenup five days before the wedding. Their prenup limited K-Fed to a million dollars (plus child support, of course). As events played out, she was fortunate to have these agreements. Given the complexity, size, and extent of today's high-income individuals; their separate property earnings, royalties, and other returns; and the fact that 55 percent of all first marriages and 67 percent of second marriages end in divorce, it seems as if everyone should now have a comprehensive prenuptial agreement. You can even pass out signed copies of your prenup to your guests as a wedding memento.

Unreasonable Prenups

Here is something to think about. One recent prenup limited the husband to watching one Sunday football game with friends per month in his own house. For a dedicated sports fan, such a restriction could be deemed cruel and unusual punishment, which is already barred by the Eighth Amendment. Mercy (what's next?)!

Now, get ready for this one: consider a prenup that includes the number of times sex is on the marital menu per week and a list of all different positions that must be tried. Any man or woman who wants a signed, legal document stating that one must have *reverse cowboy* or *out on the edge* sex positions twice a week or the marriage is off qualifies for an immediate nomination for the most unreasonable person of the year. I've heard of the *reverse cowboy*, but what in the world is *out on the edge?*

As divorce and remarriage become more prevalent and as gender equality continues to increase, courts are increasingly upholding signed prenup agreements. Recent appellate court case decisions continue to change the current law regarding prenuptial agreement requirements. Such was the case for Barry and now ex-wife, Sun Bonds, who signed her prenup in California without an acknowledgement of (formerly required) legal representation on her part.

The California Supreme Court ruling came in September 2000 and ultimately upheld the prenup signed by Barry, his attorney, and only Sun. Because the agreement was signed when Barry was a rookie earning only a six-figure income, the agreement was upheld. Sun was not allowed to share in his later higher earnings after they divorced. Competent legal counsel could have provided a salary increase clause to cover this foreseeable contingency.

The following story illustrates realities that can and should be anticipated. When Harry, a 54-year-old, short, landscape architect met Sally, a 5'10", 41-year-old Chicago physician, it was love at first sight; their relationship immediately blossomed (she called him *Shorty*, he called her *Doc*). Soon Harry realized that if he married Sally, and things did not work out, his business, his home, and his other separate property assets would be at risk. Harry diplomatically raised the suggestion of a prenup with Sally; she was not interested.

Harry finally said, "If WE don't sign a prenup, WE can't get married." Sally finally agreed and hired a lawyer. It took months before the couple completed an acceptable agreement that allowed them to be married. Last I heard Shorty and Doc were still married.

Since more marrying couples have property that they wish to protect for their children from prior marriages, as well as for themselves if things do not go well, more newlyweds are resorting to prenuptial agreements. The lingering sour taste and remaining scar tissue of a past interrupted marriage prompts many couples to anticipate and plan for all possible scenarios, obstacles, and even for divorce, the second, third, or fourth time around.

For every sublime consideration, there's a matching ridiculous one. One San Francisco couple was determined to divide all expenses equally. The couple even agreed that it would split the $6.00 toll when crossing the Golden Gate Bridge together. Nine months should be allowed for discussions, drafts, negotiations, and eventual signing; it takes time to hammer out these provisions. Most lawyers require full financial disclosure statements on both sides. As further protection, some attorneys recommend that a court reporter be present at the signing to create a transcript, and to take down questions, answers, and other evidence of competence and free will. Other lawyers suggest videotaping the signing of the agreement to perpetuate evidence of mental capacity and similar relevant legalities. This event may be a good time to meet your future in-laws and the kids. Perhaps you can also invite an ex-spouse or two to the signing. Hey, why not post it on YouTube? Besides, everyone already knows everyone else.

What about legal fees? Think about spending $3,000 to $90,000, depending on the size and complexity of your assets. As Trump would probably say, "It is far better to have a prenup and not need it than it is to need a prenup and not have it." I recall reading that Donald Trump, 59 at the time of his (third) marriage to the lovely Melania Knauss, who was 35 (24-year variance), may have had three (personal assets, corporate ownerships, and international holdings) prenups. It seems that Ivana Trump also believes in the younger spouse concept. In April 2008, Ivana (she at 59, he at 35—also a 24-year variance) married Rossano Rubicondi in a lavish ceremony at The Donald's Key Largo estate in Palm Beach, Florida. See, it pays to be nice to your ex. Perhaps he/she may one day allow you and your new spouse to marry at one of their many houses and host the reception there. Ivana's fourth marriage lasted only six stormy months. Well, as they say in New York, "Next!"

Ancillary Prenup Protection

After money, the second most common cause of divorce deals with sex *and the lack thereof.* I've handled many divorce cases that included sexual-related problems over my years of practice. I feel compelled to include some of the more common problems, along with possible prenup solutions to head off these troubles at the pass. As already demonstrated, prenups can be used for sexual-related marital safeguards (anti-cheating clauses). Many spouses are insecure, aging, and breathing; thus, the following may apply to all of us. At one time or another, most (living) married persons have had secret sexual fantasies of being in bed with someone other than their spouses. Every generation has had its leading man/woman pick, from Betty Grable/Clark Gable in the past to Angelina Jolie/Brad Pitt today.

While in bed with our beloved spouse, the following question may come up: "If, my love, you could make love to any other man/woman, whom would you desire?" Stop! Do not answer the question. This is a super-sensitive subject. You should have the right to remain silent. You ought to have the right to be represented by legal counsel. If, however, you elect to answer, then there's one, and only one, answer that can be given: "Why you, of course, my love, only to you!" Sure, and the Easter Bunny comes in spring and Santa comes in winter.

Spouses who ask this question, my psychologist colleagues tell me, are usually seeking reassurance that their spouse would want to make love only to them. Still, we must all be realistic. While you may have your secret phantom lovers, there's no way in the world he or she will unexpectedly appear in your bed. Then again, stranger things have happened ("Be careful what you wish for!").

Note: The following material may be
offensive to some. For those who are
either shocked or just not interested,
please skip the next few pages.

Because this is such a sensitive subject and because spouses usually do not reveal their deepest and darkest sexual fantasies to each other (which is why so many couples have so many sex-related issues), this topic must be approached with care, caution, and common sense, if at all. Researchers in this area suggest that the majority of women/men never discuss these subject-topics and leave them forever dormant under their marital mattress, so to speak.

First, we need a sidebar review and a little sexual psychophysiology. We already know that the brain (in most cases) is our largest sex organ. We also realize that a little spicy stimulus can enhance sexual passion, pleasure, and performance. Perhaps you and your spouse should first undergo a sexual awareness/inhibition audit. Where are the two of you on your sexual openness and sharing of your true sexual interactions?

Please answer the following six simple questions with yes or no answers:

- Do you talk openly about sex to each other?
- Do you and your spouse occasionally enjoy viewing a porno movie together?
- Are you comfortable discussing your sexual desires and other related topics with your spouse?
- Do you get kinky with each other during sex?
- Are you each comfortable with your own eroticism?
- Have you discussed whom else you would like to make love to with your spouse?

Caution again. If this bothers or offends you, please skip to the next section. Menacing dangers may be lurking in this sexual activity.

If you and your spouse mutually elect to go there, these open erotic sexual discussions may cause marriage-threatening problems for some. There are reported cases where spouses who engage in these *open sexual discussion* activities occasionally experience difficulty in differentiating between fantasy and reality. Sometimes one spouse may get caught up in his/her erotic fantasies and cross the line. Selected spouses mistakenly believe that their spouse is fine with their over-the-line behavior because it is openly discussed and promoted in *their bed*. Once this line is crossed, however, the roof can come crashing down. Remember, what is talked about in your marital bed must stay in your marital bed.

I once heard a story about a man named Mark who was married to a wonderful woman named Marsha. One night while in bed, Marsha asked Mark which of her four attractive girlfriends he would like to make love to. It seems as if Marsha was expecting the *only you* answer. Innocent (dumb) Mark, believing it was a fair question, gave his honest answer: "Oh, just to two of them!" That was it. Marsha left the marital bed and went to sleep on the marital living room couch, where she slept for the following week.

Mark was sentenced to sleeping alone, no sex, and repeated solo shower sessions. Yes, this could happen to you; many have endured such harsh sentences. Marsha further accused Mark of being controlling, stubborn, and too much of a drinker. Mark's response: "Hey, what's wrong with that (in light of my other excellent good qualities)?"

Given the controversy of this explosive subject, the following are the likely gender views on Mark's response. First, a woman's probable point of view: "Mark, as would any other selfish and self-indulgent man, would be totally out of line in wanting to talk about another woman while making love to his wife ..." From a man's likely point of view: "Mark, as would any other normal, vigorous, healthy man, was excited talking about Leslie, while having sex with Marsha ..." I know it sounds a little crazy, somewhat kinky and almost bizarre; however, such is the quasi-perverted sexual psyche of countless otherwise normal people when sexually aroused.

After repeated disagreements, disputes, and disappointments, both Marsha and Mark finally had had enough of each other.

They, too, ended up getting divorced for medical reasons: they were sick of each other. One year later, Mark ran into Marsha at a local shopping mall. He greeted her and told her that, thanks to her, he had become a changed man. He proudly told her that he was no longer [as] stubborn. He had stopped being [as] controlling and that he did not drink anymore [or any less]. He told her that he had been seeing Leslie, one of Marsha's former girlfriends, who had also divorced last year. See?

Marsha told Mark that she was glad that he had *hooked up* with Leslie and said that she, too, had changed. Marsha said that she had met Leslie's ex-husband, Elhand, at a Divorce Recovery Group meeting, that they had been dating, and that he was really good to her and for her. Marsha then told Mark that Elhand thought Marsha was a great lover, and that they were both very happy. It seems as if Elhand's sexual compliments worked better than Mark's unappreciated sexual fantasies. Frequently, divorce brings benefits to both ex-spouses and others.

Two of my university psychology colleagues (one female, one male) provided the following explanation as to one possible root for Mark's behavior:

> Women and men process sexual expressions regarding alternative partners differently. Hence, when a husband tells his wife he would like to make love to one of her attractive girlfriends, wives generally take it personally and as a tacit rejection of them.

> Men, on the other hand, are said to be more pragmatic in hearing their wives' spicy sexual wishes of sleeping with someone else, and tend to get caught up in the erotic excitement and arousal of the event, without feelings of personal rejection or intended harm to others.

I am certain that there are other compelling explanations and thought-provoking theories regarding this explosive topic. Many women and several men enjoy reading romance novels laced with love, passion, and even salacious sexual commentary. Every major bookstore and website bookseller carries shelves of romance novel selections. Millions are sold daily. But wait! This may be your answer to a troubled area. Perhaps you should become the *Fabio* of your domain. Yes, let your hair grow long, start wearing open long-sleeved white shirts to bed, and get yourself a used white pony to ride into the bedroom (low ceilings). This may help you talk to and listen to your spouse about her/his romantic desires.

Then again, there are spouses who achieve higher levels of sexual intimacy while openly sharing their fanciful sexual needs. As we age, the potential for superior sexual enjoyment increases, as we are developmentally more capable of deeper intimacy. With age, however, sexual performance becomes a greater challenge for both sexes, because Mother Nature places age-related restrictions on both spouses, via the loss of natural love lubrication and allowing our love lances to bend-in-the-middle. Some may need added excitement and new practices *to get up and away* from their routine robotic patterns and customary sexual sequences. Some spouses enjoy hearing about their partners's past sexual episodes; others do not.

When it comes to sex, women say that most men are already animals. Men seem to get turned on by almost anyone, anyplace, and at any time (what was your name again?). Reportedly 43 percent of men (and it's not just construction workers at their worksites, but this group includes presidential candidates named John) would have sex with a person they had just met, compared with only 9 percent of women.

If you or someone you're considering marrying finds alternative sexual partner discussions repugnant to hers or his beliefs, values, or standards, you can add a prohibition clause against any and all such discussions in your prenup. Wow, that's a lot of complicated heavy material; nevertheless, prenups have their place. I've included an example copy of a prenup in the Appendix. This sample is provided as such; it is merely an example of what you may need, as opposed to what you actually require, and it may not be enforceable in your particular state.

Postnuptial Agreements (Postnups)

As in the prenups above, a postnuptial agreement (postnup) is a contract between husband and wife; however, these agreements are entered into after the spouses are already married. Postnups are not new, but perhaps newly discovered by some. Just as with water and the wheel, postnups have been around for an exceedingly long time and have been used to promote health, harmony, and happiness in deflated, troubled, or flat marriages. After the Garden of Eden incident with the apple, it is said that Adam requested a postnup from Eve; however, they could not find a lawyer. Then, because of Eve's disobedience, God punished everyone by giving us all one or more of the six-audience, pre-engagement protocol warnings listed in Chapter 12 (in-laws, stepchildren, ex-spouses, etc.), along with headaches, "ED" (erectile dysfunction), locusts, and lawyers.

It seems as if the true underlying motivation for requesting a postnup is not about money, assets, or property, but rather it is a subterfuge for more serious underlying marital problems, that at least one spouse does not wish to address (at this time). In my professional opinion, as a professor and practicing divorce attorney, postnups are often mere harbingers for coming divorces, as demonstrated in the Burkle case and the Tomasino story below. Often postnups merely streamline the divorce process by preemptively eliminating spousal support, division of marital property, and other issues.

In the California appellate divorce case *Burkle vs. Burkle*, Jan was unsuccessful in her attempt to have the couple's postnup set aside. Their postnup included acknowledgments signed by the parties that they fully understood the agreement and its consequences. Attached to the agreement were signed, detailed declarations by their experienced divorce attorneys stating that they had fully explained the effects and ramifications of the agreement to each of them. Six years later, Jan filed for divorce and claimed that their postnup was invalid. She argued that, at the time the agreement was signed, she was suffering from severe depression, taking strong medications, and emotionally dependent upon her husband for her decisions.

Based upon the acknowledgments and declarations in the agreement and because of the court's determination that an unreasonable amount of time had elapsed (six years) before the wife complained about the agreement, the court held their signed postnup to be valid. Unfortunately for Jan, the agreement also contained her acknowledgment that she had been given a full disclosure of her husband's assets.

Jan was compelled to settle for the $30 million amount pursuant to the postnup (rather than the billion dollars plus controlled by her husband Ron). Needless to mention, she would have been far better off not signing the agreement, continuing to take her medications, and filing or divorce later. Ladies and gentlemen, if you have any doubt (even just one) or feel you're being pressured to *sign* any agreement with your spouse, don't sign it. You may only be postponing the inevitable. You may be surrendering valuable property rights and important benefits. Tell him/ her that you need time to think it over—five years or so. Then again, he/ she may not want to put up with the aggravation and may offer to buy you out at a higher and better price.

My good friend Tomasino told me that he had asked his wife, Therasina, to watch her weight, because he was concerned more about her health than her looks. Therasina, he said, ignored his loving requests and became contemptuous: "I don't use weighing scales anymore," she angrily responded to his modest request. Tomasino told me that the marriage was over then and there. He came to see me initially to prepare a postnup to simplify the coming divorce. Their postnup equally divided all of their property and was mutually acceptable to both; the agreement was signed by them and counsel. Six months later to the day, Tomasino filed for divorce. The rest is history, and the future was predictable. Their postnup totally streamlined their subsequent divorce, making it less far stressful and costly.

Postnups can also be used to shield community property assets from business creditors. Assume you have been married for 31 years, and you and your spouse already own seven valuable homes with an estimated current equity-value of some $90 million. Suppose further that you purchased a major league baseball team (Los Angeles Dodgers) in 2004 for some $432 million, and you were concerned about personal asset exposure to business liabilities or creditors' claims. You could have a postnup where all of your real estate is transferred to your wife (who also happens to be an attorney), and 100 percent ownership of the team (with a current estimated value of $708 million, and an equity-value of $289 million) is transferred to the husband.

Be careful, because sometimes a shield can be used as a sword. This mix-up could cost $19 million in attorney fees to straighten out! Since both husband and wife intended to protect their valuable real estate from [potential] team creditors, it would seem that their postnup agreement should not favor one spouse over the other. It's as if they had put their property into two individual trusts for a common purpose. There is an *"ex-"* vs. *"in-" clusive* "typo" in an Exhibit to their postnup; team ownership should thus remain a joint asset.

Today married couples procure postnups to help resolve troublesome issues in their stressed marriages by removing sources of disagreement over finances, assets, and other problematic matters. Postnups are also used by spouses as a way of controlling, punishing, or even rewarding certain spousal behavior, like adultery, over-spending, going back to college, preparing well-cooked home meals, or mowing the lawn.

Additional justifications for procurement of a postnup include sudden financial changes for either spouse following marriage or even after long discontented years together. These changes include career changes, receiving an inheritance or winning the lottery, experiencing a change in investment income, selling a business, or meeting Joe/Jane, the attractive new single neighbor on the block. These are all valid, fully legitimate and reasonable justifications to obtain a postnup.

For some couples, a postnup can stop conflict (for a few weeks, anyway) and promote harmony in their marriages, at least until the process server comes to their door with divorce papers in hand. Postnups seem to be the new phenomenon of our time. Granted, they can help assure that a divorcing spouse won't be giving away the entire farm to their mother, children, or new lover, as well as their old attorney, a favorite cocktail waitress, or bartender down the street. Postnups are also used to supplement existing prenups when a spouse hits a tree or runs into a fire hydrant.

Currently, the validity of postnups varies from jurisdiction to jurisdiction. It's vital that each spouse have a separate and independent lawyer representing him or her before signing any postnup. Enforcement of Barry Bonds-like prenups may apply to postnups, but no one knows for sure because each case and each court are different. I have also included a sample copy of a postnup in the Appendix. Again, this is provided as a sample only; it may not apply to what you may need. Do not use this as a model, as it may not be relevant to your individual situation and may not be enforceable in your particular state.

One- and Three-Pot Financing

Money remains the number one cause of divorce. As said, prenups can add *balance* to marriages with a financially overloaded spouse. Postnups can bring *stability* to wealthy couples experiencing marital problems. Years ago the Carpenters had a great hit, *We've Only Just Begun*. Such is the case with many couples, for they start off with little or almost nothing. Given the simplicity of their financial situations, most of these newlyweds use the *one-pot* plan. This alternative calls for all earnings and other available funds to be deposited into a single checking account. All bills and expenses are paid therefrom and remaining proceeds are saved for the next month. This safe, simple system serves their needs and usually no one challenges anything, because both are fully informed.

Couples with accumulated wealth or clashing financial goals can use the *three-pot theory*. Under this system, each spouse has her/his own separate pot. There is also one additional pot for the community. Based upon mutual agreement, each spouse contributes 50/50, 60/40, or any other agreed-upon contribution percentages, to the community pot. Contribution can be based on earnings, income, or separate property proceeds, as well as height, weight, or any other objective basis.

Contributions to the community pot are used to pay community bills: house/rent payments, utilities, insurance, and other shared expenses. Remaining third-pot funds can be used for next month's community bills. Ownership in third-pot purchased items would be based on the same percent-basis as the parties respective contributions. Each spouse would have exclusive control of her/his separate-pot proceeds.

Reality

While the one-pot, three-pot, and other shared financing systems seem to work between spouses, sometimes spousal contaminants can enter the arrangement. Selfishness, resentment, and ego, as well as self-pity and self-interest might infect a process that worked well in the past. As noted, human nature has its dark side.

Even when there is mutual agreement, sometimes the less-wealthy spouse may feel one or more of the above listed disapproving emotions. These problems are increased when the wealthier spouse *pulls rank* and asserts her/his [higher] contributions to the marital funds.

My colleagues in psychology tell me that once a couple's financial particulars are disclosed to parents, siblings, or friends, condescending commentary and judgmental criticisms are likely to follow. Many of these external salvos are usually worse and more severe than the internal-spousal complaints mentioned above.

Don't be surprised if you hear:

- "What!"
- "We need to talk!"
- "That's totally unfair!"
- "I wouldn't put up with that!"

Family and peer criticisms about money matters are common; however, other realities can also be at play. Frequently critical comments from *trusted confidants* are sometimes motivated by our innate vicious aspects, like personal envy, jealousy, or spite. Resentful of your fortunate comfortable lifestyle, your subclass comrades might prefer seeing you at their same economic level.

Beware of those who offer over whelming sympathy or implied vindictiveness, "you can do much better" advice, or are excessively judgmental of your spouse. I recall many clients coming to see me accompanied by others. Some come with a parent, sibling, or other support person; others come with an aggressive divorce manager-promoter. I have also met with men and woman who bring a newfound *friend* to help them get divorced.

Palimony

Newfound property claims for maintenance and support based on alleged oral promises have flourished between unmarried couples living together (a.k.a. shacking up). In 1976, the California Supreme Court established a new legal principle allowing Michelle Triola Marvin (the former live-in lover and chief pasta chef) to sue her actor-roommate Lee Marvin for palimony. Marvin M. Mitchelson, already known as the divorce lawyer for the stars and their exes, represented Michelle. Mitchelson was shrewd and smart in his work. He represented the ex-wives of King Fahd of Saudi Arabia, Marlon Brando, and scores of other celebrity clients.

After their breakup, Michelle moved in with her new longtime companion Dick Van Dyke (she stayed with him for 33 years, until her death in October 2009). Both homes are in Beverly Hills, California. Hey, don't knock it—same phone prefix and same zip code, and she later knew all of the waiters and chefs at *Il Fornaio*, the best Italian restaurant in the entire Beverly Hills area, by their first names. Besides, as we have said many times, everyone already knew everyone else.

The palimony doctrine is an extension of what lawyers call *promissory estoppel*. This recognized legal principle permits a party to recover on a promise, even though the promise was made without legal consideration and would thus otherwise render the promise unenforceable. Essentially it prevents the promisor (the person making the promise) from arguing that his/her promise should not be upheld. It also requires that the promisee (the person trying to enforce the promise) actually relied on the promise, that said reliance was reasonable, and that the promisee would be damaged by not enforcing the subject promise. Lawyers! Enforceable support promises must be memorialized in a written contract or other acceptable memorandum.

In *Marvin vs. Marvin* (even though Lee and Michelle were never married, clever Mitchelson used Lee's last name, which gave Michelle's case greater credibility), Judge Marshall ordered Lee to pay $104,000 to Michelle for *employment rehabilitation purposes*. Her claim for half of the $3.6 million, which Marvin had earned during their six years of cohabitation, was denied. Later the California Court of Appeals reversed this decision, declaring that Michelle was not entitled to any money whatsoever.

The court ruled that: "A *cohabitant* in an unmarried cohabitative relationship has no community property claim, but merely a contract claim." Without evidence of a contract (all love-nest pledges and pillow-talk promises must be in writing) between Lee and Michelle requiring that Lee support her if their relationship ended, Michelle could not recover any money whatsoever.

The palimony doctrine originally applied to claims for support and maintenance preceded by a breakup between an unmarried man and woman living together. In May of 1981, we had yet another case of first impression (as is common in the law) dealing with a palimony doctrine claim brought by Marilyn Barnett, a former secretary and lover who sued divorced Billie Jean King for palimony. Wow! That would ruin your whole day. The suit was based on Billie Jean's ending their serious ten-year relationship. Marilyn claimed that Billie Jean had promised (pillow talk?) to provide her with life-long financial support.

The court ruled in Billie Jean's favor (no admissible evidence of any agreement). It was: "She said/she said." Unfortunately, everyone lost. Billie Jean had $1.75 million in endorsements immediately cancelled. She was forced to play another two seasons just to pay her legal fees and costs. Marilyn was said to have later attempted suicide. She was found with a broken back below the balcony of the stilt-level Malibu home. The incident left Marilyn a paraplegic, and she is confined to a wheelchair.

Same-sex palimony lawsuits continued. In 1982, Scott Thorson filed a $133 million palimony/fraud lawsuit claiming that he was Liberace's lover, that Lee had promised to "take care of him," and that Lee might be suffering from AIDS. As such, Scott claimed that he would eventually get AIDS. The lawsuit was later settled out of court for an alleged $95,000.

But wait. If tennis is your game, we go on to the next match: *Judy Hill Nelson vs. Martina Navratilova* (Judy's eight-year romance with women's tennis star Martina). This heated palimony suit against Martina followed their harsh breakup. The lawsuit, filed in 1991, was based on allegations that Martina had an extended, serious, and loving relationship with Judy. As reported by one commentator, "It was to become America's ugliest divorce case." Judy, as Martina's wife, claimed she deserved half of Martina's earnings and property acquired during their eight-year relationship. Judy further cited a signed agreement (strong evidence), the signing of which had been videotaped (by Judy with her new remote function video camera, recently given to her by Martina). Terms of the final settlement were never disclosed. Judy was allowed to keep the house in Aspen they had custom-built. Judy's skilled lawyers asked for $11 million. The case was settled out of court. This bespeaks a probable settlement range between $5 million and $8 million. That is not bad for a six-year high-end lifestyle (with paid room, board, and travel).

After the Marvin decision, I was inundated with appointments involving unmarried couples who were living together without any agreement as to their property rights, support expectations, or other post separation ending legalities. Complexities in these living arrangements were compounded where one or both parties had already liquidated furniture, cars, or other duplication property that was not needed or would not fit in their new abode. Further complications ensue when couples purchase homes, cars or additional new items, as to ownership, division, and distribution when the relationship ends. Conflicting expectations can lead to great stress, expenses, and unhappiness. All of these matters must be addressed via a comprehensive Cohabitation Agreement, if you plan to move in with someone to whom you are not married and share living expenses.

One last troubled but incomplete divorce case without Trump Armor was the 15-year marriage of Peter Brant, 63, and his second wife, 41-year-old Stephanie. He is a $2.7 billionaire with a vast art collection and his own polo team, she a former *Playboy, Sports Illustrated* cover-person, and *Victoria's Secret* model. He claimed she cheated on him and abused alcohol and drugs; she said he was too controlling. She filed for divorce in March 2009. Somehow Peter married without listening to his good friend The Donald: "It's a lot easier to get [a prenup] done when you love each other than when you hate each other!"

After heated and protracted nuclear divorce litigation, Peter and Stephanie reconciled their differences and dropped their divorce in late September 2010. No news yet on how or why; just a request: "They ask that their privacy be respected," (perhaps a favorable postnup?).

WHAT YOU NOW RECOGNIZE, UNDERSTAND, AND ACCEPT

1. Prenuptial agreements are recognized in all 50 states.

2. Be extra careful if you're marrying a lawyer or someone who has a lawyer relative.

3. Prenuptial agreements supersede divorce laws to your benefit.

4. Pre-and postnups can include prohibitions against mentioning past lovers.

5. Never, ever, use a "sunset clause" in any agreements (ask Jack).

6. You can add a "no cheating," "no drugs," or even a "no cheesecake" clause.

7. Postnups are made after marriage, with legal representation.

8. Postnups are often mere harbingers of coming divorce storms.

9. Postnups are becoming more popular in troubled marriages.

10. It's better to have a prenup/postnup and not need it than to need one and not have either.

CHAPTER ELEVEN

Post-Divorce Dating and Other Adventures

A man noticed an attractive woman entering his plane as he sat. Suddenly, the attractive woman was standing in the aisle next to him and said, "Pardon me; I believe you're in my seat." They exchanged seats and the man said, "What will you be doing in Chicago?" She responded, "I'm going to the American Anthropologist Convention." He asked, "What will you be doing there?" She said, "I will be debunking two popular sexual myths." He replied, "And what would those be?"

"Well, first," said the woman, "there's a myth that no one male group can be identified as being best endowed. My research established that the American Indian male is the best blessed."

"What's the second myth?" asked the man.

"Well, somehow," said the woman, "French men have been considered to be the best lovers. This also is not true. Based on my research, it is Jewish men who are the best lovers." Then, red-faced, the woman turned towards the man and said, "I'm sorry, I don't even know your name." The man extended his right hand and said, "Tonto. Tonto Goldstein!"

One never knows what might happen; even taking a domestic flight has potential meeting opportunities; nevertheless, based on our faulty DNA and imperfect human nature, many of us rush to retie the marital-knot just untied. Once retied, however, it is expensive to loosen or untie again. As mentioned in Chapter Four, spousal proposals are said to be our second most important life decision. After completion of my second divorce, I waited 180 additional days to get back out into the dating scene again. Wow, what an education (a second rushed marriage, an amicable divorce, and a rapid recovery); I sure learned a lot!

For many, divorce ignites an immediate search for a spousal surrogate. Most of these *hunts* are for either a caretaker companion or rebound romance-replacement, and searchers are not concerned about appearing needy or desperate. These caretaker companion and rebound romance seekers include the separated, divorced, and even the widowed. Same-sex partners experience similar separation sequences in their relationship-ending situations and sometimes suffer more than heterosexuals. There is a lack of available professionals (in many areas) to counsel and treat non-heterosexual individuals, as well as a limited number of suitable partners available for them.

Rushed relationship replacement factors include the following:

- Seeking the comfort of a new companion
- Proving to themselves, and others, that they are still desirable and appreciated
- Missing the fact that they are looking for a clone of the person who just left

It's not uncommon to see two of the three motivations present in a single search, and all three can be present in extraordinary cases. Prevailing practices suggest that most men will often hook up with a caretaker companion until someone more desirable comes along. Other men date sporadically, while some become loners and keep to themselves.

Women, on the other hand, are said to be more cautious and not willing to take in just anyone. Women have stronger support systems, and they seem content being alone—flying solo—waiting for an appropriate partner (*Prince Charming* or Dorian Gray) to come along; however, changes are occurring here, too.

Women usually have six good, close friends, while men usually have one or none. Women frequently get together and go to movies, shows, and operas, as well as cross-country trips, foreign travel and other activities. When was the last time you saw a group of guys doing any of the above?

The former conventional wisdom used to be *don't marry on the rebound.* Wait to remarry until after you're healed from your emotional entanglements and individual injuries. Only then can you start with someone new. Sinatra, however, used to say (sorry, ladies), "The best way to get over a broad is to find a new one." This *thinking* is a common alternative for many and is not contrary to newfound research on this subject. Research by Professor Nicholas Wolfinger, Department of Family and Consumer Studies, University of Utah, concludes that:

> There is no correlation between 'the rebound marriage'—that is, a marriage that quickly follows on the heels of the end of another—and divorce.
>
> Rebounding into a fast second marriage is no more or less likely to increase the chance of another divorce than if a person waits a longer period of time.

We already know that the search for a new spouse is difficult. Second marriages are subject to greater pressures and higher divorce rates than first marriages (67 percent and 55 percent respectively). Second-time spouses are expected to have increased maturity, improved communication skills, and inalienable conflict-resolution talents. Often they do not. Second-timers sometimes come with recent exit experience. New spouses may suddenly find themselves hearing, "Hey, I don't have to put up with this crap. I'll just get divorced (again)." As would be expected, first-time marriage handicap factors also impact second-timers (divorced parents, low levels of education, and unresolved personal issues).

While I certainly exercised due care in waiting to find a spouse on both occasions, I definitely did not do so after I met and injudiciously married them months thereafter.

I may have been the greatest offender of the two mandatory marriage prerequisites in both of my incomplete marriages. I did not date either of my ex-wives long enough to get to know them and for them to understand me. I also was not engaged to them for a sufficient period to value them or for them to appreciate me. This was my error in both marriages. Here is what I did wrong, twice.

Fresh out of law school, degree in hand, and a job starting Monday, I went looking for a spouse. Fortunately, I did have the common sense to wait until *after* graduation. I realized that I would step into a higher socio-economic pool with far better spousal prospects. I was correct. Unfortunately, I observed many of my law school classmates had outgrown their spouses. Many of these highly intelligent individuals experienced profound growth spurts, fueled by newfound confidence via graduation and promising employment opportunities. Uncomfortable with and no longer appreciative of their earlier choices, many good wives and some stale husbands were left behind, as they were exchanged for new, better educated, and sometimes more sophisticated replacements. Such are the frequent and foreseeable outcomes in early marriages where one enters a new arena supercharged with intellectual stimuli, while the other remains in an intellectual time warp.

I am a man of letters. I also learn from my mistakes (or so I thought). Thirty-two years after the one-month wait to ask Apollina for her hand in marriage, I waited twice as long before asking Aida to marry me. The second time around, I was wiser—I waited two months! Boy was I smart. Still, this *doubled* dating duration was too short, and the engagement period not long enough; both resulted in the same spurious outcome. My second marriage lasted only 27 months.

In reviewing my incomplete marriages, I've come to realize and admit that I just did not know my past wives (nor did they know me). Even if my first marriage lasted 22 years, it did not last a lifetime. We were lucky for the good years, but it did not endure. After being single for 11 years and dating scores of interesting and accomplished women, I met Aida. Somehow, I fell into my past pattern of taking a long time (11 years) to meet someone only to experience the same uncontrollable propensity to propose to them an average of 45 days later.

After my spontaneous proposals, I married the women (on average of) five months thereafter. Why? It's now clear to me that once I found a *keeper*, I rushed to propose (as if they were not going to be available next year), and then I hastily married them. Why? It's not as if they had to be engaged by midnight or married by the end of the month. Why? Well, lessons learned; never again! Next time, a two-year dating duration, followed by a three-year engagement (as they say down South: "Good luck with that!").

Post-Divorce Dating

Perhaps you should go online. The advent of Internet dating has launched a cottage industry of successful, selective, and specialized dating services. For a modest fee, you can find *Mr. or Ms. Al Most Right*, sometimes within your same zip code. Match.com, eHarmony.com and many others have saturated the landscape. There are also gay/lesbian, religious, and ethnic sites. Some sites provide services for herpes and HIV/AIDS-infected individuals and others for ailing and challenged persons. Since 2010 was also an election year, there are also Republican and Democratic online dating sites for those who may want *political compatibility* from the start.

There's a plethora of established dating services (EDS) in major cities awaiting you. Just Google your local areas and you'll discover what dating services can provide; some focused selections include:

Professionals
Professional millionaires
Professional millionaires
who are extremely old

Several EDS charge huge fees—anywhere from $5,000 to $100,000. These commercial services supplement the traditional places where everyone used to find love: church, school, work, and other unique venues like art museums, opera houses and theaters, as well as specialized lectures, and even Home Depot, Costco, or the airport. Naturally, men and women should frequent forums of preference to find suitable partners with similar interests. Do not expect to find any Puccini aficionados at a monster truck show; the reverse (thanks goodness?) is also true.

The reverse is also true: avoid bars, addiction recovery meetings, prisons, and other such places. Don't be surprised if you're approached while shopping at Home Depot. Many well-dressed women shop there and feel comfortable asking well-dressed men innocuous installation or product questions. Naturally, I still wear my tuxedo while shopping at Home Depot and other places frequented by quality, eligible women.

Frequently, second and third would-be spouses come with newfound support obligations via ex-spouses and minor children. At the same time, by our second and subsequent marriages, we are usually more financially grounded and emotionally mature. It's as though you had both feet on the ground rather than just one. Would-be spouses who come with personal agendas, demand lists, or excess baggage should be avoided. Those with drug or alcohol problems, excessive debt, two or more bankruptcies, or other such luggage should be avoided immediately—*no second dates here.* But wait! Who's left? There are always far better prospects waiting for you. Why start off with a load on your shoulder when you can find someone less burdened and more suitable for you?

Remarriage Prerequisites

The first mandatory prerequisite for remarriage is a one-year (going steady) dating experience. Good marriages and lasting friendships are based on acceptance. We date, dine, and spend prolonged periods of time together; we travel and eventually share intimate moments, which bring us even closer together. The dating process is where two people really get to know each other and learn each other's deep-seated personal values, public virtues, and private vices.

The second mandatory prerequisite is a one-year engagement. This cycle is just like the dating phase but with mutual exclusivity, greater intimacy, and planning for a future together. The engagement period is where couples really get into life-long expectations and life goals. This next level allows us to discover each other's hidden characteristics and intimate details. We realize individual idiosyncrasies and personal proclivities via honest and open discussions necessary to reveal material differences in life goals and remarriage expectations.

Still, you need to spend time together to experience each other and each person's suppressed behaviors, which may only surface under special circumstances or conditions, like a blue moon (which only occurs once every 19 months on average) or during leap years.

Marriages without prerequisite satisfaction can lead to disappointed and dissatisfied spouses, who later become *roommates*. Couples who rush into remarriage without prerequisite completion become stressed, strained, and stretched individuals who frequently move onto Victor Hugo's *Les Miserables* standing; many eventually divorce. But wait, who's to blame? It's like walking into any restaurant and randomly ordering *Number Five* without looking at the menu, asking what number five is, or anything else about it, and then complaining later. The purpose of dating and being engaged is to find and discover obvious, as well as latent and suppressed flaws, fractures, and failures (hey, we all have them; it's part of being human). If troublesome defects, deficiencies, and disparities are not discovered, resolved, or reconciled during the dating or engagement periods, the foregoing may cause major conflict later.

Couples contemplating second or third marriages will, hopefully, come into their new engagements with expanded experience, improved maturity, and a better understanding of what is really important to them and to their new partner. This period is a time of discovery. If we rush and combine the two different periods (dating and engagement) into one, *datgagement*, we shortchange ourselves and our partners in the important sequential processes needed to learn about who and what lies ahead.

As simple as it sounds, to love someone truly is to accept them totally for who they are. Even if this person suffers from follicle regression (is bald), has developed an excessive abdominal liquid grain capacity (has a pot-belly), and is body-mass imbalanced (is a little on the heavy side), along with being uncouth (lacking in social graces), has acute cosmetic surgery requirements (needs work), or requires immediate dental seeding (has missing teeth), this person could be your soul mate (or perhaps even a cell mate).

> As my father used to say:
> What you see is what you get,
> and it's not going to change.

As first-time spouses, many of us were at a disadvantage. We lacked the wisdom, maturity, and the necessary conflict resolution skills to discuss and resolve complex issues in a loving manner. Still, many come with super-charged sexual needs and physical wants that helped them stay together.

First-, second-, and even third-time spouses wrongfully assume that any undesirable characteristics of their newly found future spouses can be changed, modified, or eliminated. Granted, there are some habits, propensities, and behaviors that can occasionally be altered, but, as a whole, we should be happy with what we have, or we should go elsewhere. Former First Lady Laura Bush told George that if he did not stop his drinking, she would leave him. He understood, and he stopped drinking altogether. There are hundreds of other viable examples of such ultimatums that have worked; there are also thousands that have not. By all means, if you ever intend to tender such a challenge, be sure you're prepared to follow through, for if you do not, we are told, the consequences can be severe and long lasting.

Both men and women may find Mr. or Ms. Almost Right but for his/her smoking, drinking, or sloppy attire. Still, there are other complaints: his/her lack of interest in playing bridge, dancing, or going camping with the in-laws, kids, or church members, along with not traveling to Africa and other incompatibilities. Unmet wishes and unchanged behaviors may cause indirect isolation, repeated irritations, and bottled resentments. If there's a failure in achieving any of the desired changes or expectations and if failure to attain the anticipated change or expected goals would result in a deal breaker, then look elsewhere. It's not as if you didn't have a choice. If you stay, pay and pray that change will somehow come; often it does not.

But wait! Even if you take sufficient time and effort to discuss and agree upon mutual goals and objectives, individuals change their minds thereafter. Yes, spouses agreeing to and planning for *Plan A* often experience changes to *Plan B* by the other spouse. It does happen (ask Aida). Spouses who do not adjust to these changes often end up not being spouses. Selected spouses have *universal adaptability*, which amicably allows them to adjust to career, location, and other significant changes with comfort and loving mutual respect.

DMRM

Men and women have different and declining standings in the dating, marriage, and remarriage (DMRM) arenas. Men, nevertheless, seem to have the odds in their favor in all three areas because there are greater numbers of eligible quality women for the smaller numbers of eligible men. Once again, add in the word *quality* and the pool of eligible men shrinks even further. All must keep in mind that, if they do not first find what they are looking for, they must move on and look elsewhere. Often, better partners and healthier choices await you. Why stay with someone who does not fit? It's as basic as trying to put a size 12 foot into a size 10 shoe. Eventually you may get that foot into that shoe, but there will be blood, pain, and future foot surgeries (divorces).

Based on these logical conclusions, men should realize that there are many other fish in the sea. There are also many male fish for the ladies. Just keep fishing. Sooner or later you may catch a good one, and don't let yourself be subjected to the agony and lasting lament of the big one that got away!

Several men's and women's publications and their prolific writers tell us monthly that women and men may need to realize and appreciate certain DMRM facts. Because of the greater competition in finding and keeping a quality eligible man/woman, women/men may need to work a little harder to improve their eligibility. Most of us are familiar with the repeatedly-voiced common complaints about the sexes by the sexes (see Chapters 3 and 12). There are currently several good books available for both men and women to enhance and improve their respective DMRM batting averages in getting hit-on more often by members of the opposite sex.

Logic and reason support the valid conclusion that we gravitate to persons in whom we find similar qualities, values, and interests, as those we ourselves already possess. In troubled marriages, spouses often have good character, shared values, and common goals. Others are even more blessed and also enjoy mutual interests, similar spiritual beliefs, and other common threads that hold and bind them even closer together. Still, all of the foregoing points are still not enough! Why?

The primary reason most marriages are interrupted is that somehow, petty indifferences and cumulative resentments infect the relationship. These contaminants, if not addressed and resolved, are compounded and eventually erode the mighty pillars that once shored up the spouses and their once invincible marriage. Relationships, marriages, and sometimeseven solid friendships often end in sorrow and scorn.

Marriage is a toll road. We pay as we go. Sometimes we do not go that far; nonetheless, the toll is expensive. One never really knows what the future will be in post-divorce dating or even in well-established marriages (ask Al or Tipper Gore!). Men and women have different criteria for marriage and remarriage. Women used to be more concerned about financial security and stability, as well as dancing, traveling, and other social activities they enjoy. These now seem to be fading concerns. Continued financial gender equality provides women with the security and economic stability they used to seek from men. Social activity is available via church, club, and community functions; there are also various vacation purchase options, which more women can now easily afford. Still, women (and men) seek companionship.

Men, on the other hand, operate with totally different decisive platforms. While some men may disagree, most (those under 81) are still concerned about looks, breasts, waistlines, and legs. As superficial as we men seem to be, we are still men. Many like to astound others with their impressive partners. Nevertheless, despite being specious, silly and shallow, many of us are still darn good husbands, fathers, and lovers, as well as good providers, companions, and life-long friends (even after divorce).

Post-divorce dating is life's secondary crucible, where we again observe the actions, interactions, and reactions of our newfound post-divorce loves, but with a sharper eye and a better ear. I proposed to Apollina after knowing her for only one month. I recall that, while dating, we never had a fight, serious argument, or even a heated dispute. How could we? We were all love and kisses. We never experienced anger, disappointment, or even a mild disagreement. How come? We dated for only 30 days; nevertheless, I asked her father for her hand in marriage. I still remember his answer: "What's the problem? Don't you want the rest of her?"

After that, we had a (very short) 138-day engagement that was not an engagement. The next thing I knew, I was standing before my parents and good friends saying, "I do." I did? Following the wedding and reception, we were off to San Francisco to start our lives together as husband and wife. Months later, my new bride had worked all day fixing dinner (my mother's lasagna recipe). I innocently (but obviously not innocently enough) commented that the radishes in the salad were a bit large. Apollina exploded and threw the entire pan of untouched lasagna into the sink. Then she stormed off to the bedroom and slammed the door! Wow! I had never seen her like that. Had I known this side of her, there may never have been a wedding.

Months later while at home and sound asleep, we heard disturbing noises downstairs around 3:00 a.m. "Go look," Apollina said. "You go," I replied. We went down the stairs together. Bravely, I held her in front of me as we carefully stepped down the stairs, entered the kitchen, and found the cats mating. The preceding was placed here to remind you that sometimes couples who rush through the dating and engagement periods (as we did) do not even discuss who goes down the stairs first.

The moral of the story is that rushed dating and short engagements yield no clues, signals, or warnings of forthcoming train wrecks ahead. Everyone has them, but we're just not all prepared to handle the carnage. It's not easy to walk away from a relationship, and it is even more difficult to end a marriage. Although we all want to hang in there, hoping things will change and eventually become better, often they do not. Difficult days and stressed nights require delicate discussions, recalling that said conversations are with the person they once could not stand to be apart from. This person is the one you married and the one with whom you need to communicate civilly at all times. If you were not good at this in your last marriage, you can practice for your next relationship or marriage.

Controlling Personalities

One of the greatest laments frequently heard in divorce clubs (and they have many members) is "He/she became controlling after we were married." Usually this behavior does not start overnight.

Excessive controlling behavior does not start just the first year, the first month after marriage, or even the night after the honeymoon. If you're honest with yourself, you saw early shades of his/her controlling personality before, maybe as early as on your second date, which may have been the night after your recent honeymoon. Clear manifestations of excessive Controlling Personality Disorder (CPD) appeared early in your dating days; perhaps you did not want to see them. Yet, looking back, you now can recall various warnings.

Some individuals are fortunate because frequently a friend of the person they are about to marry will warn them that their good friend is "really bossy." As mentioned before, however, when we are in love we do not listen to the important warnings provided. Many have the misfortune to marry those who are *later* discovered to be controlling. But wait! How can you determine when a person has this personality disorder? No one comes with an imprinted barcode or warning label, yet the signs are there from the beginning.

Blessed are they who look, for they shall see. Many catch sight of the telltale signs before them, not lit up in neon but, nevertheless, there and quite noticeable. Think back. Were movies, restaurants, and other selections made or suggested by him/her? Were you asked for any input whatsoever? Far worse is the individual who asks for your input, then totally ignores it. You may ask yourself, "How did I not see this?" Your former/future spouse may have been comfortable with you in the beginning; later, you recall his or her frequent questions about your whereabouts. Soon he/she started telling you what to eat and how far you would need to walk to burn off the calories from the chocolate cannoli you may have just ordered.

My psychology PhD colleagues say:

> Individuals who date and plan to marry
> persons with adult children should look
> at their marquee for his/her coming control
> attractions. Persons who treat their adult
> children *as children* are not anxious parents;
> they are board-certified controllers.

I saw this in my very own condo building. My neighbors, Mathew and Martha, had become embroiled in a major dispute. Martha was fine with Mathew's son Howard's recent engagement to *The Great Helena*, but Mathew was not. Mathew strongly objected and refused to accept her because "she was too old, and she was getting older." Martha was beside herself trying to keep the peace between her husband and his son, as well as between her husband and herself.

Mathew even recruited me *to talk sense into* Howard. I did. I told him to follow his heart and do what he thought was right. Soon after, Mathew gave in and Howard married *The Great Helena*. Spouses who continue to control their adult children's decisions are likely to move into the marital theater, too. So do not lament later, "He/she became controlling *after* we were married."

After Martha's battle with Mathew over his son's spouse selection, Mathew told me about a serious snag involving Martha. Prior to marrying, they discussed finances (at least, he did). Except for house and car payments, neither had any debts. Mathew told me he provided Martha with a detailed spreadsheet of his assets, income, and investments and that Martha was impressed by his openness. His spreadsheet conservatively projected his income returns and anticipated asset growth for the next 20 years.

Mathew also informed me that he did not request (his mistake), and that Martha did not provide (her mistake), any corresponding financial information or such disclosures to him. Mathew stated that neither one had given the other any information pertaining to their expenses. Suddenly, however, Martha felt as if she had some kind of inalienable divine right to have received Mathew's expense information.

This demand started when Martha discovered that Mathew was helping his older brother, Lucky, with modest, monthly $320 two-year pre-Social Security contributions from his separate property savings account. Lucky had lost his left eye in an industrial accident while working at Happy Industries. One year later, he was crossing Hope Street and was hit by a car he did not see, and lost his left leg. Last year, Lucky was in yet another automobile accident on Grand Street and lost his right arm. Even when you have worked at Happy Industries and have been on Hope and Grand streets, things do not always go well.

After this innocent discovery, Martha continuously complained about Mathew's moderate financial assistance (from his separate property savings) to his disabled 60-year-old brother. Mathew said that Martha further chastised him for failing to show her any respect in not providing her such *vital information*. Martha also told Mathew she never would have married him, had she known about him helping his older brother. It would seem that Martha had no basis whatsoever to grumble about Mathew's modest separate property contributions to his brother. Repeating these unfounded criticisms only made matters worse for both of them. Telling your spouse that you would not have married him or her (for any reason) seems to be totally counterintuitive, and a felonious act of marital sabotage via an expressed *go away* directive. Still, perhaps Mathew should have disclosed his modest assistance to his brother (then, some other compliant would have [likely] surfaced).

As we have noted before, marriage is never perfect. It's painful to be subjected to repeated criticisms and unfounded complaints. The schism between Martha and Mathew continued, until Martha finally told Mathew to move out and she filed for divorce. Mathew told Martha he was glad to go! Martha later told me that she had reached her tipping point and that she just could no longer live with Mathew. Martha could not accept Mathew's lack of respect and his (sparse separate property) benevolence to his brother Lucky, and Mathew could not tolerate Martha's continual complaints and lack of respect. The last I heard they were both back on the dating scene, looking for new partners and for much needed individual respect.

Oh, but beware when dating, for many are not honest in responding to questions asked; here's a few to look for:

> Question: "How old are you?"
>
> Answer: "How old do I look?"
>
> Question: "In what year did you
>   graduate from high school?"
>
> Answer: "In my senior year."
>
> Question: "Have you done this before?"
>
> Answer: "Oh no [not with you]!"

But wait, some spouses never get any respect! Late one night on television, Rodney Dangerfield told Jay Leno that, one night last week when he had come to bed, his wife started talking about wild sex and about all of the wonderful things she was going to do to him. "Jay," he said, "I get no respect, not even in my own bed." "Why?" asked Jay. Rodney said: because, "She was on the phone talking to someone else."

Poor Rodney passed on after years of no respect! Even Rodney would have agreed that the universal prerequisites to marriage and remarriage are respect, a year or two of dating the same person, a one-year engagement, and then marriage. This format could be followed by a time-out and then remarriage to the same person again. Rodney dated, married, divorced, and (after a one-year time-out) remarried his first wife Joyce Indig. Later, after seven additional years of no respect, they divorced for a second time (as did Elizabeth Taylor and Richard Burton, Steve and Elaine Wynn, Larry King and Alene (Akins), and many others).

Perhaps it was the jokes Rodney told about his wife; like most celebrated comedians, Rodney also used his spouse as a fair game.

Who can forget Henny Youngman's:

"Take my wife, please!"

Rodney repeatedly talked about his wife's poor cooking (something about flies not coming into the house). He talked about his wife's supposed unfaithfulness (occasionally finding her undergarments in a cab), and about her being with other men. He also talked about her mother, their dog, and especially about himself (always in a self-deprecating manner).

Twenty-three years after his second divorce, Rodney married Joan Child. Others wait longer yet. Barbra Streisand waited 27 years after divorcing first husband Elliott Gould to marry James Brolin. *Why rush?* And speaking of Rush, let's look at Rush Limbaugh. Whatever your opinion of Rush, there's no doubt that he is smart, shrewd, and successful. You may not agree with everything he says; however, you must concur that he knows how to say it.

Like so many others in the front-page listing, Rush has not enjoyed the same stellar success in his marriages as in his celebrated career.

Given the facts and backgrounds of other divorced individuals in this book, Rush's four marriages and three divorces seem to be within the norm and consistent with those of Johnny Carson (four marriages, three divorces) and Larry King (eight marriages and seven divorces). These talented individuals had 16 marriages among them. It appears as if these highly successful, hard-working, and creative individuals seem to run at higher temperatures and on troubled marital tracks.

Sex, Drugs, and Divorce

Incompatible sexual practices will add stress to any marriage. We already reviewed men's wandering ways and have provided extensive examples of male deviations; however, we have not looked at the female side of this issue. While much can be said, perhaps the following details from Jane Fonda's 2008 television appearances where she discussed her well-written and interesting autobiography, *My Life So Far*, will help.

Jane tells how she was married to three remarkable and interesting men. In Chapter 11 of her book, Jane tells us how she engaged in threesomes to please her womanizing first husband Roger Vadim, because *"he liked to bring other women into our marital bed."*

Drugs, marriage, and remarriage just do not seem to go together. Many a good marriage has been derailed because of illicit drugs and the problems that follow their use and abuse. Menacing comments can also be made about how divorced men and women become addicted to drugs, not only the illegal drugs sold on the streets, but also those prescribed by local physicians.

Many divorce-bound men have had problems with prescription drugs. Elvis Presley, Rush Limbaugh, and Michael Jackson are prominent examples. Elvis and Michael both divorced, Elvis once, and Michael twice. Were Michael's controversial 11-month marriages for convenience or possibly a cover? We may never know. Both Elvis and Michael met their untimely deaths, at 42 and 50 years of age respectively, via the use and abuse of ethical drugs prescribed for them by what are now referenced as unethical doctors. Their drug abuse certainly did not help their marriages.

In April 2006, Rush turned himself in on various prescription drug possession charges; these allegations preceded a long investigation, which included the stressful months preceding and during his last divorce. Rush later admitted his addiction to painkilling medications.

Prescription drug abuse and untimely death are not exclusive to divorced men, for many divorced women have also been subjected to the same addictions and accidental deaths. Anna Nicole Smith died at the young age of 39. Anna's death was determined to have been due to an accidental overdose of as many as nine medications. Her prior addictions and abuse of ethical drugs seemed to have been aided and abetted by several physicians and others who have been charged with various offenses.

Many other divorce-destined women have acknowledged addictions to prescription drugs. Judy Garland (who married and divorced five times) died at the age of 47. Her 12-year drug addiction impacted her marriages. Judy struggled to overcome other personal problems, including heavy drinking; she attempted suicide several times and was plagued by financial instability, often owing hundreds of thousands of dollars in back taxes and other obligations. Studio doctors had her on uppers to keep her going during the day, downers to sleep, and then various weight-control medications to maintain her in stage readiness. These lengthy and lethal combinations took their toll.

Her five marriages and drug-impacted, acrimonious divorces were devastating. Judy had numerous flings with married men and several women. She died in 1969 in a rented house in London from an accidental overdose of barbiturates.

Marital Diversity

One of the great benefits of having spent 36 years of my life at CSULB was having had the opportunity to have lunch at the faculty dining room—*The Chartroom*. Where else can you sit and have an enjoyable lunch with diverse PhDs sitting with you? Where else can you dine and discuss dissimilar topics with readily available expertise already seated among you? It's like being at a board of directors meeting, but without being bored.

Once we had a fascinating lunch discussion on marriage, divorce, and remarriage. Several of us stayed long after we finished lunch because it had turned into a dynamic graduate seminar, with others joining us. It started with comments from an anthropology professor who said:

> "There's now a greater diversity among dating, married, and divorcing couples than ever before. There are some 52 million multi-racial individuals in the United States today. Most are in Hawaii, California, Texas, and New York, and there's one in the White House. Many of us are products of diverse parents who are not from the same cultural, racial, or religious backgrounds."

The foregoing was certainly true for me, because I came from two different ethnicities, my children from four and my grandson from seven. The professor went on to say, "Among Asians today, 50 percent marry non-Asians. A recent survey reported that in the year 2008, 36 percent of Asian women under the age of 35 dated only non-Asian men." At our table, we had Dr. Galileo Galilei Schwartz, a Caucasian physics professor who had a 12-year history of exclusively dating Asian women. When asked why, he commented, "I like the culture, their health consciousness, and philosophy of life." Suddenly, a music professor jumped in and said, "No! It was because of Puccini." "Puccini?" someone else said. "How can that be?" Now things were getting interesting; several other professors joined our discussion.

The music professor requested more coffee, sat back in his chair, took off and folded his glasses, as if in class, and said:

> "Puccini's *Madama Butterfly* started it all. You see, this was the very first literary operatic dramatic composition that presented an extended narrative musical story celebrating a heroic

relationship between a Caucasian male hero and an Asian female heroine. Yes, it started there, and it was picked up by Hollywood in the early fifties after the war. *Tea House of the August Moon* (the novel, play, and movie) in 1951-1956, *Sayonara*, and *Suzy Wong* in 1957.

"The idea of American soldiers dating and marrying Asian women increased during the post-war occupations of Japan and Korea, and the war in Vietnam. Then, suddenly, the idea really took off. Hollywood again advanced the theme: first *Rambo*, then *James Bond*, and several other movies in which Caucasian leading men promptly all had beautiful Asian girlfriend co-stars and it continued on to other productions from there."

Outstanding! Our opera aficionado really explained that one. I now see the connection or possible motivation for others. Dr. Schwartz, our physics professor, later admitted that he had seen *Madama Butterfly* five times by the time he was 26. Professor Schwartz, it seems, had also fortuitously discovered that university professors were held in high esteem in Asian cultures, unlike America, where they experience lower levels of appreciation, and pay.

As was often the case at *The Chatroom,* ask a question and you get a dissertation! The anthropological and operatic anecdotes above led to later discussions on the topics of intercultural, interfaith, and interracial marriages and divorce. Needless to state, marital diversity in one or more of these controversial areas can lead to internal stresses and external difficulties that can cause a couple to endure unexpected problems, and even to divorce. Here is one that happened long ago.

On January 17, 1961, Mrs. Lincoln, JFK's personal secretary, called Sammy Davis, Jr. to disinvite him and his white fiancé from Kennedy's presidential inauguration (a black man with a white woman [May Britt] would upset Southern congressional representatives). After this snub, Sammy and Frank Sinatra divorced the Democratic Party and became loyal Republicans. Sammy and his third wife Altovise may have been the first African-American couple to spend the night in the White House, via President Nixon invitation in March of 1974.

Sammy and Altovise slept in the Queen's bedroom because he did not want to stay in the Lincoln bedroom out of fear. Sammy himself said,

> "I thought to myself, now I
> don't want [Lincoln] coming
> in here talking about, 'I
> freed them,' but I sure
> didn't want them to sleep
> in my bed."

Like many others on the list in the beginning of this book, Sammy, too, had three marriages and two divorces, along with many other interesting life experiences. Others have also had interracial marriages. Here is an interesting comment from a sociology professor regarding a black man who appreciated white friends and women over black ones:

> After his divorce from his
> African-American, first wife in
> 1979, O. J. Simpson seems to
> have exclusively dated white
> women.

> He dated, married (1985)
> and divorced in 1992 (killed?)
> a white woman. He had far
> more white friends than black
> ones. He now has a white
> cellmate, white prison guards,
> and a white warden.

Still, things have changed in the last 50 years. Today, 23 percent of African-American men marry nonblack women, while only 10 percent of black women marry nonblack men. Fifteen-percent of all recent marriages are between interracial couples.

Now, a few interesting words about married people and individuals who date them. There are significant numbers of men and women who date married people. Years ago, society considered these individuals to be insecure, desperate, and lacking confidence and other virtues. Past conventional wisdom equated having an affair with a married person to playing Russian roulette with a revolver having two bullets in the cylinder rather than just one. Affairs with married persons and playing Russian roulette each have marginal success rates at best; both were deemed to be dangerous and deadly short-term events.

There are, nevertheless, noted cases of long-term affairs. Married Spencer Tracy had a 26-year affair with divorced Katharine Hepburn, which lasted until Tracy's death. Katharine and Spencer became one of Hollywood's most recognizable couples on-screen and off and at select secret rendezvous locations; she even took care of him during his prolonged terminal illness. There are many others, however, who date married partners; most of them end up alone, after lost years of invested time, money, and energy in a dead-end relationship with a married person, who elects to remain married.

Enjoy your post-divorce dating and other adventures that await you. Do not become a recluse and give up on the other sex yet. Besides, there's more to life than sleeping single in a bed for two, and one can only watch so much television.

Remember: we always appreciate favorable qualities in others we ourselves already possess, and we also react negatively to (what we consider) undesirable characteristics of others. Simply said, it's all a part of our complicated and unique attraction calculus. This formula includes neurochemical, physical, and emotional (positive and negative) reactions, as well as selective logical imputes, that brings us to our selected partners.

WHAT YOU NOW RECOGNIZE, UNDERSTAND, AND ACCEPT

1. Welcome to the world of "caretaker companions" and "rebound romances."

2. Men more frequently hook up with someone new faster than women.

3. Don't marry on the rebound. Why not? Because the odds for success are not promising: 67% of all second marriages, and 74% of all third marriages end in divorce.

4. Good marriages are based on total acceptance.

5. Frequent places you enjoy to find someone with similar tastes.

6. What you see is what you get, and it's not going to change.

7. Sometimes ultimatums work: be prepared to follow through.

8. There are fewer eligible men than women; add in the word quality and the number becomes even less.

9. Marriage is a toll road. You pay as you go; even short trips have expensive tolls.

10. You can put a size-12 foot into a size-10 shoe, but there will be blood.

CHAPTER TWELVE

Eat, Drink, and [Should I] Remarry?

A man walks out to catch a taxi just going by. He gets in, and the cabbie says, "Perfect timing. You're just like Franco Bollo."

Passenger: "Who?"

Cabbie: "Franco Bollo. He's a guy who did everything right all the time, like my coming along when you needed a cab. Things happened like that to Franco Bollo, every single time. He was a terrific athlete. He could have won the Grand-Slam at tennis; he golfed with the pros. He danced like a Broadway star and you should have heard him play the piano. He was an amazing guy."

Passenger: "Sounds like he was something really special."

Cabbie: "He never made a mistake, and he really knew how to treat a woman and make her feel good. He would never answer her back, even if she was in the wrong. He was the perfect man! He never made a mistake. No one could ever measure up to Franco Bollo."

Passenger: "An amazing fellow. How did you meet him?"

Cabbie: "Well, I never actually met Franco. He died. I'm married to his widow."

As we can see from the story above, sometimes remarriage brings its own standards and benchmarks. The cabbie was well familiar with Mr. Bollo's impressive and ideal practices (by which his new wife measured him daily).

After my second graduation from Divorce College and receipt of my second P4hD (Paid 4 her Divorce), I was alone again. Being alone was nothing new, for I was well-accustomed to fending for myself and comfortable with my sudden return to single status. My feelings after the first two months after both separations, and specifically after entry of the Final Divorce Judgments could be summed up as relief, release, and rebirth. Both were like having an effective emotional catharsis.

A year after my first divorce, I started dating again. I returned to the local Catholic church. As in years before, my motivation for attending church included meeting single women. It seems as if today most parishes have Church Divorce Recovery Programs (CDRP), which for the Catholic Church, seems oxymoronic. An institution with a history of being anti divorce, dating back to King Henry VIII's first divorce in 1533, now embracing divorce recovery programs?

Well, change does come. I attended several of the CDRP sessions and discovered that most of the people there were coping with their situations. There were several other beneficial aspects for CDRP participants. One was in gathering the attendees into small specific sub-groups, which concentrated on common issues. There were custody, visitation, and support discussions, two groups dealing with lawyers (one for lawyers who were not getting anything done and one for lawyers who were doing too much), and one group for financial planning during and after divorce. Healing is compounded in a community of common concern and collective communication.

Whom to Look For and Where to Find Them

My first post-divorce dating venture was to check out the local arts groups for clusters of eligible, quality female members. It did not take long to discover that the local art museum had a singles group with several interesting eligible women. I joined in April and was invited to attend their June 30th year-end party. But wait, how could this be?

One woman had previously told me she had to wait a full year to attend the year-end party; yet, I was invited just after two months? The answer soon became apparent. The party was held at the beautiful ocean-view home of a member whose husband had passed away two years before. When I arrived, I immediately noticed that there were several more women than men. As the evening progressed, the ratio of women-to-men continued to increase. At final count, there were 29 women to 18 men. Now I realized why I had been invited.

Just as in math, science, and business, there are certain axioms that must be accepted in and about post-divorce dating adventures. Here are a few that will help you:

- Activate yourself and circulate.
- Get involved in new activities.
- If you don't succeed at first, try again.
- Frequent places you enjoy to meet people with similar interests.
- There are far more single women than single men (5:1 in New York, NY).
- It's truly a matter of numbers.

Before you reject your next prospect, take a good look in the mirror. Unless you see Brad Pitt or Angelina Jolie, why not take a chance and meet someone who is obviously interested in you? Most of us are far too superficial, picky, and unrealistic. By gender, the following seem to be the top 12 reasons to just say, "Next!"

Women's unacceptable characteristics in men:

1. Not tall enough
2. Not enough hair
3. Not enough class
4. Not physically fit
5. Not enough money

6. Not as smart as she

7. Not willing to spend his money

8. Not interested in exotic foreign travel

9. Not secure financially, emotionally, etc.

10. Not interested in dancing or in dance lessons

11. Not interesting enough, does not do anything

12. Not humble (brags excessively about himself)

Three, six, and nine, are not deemed to be superficial by some commentators but are considered valuable relationship prerequisites for companionship longevity.

Men's unacceptable characteristics in women:

- Too old

- Too tired

- Too smart

- Too bossy

- Too heavy

- Too talkative

- Too many plans

- Too many wants

- Too heavy (again)

- Too much baggage

- Too many of the above

- Too many (you fill in the blank) _____

If you have not already done so, perhaps you should make a priority list of required and desired attributes and characteristics for your new dates. Long after my first divorce and after careful consideration, I developed my own detailed list for desired qualities for my future dating prospects.

While Aida scored extremely well on my list, I realized after my second incomplete marriage that certain adjustments and additions to my list of priorities were obviously needed.

Dave's New Top 20 Dating/Spousal Ss

- Smart
- Sense of humor
- Smiling and positive
- Settlement conflict skills
- Spiritual and scrupulous
- Similar values and expectations
- Self-confident, yet steadfast
- Schooled, but not sophomoric
- Sociable
- Sophisticated
- Skilled in the culinary arts
- Systematic (neat and organized)
- Sensitive and supportive
- Serious, yet sympathetic
- Sharing and giving
- Successful and secure
- Sensuous
- Stylish
- Sexy
- Still thinking about this one ____

These women and men do exist; they are known as angels and saints and are all in heaven. Dream-on! Most of us already know that such persons do not exist here on earth.

While almost impossible to quantify individual variables and spousal preferences, an incomplete list may be better than no list at all (I originally had 14 items on my list). Just as in any goal, mission, or voyage, you need a plan to reach your destination and charts to keep off the rocks. Start with the bookends of your must-haves and then work down. Next, work on the could-haves and discuss your list with people who know you well. This group would include your siblings, children, and best friends (What about your ex?). Once your list is developed, prioritize from most important to least important among your chosen criteria.

I've recommended this plan to many people. The number one item on everyone's list has been (or should be) intelligence of a similar level. You must be able to talk to each other on diverse topics with a common vocabulary. Most would agree that having meaningful mental intercourse is a prerequisite to having satisfying sexual intercourse. Besides, it's also fun to talk after sex, especially if you don't smoke; nevertheless, a final list for male or female selections may require additional tweaking as necessary. Your final list should be qualitative and not quantitative.

There are also various "S" characteristics, which should be avoided; the top ten (in alphabetical order) could possibly include persons who are:

- Sanctimonious
- Sarcastic
- Self-centered
- Selfish and stingy
- Shallow and superficial
- Snotty and arrogant
- Spoiled and snobbish
- Stubborn
- Sullen
- Surreptitious and secretive

Men and women dating back to Adam and Eve have dealt with the foregoing ten characteristics. Some have been married to individuals having three, five, or more of these ten traits. These women and men also exist; they are known as Diane, Denise, and Delilah, and Sean, Steve, and Samson, and they also are here on earth.

I am certain that your dating experiences will be far more enjoyable if you go into them with low expectations and without the hope and prayer that this could be Mr. or Ms. Right. Post-divorce dating must be approached as a search-and-discovery mission rather than as a search-and-rescue effort. Search and discovery applies to you even more than your potential partners. Learn about yourself as you go. When you're ready, get out there and search for yourself. Discover how you act, interact, and react with new, interesting people and why. Take sufficient time to learn about your new dates (and especially about yourself). Practice asking questions you may have failed to ask before. Learn to answer questions being asked of you with a reciprocal question to your interrogator, and stay with your question until it is answered.

If you find something unacceptable about your new friend while dating, shift the problem onto yourself and do not criticize him/her. If you cannot stand the problem, tell him/her that you do not do well in such situations. If nothing is said about your objections or concerns, this problem will only fester and could later become an infection, just as if you had an unattended small pebble in your shoe, which eventually may require an amputation (divorce) to cure.

This next paragraph is important for the male readers. Men like to rescue women from their predicaments, which can leave them feeling vindicated and accomplished. Mistakenly, these champions trust that their valiant efforts will cause these rescued women to feel beholden to them. Such is not the case, for women rarely fall in love with someone who happens to come with a gallon of gas or changes a flat tire.

Women have also been known to rescue men. It seems, in many of these situations, that the rescued male may depart soon after being paid female financial benefits ($50 million divorce settlement, as Tom Arnold possibly may have received from Roseanne Barr). But wait; Roseanne herself recently admitted to putting laxatives into all three of her ex-husbands' food and drinks. No wonder they were all on the run.

The reverse is true. Women who gain from their male associations sometimes leave after reaping financial benefits. Evita surely benefited from her short association with Agustin Magaldi, the handsome tango singer and former used car salesman at *Automóviles de Argentina* (adaar. com). She stayed with Juan Peron, however, and reaped even greater rewards, including immortality and a new CD.

Relationship rescues are far different from flat tires, running out of gas, or plugged sinks. All of the foregoing can be remedied by merely calling the Auto Club or Joe the plumber. But wait again! Beware of persons seeking cash-flow rescues due to pressing credit card bills, car payments, or mortgages they cannot pay when they're asking you for help: "Oh, just this one time!" If you're making someone a loan, make it absolutely clear that it is a loan and not a gift. Request and get a signed promissory note. Better yet, just don't make him/her a loan. Chances are you'll never be repaid. If the relationship goes well, both of you will forget about it. If the relationship does not go well, the debtor will surely forget, and the lender may not be paid unless he/she presses the matter via small claims or other legal action.

Beware of those who tell you of others who have made financial gifts to them in the past. Whether you realize it or not, this is a loaded guilt bomb and a post-hypnotic suggestion, telling you how others considered them worthy of economic sponsorship. This *NOTICE* lays the groundwork for you, too, making a contribution to them. Don't do it!

When Not to Date

As you consider entry to the post-divorce dating scene, remember that it can be difficult and daunting. It takes time, money, and energy as well as patience, practice, and more patience. Many of you now reading this book may be short on two, three, or all five of these requirements. If you fall into one of these groups, perhaps you should take a breather and wait until you're better prepared to pursue or be pursued. If you find yourself tired of the dating scene, which has only yielded repeated disappointments and rejections, then possibly you are the problem.

Are you unreasonably demanding and picky? Are you someone who must have most things your way? Then perhaps you should remain alone. Maybe you should write books about chopped salad, proper table settings, and when not to sell your troubled stocks. You could even change your name to Martha.

Some divorced women never remarry, and go on to become extremely successful. Such was the case with Martha Kostyra (the future Martha Stewart). While at Barnard College, Martha met, dated, and later married Andy Stewart, a Yale law student, in 1961. Six years later, after the birth of their daughter, Alexis, Martha went to work in New York as a stockbroker. Martha and her husband divorced in 1990 after a bitter three-year separation, initiated by Andy, who elected to move out to live with Martha's younger, more attractive former assistant. As I keep repeating, in many of these unions everyone already knows everyone else.

The divorce launched Martha into commercial stardom. Yes, one success after the other and then off to prison for four months. Amazingly, she survived that as well and came back even commercially stronger than before. Today we see more professional women electing to remain single after an interrupted marriage. We've also noted that many women are postponing marriage until their careers are well-established. Diane Sawyer married for the first time when she was 42. She married Oscar-winning director Mike Nichols, who was then 56 and had been married and divorced three times. Many of these late-first-time-married women seem to marry divorced husbands. Hey, who else is left? Interestingly, women sometimes perceive men who have never married as too peculiar or as being flawed in other ways. Men, on the other hand, seem to be less concerned about this reality (Warren Buffett, et al.).

New social trends have emerged, as women (and men) are no longer subject to pressure and prejudice of remaining single; both are now taking longer to complete their educations and marry. The education cycle has been extended well into the 30s, and the median age for first marriages is now approaching 28 for men and women. Today, 22 percent of women in their 40s have no children; 41 percent of all births are to unmarried mothers, and the new national median-age for first-time mothers in the U.S. is approaching 26 years.

As skilled and seasoned divorce war survivors, many of us will re-enter the post-divorce dating and remarriage arenas with high hopes. One fascinating fact is that eligible men just do not last long. There are several valid and pressing reasons for their short-lived single Sundays. First, men are generally not as functional or self-sufficient as women when it comes to living alone. Men sometimes need, and always enjoy, being cared for by a good woman. Perhaps it starts with Mom and continues with the first wife. Whatever the true reason, having a clean and tidy place to come home to, a good home-cooked meal, and a clean and fresh pressed shirt are common expectations for most men. Men enjoy the warm and close companionship of a good woman, be it at a car show, going to Home Depot, or even just going to Costco for mundane purchases. Women enjoy a good man's presence at the mall, movie, church, and other such places.

Necessary Time Together

Your past marriage may have suffered from what is generically known as Not Enough Time Together (NETT). Perhaps your past spouse needed and required more of your time, attention and individual companionship, which may have been missing in your past. Sometimes just a three-day getaway or some other just-the-two-of-you activity can do wonders for your relationship and for both of you individually. When was the last time the two of you took a simple barefooted walk together along the ocean, a lake, or river, or shared a quiet romantic dinner and a bottle of good wine, or just sat (no TV, phones, or other distractions), held each other and talked about how much you appreciated and loved each other?

Even Johnny Carson acknowledged this:

> If I had given as much to marriage as I gave to The Tonight Show, I'd probably have a hell of a marriage. But the fact is, I haven't given that, and there you have the simple reason for the failure of my marriages: I put my energy into the show.

My former mother-in-law once told me, "Showering your wife with gifts is not as good as giving yourself to her." She was right. I did not realize that spending more time with Apollina might have helped our troubled marriage until it was too late and we were already apart.

If a lack of necessary time together affected your past marriage, and you see it missing again, perhaps you need to discuss this matter openly with your newfound friend. Every relationship and marriage should have a scheduled date night. Perhaps candlelit dinners: he goes to dinner on Tuesdays; she dines on Thursdays.

What and Whom to Look For

If you're still looking for Mr./Ms. 100 Percent Right, you have not done your homework; this mythical person just does not exist. Then again, there may be an answer to this dilemma:

FIVE RULES FOR A HAPPY LIFE

- It is important to have someone who helps at home, who cooks from time to time, cleans up, and has a job.

- It is important to have someone who can make you laugh and can also laugh at him/herself.

- It is important to have someone who is honest with you at all times.

- It is important to have someone who is good in bed and who likes to be with just you.

- It is extremely important that these four people do not know each other.

Given the realities that one cannot have four spouses in most countries, we go on with our searches. Unlike blending good red wines, people cannot be blended; nevertheless, when making final spousal choices, we sometimes get down to the last two individuals being considered and wish we could somehow take a certain characteristic from one and add or remove it from our almost-perfect person.

Many of the wished-for items seem to be for missing physical characteristics rather than unseen attributes of character or integrity. Too often we make our rushed proposals and hurried acceptances as if we were out buying a new car. We look at the appearance and the lines of the car (body) and at a few other random features (characteristics). We carefully look at the engine (income and assets they have), check out the (financial) specifications and glance at the interior (person). Still, we often fail to look at the brakes (character) or the safety features (trust and honesty) before making our purchases.

People who plan to remarry must choose wisely. Find someone to whom you're not only physically attracted but someone you respect and who respects you. Similar values, morals, and expectations are important. Take the necessary time to find someone who knows how to share, is honest, and tells the truth all the time. I am reminded of the story of a suspicious husband who feared that his wife might be seeing someone. He sent her flowers to her at her office, but did not include a card. The next day, his wife mentioned that someone had sent her flowers and asked if it was he?

Had his wife said nothing about the flowers, there might have been an inference that she may be seeing someone else. Even an innocent mistake at the flower shop could be verified and not leave the wrong conclusion. Because of her honesty, her husband admitted that he had sent the flowers. Moral of the story: *always tell the truth*, even when not under oath.

Several remaining remarriage realities must be addressed. Granted, ours is not a caste society with compelling social stratifications defined by preexisting requirements for marriage/remarriage. It seems, however, as though many of our modern-society marriages have become economic unions, mergers, and acquisitions, where spouses consider each other's earning capacities, assets, and other material accumulations ahead of their future spouse's character, trust and honesty. There are circles of men and women who retain ridiculous requirements and superficial standards for even meeting someone.

Current data suggest that as many as 81 percent of American women marry up: that is, they marry a man who has more and earns more than they do. Women sometimes choose wealthier men subconsciously (automatically having already eliminated less successful men without admitting it). This phenomenon, known as *fortune dating* only allows women to date and fall for men who meet their preset values regarding success, assets, and income. The other men, no matter how good their character, intelligence, or compatibility, get screened out long before they are ever seriously considered. Only a small minority of women (18 percent) marry men who have less or earn less than they do. They are the ones who eliminate the financial aspects for the men they choose.

Men are said to have their *preset T-and-A perfect 10 parameters,* by which they subconsciously allow themselves only to date and fall for women who meet their specious appearance and physical standards. Most men have not yet accepted the reality that we all gain weight with age and that many of us will one day need facial ironing. Men overlook and leave many good women behind, notwithstanding their good character, creditable compatibility, and other advantageous attributes.

In later life, many divorced individuals (men more so than women) want to remarry. Some of us do not seem to realize that *whomever* we marry is more important than *being* married. We search for companionship and (possible) happiness. After all is said and done, we must realize that marriage, and markedly remarriage, are really about self-development; they are love nests of commitment. Marriage requires mutual loyalty, coupled with a lasting forbearance of your spouse's faults, a continued capacity to compromise conflicts, and the willingness to honor the needs of another as well as your own. Wow! That is a tall order. Sharing your life with one particular person requires hard work, full acceptance, and respect, along with trust (and for men, control of the TV remote). Still, vibrant marriages have their challenges and demands, as does living alone.

As we date again after divorce, we already know that no one sells happiness insurance (divorce insurance is now available). Not only do the standard risks remain but also all of these hazards are now compounded because of increased age factors. Many of us in the remarriage market are not in our 20s, 30s, or even our 40s. Many of us going through the re-dating process after divorce are in our 50s, 60s, and even in our 70s. The risk factors in midlife dating now include general heath (emotional, mental, and physical) issues and will one day involve medical care and repeated visits to doctors, labs, and even hospitals. Thank God for Medicare.

The following could happen to you:

> A couple had dinner at another couple's house, and after eating, the younger wives left the table and went into the kitchen. The two older gentlemen remained talking, and one said,
>
> "Last night we went out to a new restaurant and it was really great. I would recommend it very highly." The other man said, "What is the name of the restaurant?"
>
> The first man thought and thought and finally said, "What is the name of that flower you give to someone you love? You know ... the one that's red and has thorns."
>
> "Do you mean a rose?" said the other.
>
> "Yes, that's the one," replied the man.
>
> He then turned toward the kitchen and yelled, "Rose, what's the name of that restaurant we went to last night?"

There's still one unique and special person who deserves further comment regarding marriage, divorce, and remarriage. Howard Hughes first married Ella Botts, and they soon moved to California. Howard kept his wife isolated at home for weeks at a time without any cash. Four years after they were married, she returned to Houston and filed for divorce. Howard was a notorious ladies' man who spent intimate time with many famous women and a few famous men. Except for Lassie, Hughes pursued, dated, hired, and bedded more attractive female Hollywood starlets than many others combined. Hughes was absolutely ruthless in his pursuits. He sought the married, teenaged, and others who caught his wandering eye. Hughes once said, "I have never met a man I could not buy or destroy!"

Twenty-eight years after his first divorce, Howard married Jean Peters; they spent most of their four-year marriage in separate quarters (she in California, he in Nevada), and they, too, later divorced.

Now a few comments for the men and women who feel they can follow Howard's lead. For the men who feel they must emulate Howard and follow his run (assuming you have the financial resources, charisma, and charm, as well as the intelligence and ability to make endless marriage proposals), it's a difficult and lonely road. For the women, assuming you have the looks, legs, and other necessary attraction factors, things do not look good for your group, either.

Given today's list of available, beautiful women and the longer list of wealthy men who pursue them, the foregoing is not a promising platform from which to start looking. If there's one thing that should be realized from Hughes's glamorous march through life, it's that men/women of power, wealth, and success seem to enjoy the chase far more than the catch. Even when you have everything, sometimes the world is still not enough.

It's Never Perfect

Bear in mind that it's *never perfect*. We live in an imperfect world, filled with imperfect people; we search for and find imperfect partners who have suitable, compatible, and promising potential to become future spouses. With our past marriage interruptions behind us, and our new insights before us, let's hope that better relationship and spousal selections follow.

Finding someone with 70-74 percent acceptability (14 of the top 20 items on my list) is actually quite good. You and your newfound friend must then work together to build and create the remaining three to six percent to make your relationship even better. The engagement phase may add an additional three to five percent, and if things continue to go well, this may lead to marriage with an 81 percent compatibility factor. Folks, that's as good as it gets; because when we come upon the usual 15 percent of irreconcilable differences that every couple has to confront, we must give more respect to the marriage and ourselves by making every effort to ensure its, and hence our own, survival under the best circumstances possible. The rest is up to you. Recall that the most difficult year of marriage is the one you're in. Working out problems will strengthen your marriage and help it grow even more. With a little luck and wisdom gained here, better days, months, and years should await you.

But wait! Is 80 percent no percent? The answer may depend on several factors. Relationships can be difficult, marriages are demanding, and remarriage can be mission impossible. For these reasons and more, try to pick someone with whom you can commit to working through whatever life brings to you. Mutual premarital expectations that "you are the one for me" will help you navigate the usual upheavals that unfold in all marriages. This may help provide a solid foundation upon which to deal with the difficulties that confront all spouses. If you don't have that passion for each other at the start, your challenges may overcome your coping resources and the process of disengagement begins—in which case it is likely that both of you will become additional divorce statistics.

Persons under 40 remarry within three years after divorce (81 percent of men and 63 percent of women). Individuals under 50 years of age remarry less (72 percent for men and 48 percent for women). Remarriage rates for women decrease significantly thereafter (see Appendix). Date while you can and be alert to health and medical considerations among your prospects. Enjoy the journey, for there are many interesting men and women out there who would love to get to know you. Keep in mind what you have learned along the way and enjoy your ventures, be they solo, with a new friend, or even a new spouse. Maximum satisfaction is more meaningful when you share it with a special person and you feel a part of some greater purpose in life. Find someone who will love you and whom you can love in return. Who knows, you may find someone who is almost perfect.

Pre-Engagement Protocols

Some suggest that your pre-engagement protocols include the following:

- Audience with/about stepchildren
- Audience with a neutral therapist
- Audience with a sex therapist (if necessary)
- Audience with friends, family, and relatives
- Audience with any and all previous spouses

- Audience with court staff to review his/ her divorce, criminal, and civil files (public information)

Audience with/about Stepchildren

Stepchildren require close scrutiny: minors, teenagers, and adult children may all affect your life in different ways. Will you be expected to become a parental figure, with disciplinary authority, for your soon-to-be minor stepchildren? If so, find out what will be expected of you, and what you may and can not do. This answer can present a plethora of possible problems for some individuals (particularly for those who have not been parents).

Determine the nature and scope of your beloved's involvement and extent of obligations with his or her children. Teenagers bring their unique demands, difficulties, and special challenges. Even adult children can be a burden, which may be more than you may wish to take on.

Audience with a Neutral Therapist

Perhaps a few sessions with a neutral therapist may be in order. House purchasers include expert inspections to look for latent defects and potential problems. Most used car buyers will ask their mechanic to look for similar findings. You, too, may benefit from having a professional look at your (new/used) future spouse. If you've noticed attitudinal or control issues, an absence of listening patience, and no compromising skills you may need to book additional sessions. The foregoing concerns should be addressed prior to ordering your wedding announcements. Perhaps a few additional sessions with your therapist would be a better investment than an expensive honeymoon.

Audience with a Sex Therapist (if necessary)

The *sexualization* of America started in the mid-1960s with a revolution that embraced our music. Then came the 1967 summer of "free love" in the Haight-Ashbury district of San Francisco followed by the 1969

Woodstock music and art fair at the township of Bethel, New York, where it was more "free love" and "Make Love Not War!" This new mantra was followed with sex on the screen via our movies and the media. Next, Viagra bought airpower *(lift-off)*, and the revolution that continues to this date.

Given the foregoing, it's easy to understand why almost everyone has high marital-sexual expectations and why many are disappointed with their spouses' performance, attitudes, and limitations. Intimacy incompatibilities, sexual anxieties, and performance unhappiness are all common in today's super-sexualized world, all of which may require premarital professional attention. If you have noted apprehensions, unreasonable limitations, or a failure to receive what you give and expect, then perhaps a few sessions with a sex therapist may be in order. Find out what you may be in for before you get married.

Audience with Family, Friends and Relatives

In-laws, family, and relatives all require extra examination. You must determine your beloved's degree of involvement and participation frequencies with all of these persons. All of them may be joining you for more than going to church; they may be coming with you on your vacations, cruises and other getaways. Moreover, you may be joining them on mandatory family camping trips and other scheduled activities. Is this more than you bargained for or were expecting? Will his/her or your parents be moving in with you in the future? Better ask now so you can order extra sheets and other necessaries, if required. If you do not do well in these familial situations, perhaps you should pass and exit stage left. Why complicate your life with activities that are incompatible with your expectations, or even repugnant to your personality or lifestyle? Then again, this reality may help explain why you are still alone.

Next, take the necessary time to meet and greet his/her friends and acquaintances. You can learn much about someone by meeting people whom they associate, even if you have never met them. Birds of a feather flock together. Again, listen (with a sharp ear) to what they have to say about your beloved. Chances are that if you hear or see something you like in his/her friends you'll also see this in your new friend.

Audience with Any and All Previous Spouses

An audience with an ex-spouse or two can be invaluable. Buy lunch or dinner and wine for them, and get the good, bad, and the ugly about whom they used to be married to and about who you're considering marrying. Start by listening to what they have to say, then order more wine. Allow them to talk as long as they want; then you get out your list of prepared questions. Ask what caused their marriage to be interrupted. Ask them about the best and worst thing about your common person. Ask for and arrange a second or third meeting if necessary. Caution! If a troubling concern, which happened 14 years ago was mentioned, and has not been repeated, you should not be concerned. If it was 14 months ago, you might see it again.

You also need to know if any of his/her ex-spouses was/is erratic, unstable,and deranged, because he/she may impact your life. Ask and find out what is going on with all exes. Ask how your beloved feels about them. Ask how he/she treats and interacts with them. If there's lasting anger, hate, or hard feelings, your beloved may not be a forgiving person. You could be next; be careful!

Audience with Court Staff to Review Divorce Files

Court records are public information and are available to everyone (I've visited many courthouses and reviewed various divorce files in preparation for this book). If there's troublesome information buried in your newfound lover's divorce file, get it out on the table now. This information can be your program guide to the play, opera, or movie you're about to star in. Just as a performance program explains the characters, plot, and outcome of what you are about to see, divorce files often include declarations under oath regarding marital behaviors and other interesting information that may be distasteful to your beliefs, values, or expectations.

If you have children, you may find information relative to support, custody, and other relevant issues. Divorce files may provide you with confidential secrets about your future spouse's character, past behaviors, and the (hopeful) plot and outcome of your marriage. This information should not be overlooked.

Criminal and Civil Indices must also be checked; who knows what illegal or irresponsible activity or conduct may surface? Collection matters, DUIs, and other such conduct may be inconsistent with long-term happiness based on represented honesty, good character, and claimed responsibility. Better to look now than be shocked later.

When it comes to considering remarriage, all worrisome issues must be aired before going further. Asking for and accommodating these modest requests provides both parties ample opportunity to change their minds if responses are not to their standards. All six listed audiences can be informative and revealing. Fairness, however, dictates that if one asks for the foregoing, one should be prepared to proffer the same to their provider. Fair is fair. Future spouses must both be on the same page, same paragraph, and same sentence on all six serious subjects. Remember: remarriage can be a rose garden; however, showcase gardens require loving care, time, and lots of attention.

If scheduling, discussing, or dealing with any of the listed six items presents a problem, heed the warnings and leave now. Life is too short to take on someone else's problems and obligations. This *reality* is especially true in interracial, intercultural, and interfaith situations (where one person may not fully understand and appreciate predetermined family expectations, customs, or traditions). If his/her ex-spouse, children, or relatives are estranged or incommunicado with your new special someone, perhaps you should be, too. Any kind of heated, angry, or super-surprised reaction to any of these modest, mutual and mundane requests may be God's way of telling you to fold your tent and go elsewhere.

If your soon-to-be *engagee* refuses any of the foregoing, you could say, "I understand and fully respect your response. I want to wish you the very best in your continued search for happiness and companionship. Farewell!" Even if you're about to walk down/toward the aisle, it is always easier and far more economical to stop a wedding than it is to dissolve a marriage. Besides, you and your friends will talk about it for years to come. If your findings are not to your expectations, it may be time to look elsewhere. Meanwhile, becoming more selective will elevate your DMRM standing. Others will soon hear about your wise judgment and sound decisions and the good word will spread.

As I was finishing my book one day, I sat in my rocking chair gazing at the ocean, searching for a salient strong finish to bring my chapter characters to a coordinated ending. Two days before, I had attended a university lecture on John Bunyan's *Pilgrim's Progress*.

Unexpectedly, I fell asleep; suddenly like Bunyan, "I slept, I dreamed a Dream. I dreamed, and behold I saw" myself leaving my hotel room in New York after the 2011 Super Bowl. Somehow, I jumped into a cab with four other passengers. The cab was driven by the same cabbie mentioned at the chapter's opening. All five of us were headed for the airport. I was in the cab with Mark, the distressed [dumb] husband who truthfully answered his wife's questions in Chapter 10; Mathew, the troubled father of the groom in Chapter 11; Luke, the battered husband in Chapter 2; and John, the dutiful husband who built the one-bedroom house overlooking the ocean and resented his wife's son's staying extended nights in Chapter 1.

Since I knew the cabbie, I asked him, "How is married life with the former Mrs. Franco Bollo?" He turned towards me and replied, "Funny you should ask. We're getting divorced."

The cabbie continued:

> "I just couldn't take it anymore.
>
> "You would not believe what I did for this woman!
>
> "Man, you guys have no idea what I put up with!"

All of us, total strangers, looked at one another other as if we somehow knew one another as teammates who had just played in the Super Bowl. In unison we said: "Oh yes, we know exactly what you mean!"

I awakened and ran to my computer to record my dream and end my book. Well, you've now heard it from Mark, Mathew, Luke, and John, all great sources. Even though they all ended up getting divorced, it seemed as if I was lucky, for I was spared the trauma and turmoil in my past divorces that had been suffered by them.

WHAT YOU NOW RECOGNIZE, UNDERSTAND, AND ACCEPT

1. Again, there just are more single women than single men.

2. It's truly a matter of numbers; therefore, activate and circulate..

3. Unless you're Brad Pitt or Angelina, don't be too picky.

4. Make up your list of required, desired, and acceptable attributes.

5. Ask people who know you well to review your list for accuracy.

6. Date with modest expectations; do not expect Mr./Mrs. Right every time.

7. Review all six pre-engagement protocols. Give in where necessary.

8. Do not let resentment contaminate your next marriage or relationship.

9. No one sells happiness insurance—yet.

10. It's never perfect! Every marriage has 15 percent of irreconcilable issues.

In Response to Henny Youngman

A man and woman had been married for more than 63 years. They had shared everything. They had kept no secrets from each other except that the wife had a shoebox in the top of her closet that she had cautioned her husband never to open or ask her about.

For all of these years, he had never thought about the box, but one day the wife became very sick and the doctor said she would not recover. In trying to sort out their affairs, the husband took down the shoebox and took it to his wife's bedside. She agreed it was time that he should know what was in the box. When he opened it, he found two knitted dolls and a stack of money totaling $95,000.

He asked her about the contents.

"When we were to be married," she said, "My grandmother told me the secret of a happy marriage was never to argue. She told me that if I ever was angry with you, I should just keep quiet and knit a doll." The husband was so moved; he had to fight back tears. Only two precious dolls were in the box. She had only been angry with him two times in all those years of marriage. He burst into tears.

"Honey," he said, "That explains the dolls, but what about all of this money? Where did it come from?" "Oh," she said, the ailing wife, "that's the money I made from selling all the other dolls I knitted."

My prayer ... "Dear Lord, I pray for Wisdom to understand my man; for Love to forgive him; and for Patience for his moods, Because Lord, if I pray for Strength, I'll beat him to death, since I don't have time to knit any more dolls!"

This *Capstone* section brings into logical order and summarizes the divorce recovery chapters presented in this book. Occasional reviews of this section may assist in your healing and recovery from the loss of your marriage. As I completed my manuscript, I invited three divorced psychology professors (two female professors: one in her late 30s, the other in her mid-50s, and a male professor in his early 40s) to join me (in my 60s) for lunch to discuss the capstone chapters of my book. I had provided each of them with drafts of the six chapters listed below. I asked them to critique my material.

Here are the "divorce recovery" chapters:

> Chapter   3 - Healing Yourself: Getting Over Him or Her
>
> Chapter   4 - Looking Back and Looking Forward
>
> Chapter   5 - Spending Time with [Just] Yourself
>
> Chapter   6 - Reconciliation: Answers and Attitude Adjustments
>
> Chapter 11 - Post-Divorce Dating and Other Adventures
>
> Chapter 12 - Eat, Drink, and [Should I] Remarry?

Here is a consolidated summary of what they provided:

> After reading *Divorce Stress Syndrome*, you realize how your once-vibrant marriage somehow died. Once the dust settles you acknowledge that various dynamics were at play. You came to grips with the reality that your marriage collapsed and this helps you to accept that once you might have been romantically suited for each other, but you changed and he/she did not; or she/he changed, but you failed to do so.

Chapter 3

Healing Yourself: Getting Over Him or Her

Your lifelong partner was suddenly gone and the love and passion that once bound you tightly together turned into indifference and resentment; and like water and oil, you and your ex-spouse are now separate and apart. At first you may have faulted your spouse and others for what happened As you later discovered, such was not the case. Whatever it was, you realized that life's regretful experiences require acknowledgment and acceptance of your mistakes and those of others; both must be forgiven. This brought valuable lessons learned as you navigated the sequential stages of divorce recovery and your return back to emotional good health. Accepting responsibility brought closure to the reality that your separation and divorce were likely caused by events or circumstances created by you or your spouse and that the two of you simply could not live together any longer, and one of you moved out. After she/he was gone, you followed the 12 steps listed below and improved your wounded status as you progressed in healing yourself by:

- Accepting that separations usually lead to divorce.

- Respecting yourself and not groveling for his/her return.

- Admitting that there was nothing you could do now.

- Arresting blame upon yourself for what happened.

- Forgiving yourself for what you did or failed to do.

- Preventing yourself to wallow in the past.

- Denying yourself the Poor Me Syndrome (PMS).

- Forgiving him/her for leaving you and hurting you.

- Letting him/her go and saying goodbye.

- Avoiding "chance" attempts to see each other.

- Becoming involved in new activities with new people.

- Keeping a firm, positive, and forgiving attitude.

You continue overcoming sadness and emotional mayhem. Even though your world had been abruptly turned upside down, you accepted the realization that grieving was a normal and necessary part of divorce recovery, as you dealt with these mandatory steps essential to your healing.

Responding to your sudden chaos may have pushed you to find a psychologist or other counselor to help you work through your painful problems and troublesome reactions. You agree that being controlling, demanding, and needing to have most everything your way may have caused your past marriage to be interrupted. On the other hand, if you were meek and never spoke up to object to things your spouse wanted, you likely stored vessels of resentment that eventually exploded and finally pushed you to be divorced. You consequently worked with or without a counselor toward understanding the probable sources of your imperfections and you followed the helpful recommendations to correct your issues. Therapy, spiritual guidance, and educational formats helped you become a better you. With the passage of time and the final settlement of remaining divorce issues, you are beginning to accept that your ex-spouse was a decent person but just not the right wife/husband for you, just as you were a good person but not the proper husband/wife for him/her.

WHAT YOU NOW RECOGNIZED, UNDERSTOOD, AND ACCEPTED

1. When you lost someone you once loved, you grieved over that person's absence (someone who is never there).

2. This behavior was a normal, natural, and often necessary as part of our recovery.

3. Accepted and respected the farewell decision and went forward without groveling.

4. Forgave yourself for whatever you did or failed to do.

5. Forgave him/her for leaving you and for hurting you.

6. Started a new life for yourself, with new people and activities.

7. Realized that you were a good person, just not a good husband/wife for him/her.

8. Did not get into the PMS situations, because no one would want to be around you.

9. There were many good men/women out there who loved to be with you.

10. The sooner you let go, the sooner you recovered.

Chapter 4
Looking Back and Looking Forward

Overcoming your challenges is bringing you the necessary strength to deal effectively with denial, anger, and/or your former partner's depression and despair. You have discovered that successful marriages appear to require coordinated combinations. One that seems to work is the one-chief, one-Indian combo. Marriages lacking this mixture are sometimes destined for stormy seas, separations, and eventual divorces. You realize that marriages with two chiefs (or without one) are just not likely to last, even though two individuals truly love each other.

You have discovered that it is not uncommon to find that what attracts us initially (like powerful magnets) can also become the same forces that later destroy a marriage. It's as if the same powerful magnets that once pulled you together were suddenly rotated. Unexpectedly, these attraction forces later function as repelling incompatibilities pushing you away and apart from one another. Moreover, similarities in attributes, backgrounds, and characteristics yield the same disappointing results.

You recall that divorce recovery could also be impacted by attitude and expectations. You realize that if you regarded your loss as an unalterable tragedy, your present days and future nights would conform to your expectations. Accordingly, you are beginning to accept what happened, taking responsibility for your contributing share, and working toward becoming a more loving, compassionate and caring person. In time, you [actually] came to like yourself even more.

Having compassion for a former spouse and oneself is instrumental in any recovery. We heal ourselves by healing others with mutual acceptance and forgiveness. Others are noticing your altruism and desire to find fulfilling companionship and lasting happiness. Your new goals and expectations have the potential to become a self-fulfilling prophecy that allows you to go forward with a new attitude, improved behavior, and positive expectations that help you towards your new salient goals.

Looking back, you are discovering that your failure to fix past problems could cause subsequent marriage interruptions. Not addressing your problems might also result in dragging them with you on to new relationships or your next marriage.

WHAT YOU NOW RECOGNIZED, UNDERSTOOD, AND ACCEPTED

1. Looked at the people you have dated and married.

2. Looked for repeated patterns and attractions that may not be healthy for you.

3. What stood out? Is this person a clone of your last spouse?

4. Remembered that when we are in love we do not listen to the advice of others.

5. There were certain individuals whom we just should not marry.

6. Did not despair; new people come in and out of our lives all the time.

7. Was wary of someone who has opposite views, values, or needs.

8. Was wary of someone who has the same views, values, or needs.

9. Looked at your ABCs to determine that they are compatible and cool.

10. Discussed travel needs and wants, and agreed to take a trip or two together before marriage.

Chapter 5

Spending Time with [Just] Yourself

Through all of this, you are recognizing your failures, faults, and fractures which are becoming apparent through the lifting fog of being alone. You are transitioning to the next stage of divorce recovery, described as cocooning, where you keep to yourself and weather your divorce storms alone, the time needed to become a single person again. Your goal is to protect yourself and avoid further emotional suffering and physical pain from re-entry to the predicament that caused you such agony.

You notice that many going through divorce become antisocial and see some solo flyers retreat inward to deal with their anguish. You observe others seeking ethical medications from physicians. Several divorcing persons self-medicate with alcohol, drugs, or other harmful substances, behaviors, or persons to deal with their problems.

Numerous divorcing individuals, you notice, seek validation about their still being desirable persons, via rushed sexual encounters that nonetheless leave them feeling disappointed, empty, and still alone. As you find yourself dealing with your sudden single status, you adjust your priorities to survival mode. You function and discover how to socialize as a single person as you appreciate the sounds of silence and engage in a host of other solo activities not previously known or enjoyed by you.

Being alone after filing for divorce or having been served with divorce papers, you discover, was not that bad; it actually was beneficial. This period allowed you to look back at your marriage and to reflect upon your needs, wants, and fulfillment ratios. You determined who had the better deal, and this will help you plan for next time. You examine what you could do to keep the home fires burning in the future, and you used this precious time to further develop your character and regain the confidence lost along the way.

This valuable time is not wasted. It helps prepare you for whatever greatness awaits you beyond self-imposed limitations. These solo periods nourish your spirit and lay the groundwork for great things to come; it prepares you for future experiences. Your separation and divorce may be stepping stones toward that place where you're destined to be.

WHAT YOU NOW RECOGNIZED, UNDERSTOOD, AND ACCEPTED

1. There is a difference between being alone and being lonely.

2. This precious time was used to learn more about yourself and others.

3. Discovered your deficits and started rebuilding your self-confidence, self-esteem, and self-worth.

4. Learned how to do and enjoy things on your own: movies, plays, books, and travel.

5. Remembered that you are your own best company.

6. Took up a new hobby, interest, or activity.

7. Worked on your emotional, mental, and physical health; they are all interrelated.

8. Took a trip, vacation, or a cruise just for the adventure of it.

9. There are many far worse off than you, yet they cope and still function.

10. Volunteered your time, energy, and spirit to help others; it pays well.

Chapter 6

Reconciliation: Answers and Attitude Adjustments

In due course, you come out of your cocoon as you gradually re-enter the world you had left months before. You read about successful reconciliations and the favored circumstances that usually preceded them. You adopt recommendations that you had failed to practice in the past as things continue to change before you.

Acknowledging a problem is the first step necessary to the prevention of repetitive harmful behavior. Finding hidden defects that you never had addressed and admitting shortcomings that were always denied will lead you to the source of problematic behaviors that may have caused your marriage to be interrupted. After finding your emotional equilibrium, you will even consider other necessary alternatives.

You and you ex-spouse considered reconciling and looked at the recommended prerequisites listed below:

- Couples seriously contemplating reconciliation should first meet jointly with their therapists to review past issues that caused them to divorce in the first place. Meeting together is more powerful and productive than doing so individually.

- Couples could list the desired/required changes they need to see in the other ex-spouse, as well as concessions and compromises they would be willing to make toward their reconciliation objectives.

- Couples must honestly and objectively review and discuss their lists to determine if common ground may exist on negotiable issues or whether it's hopeless and unachievable wishful thinking.

You (finally) come to realize that certain things must be accepted as unchangeable and that even therapy can't change all unacceptable factors. You discover, however, that some behaviors could be modified and that you have something worth pursuing. Later, you find that success does come with attitudinal adjustments and behavioral modifications based on compassion and compromise, making almost anything possible.

Patience helps you accept that the reconciliation process requires overcoming past problems. You note that the ex/estranged spouse requesting the change had to be sympathetic, supportive, and supersensitive to the other spouse's efforts and commitment. The ex/estranged spouse attempting the modification had to be committed to the change, dedicated to the necessary behavior modification, and tenacious in his or her efforts to reach his or her goals.

Still, after all of the foregoing, reconciliation was not in the cards for you. As you stand back and away from your ordeal, you realize that you needed to look deep within your soul to find, accept, and repair other long-ignored inadequacies and imperfections. As with the warning dashboard lights in your car, divorce becomes your fix-spouse light that you finally come to observe in the divorce papers filed or served to you. All of this will assist in undertaking the required plan and the lasting commitment to a changed and improved new you.

WHAT YOU NOW RECOGNIZED, UNDERSTOOD, AND ACCEPTED

1. As Pattie LaBelle says: "Perhaps you, too, can get a new attitude."

2. Reconciliations are few; successful reconciliations fewer yet.

3. External-factor marriage interruptions provide the best odds for reconciliation.

4. Post-divorce civility by your former spouse is a big plus.

5. Altruistic and economic reasons/needs are not good reasons to reconcile.

6. Couples must first write down what they need, expect, and what they will give up.

7. You should have a competent psychotherapist to coach and guide you.

8. Your estranged spouse may still be strange: be alert and cautious.

9. Money, sex problems, and lack of communication cause the majority of marriage interruptions.

10. Beware of MFS (me first syndrome) and passive-aggressive reconcilers.

Chapter 11

Post-Divorce Dating and Other Adventures

As you progress with your recovery, you note that divorce veterans seem less willing to forgive marital infractions and are more likely to call it quits because they have divorced before. Still, most would agree that starting a new marriage with lingering anger, pain, and distress from a previous divorce still smoldering is like building a new house before finding out why the last one burned down. Divorced individuals still carrying burning embers from a past marriage are more likely to ignite a subsequent divorce when re-experiencing similar stresses; thus, marriage veterans who have not learned from their mistakes are not statistically suited for re-marriage. The remainder of those who do not remarry may have elected to stay single for interim periods or cohabitate with a new partner as they continue their personal growth. Still, whether you're married, single, or divorced, life is a struggle. Financial, health, and personal problems are all equal-opportunity visitors; no one is spared.

As you enter the post-divorce dating scene, you realize that practices have changed dramatically since your single Saturdays. Suddenly a fresh smorgasbord of dating choices awaits you; wiser and smarter, you now know what to look for and what to avoid as you consider dating again. Modern dating now includes professional matchmakers, Internet dating providers, as well as traditional introductions:

- Activate yourself and circulate.

- Become involved in new activities.

- Try again if at first you don't succeed.

- Frequent places you enjoy to meet people with similar interests.

- Accept there are far more single women than single men.

- Understand it's truly a matter of numbers.

You realize that many couples contemplating second or third marriages come to their new engagements with expanded experience, improved maturity, and a better understanding of what is really important to them and to their new partner. This reality, they soon grasp, is a time of discovery. If they rush and combine the two different periods (dating and engagement) into one, *datgagement,* they shortchange themselves and their partners in the important sequential processes needed to learn about who and what lies ahead.

As simple as it sounds, to love someone truly means to accept them totally for who they were, with all of their faults, fractures, and failures. Once accepted, this person could be your soul mate. You remember that post-divorce dating requires caution and concern in getting to know someone new. Wounded warriors from past marriages can come across as hurt, harsh, hungry individuals. You recall that it is wise to start off with simple topics and general interest. You do not get into your past too soon and don't bring out unabridged versions of your past failed relationships or sexual experiences and preferences. You are especially careful about herpes, STDs, and other health hazards; both of your being tested are prerequisites to foreplay. Still, self-protection, safe sex, and vigilance bring new concerns via cohabitation arrangements, palimony, and shared living expense agreements.

WHAT YOU NOW RECOGNIZED, UNDERSTOOD, AND ACCEPTED

1. Welcome yourself to the world of "caretaker companions" and "rebound romances."

2. Men more frequently hook up with someone new faster than is the case with women.

3. Don't marry on the rebound. Why not? Odds for success are the same.

4. Good marriages are based on total acceptance.

5. Frequented places you enjoy to find someone with similar tastes.

6. What you see is what you get, and it's not going to change.

7. Sometimes ultimatums work; be prepared to follow through.

8. There are fewer eligible men than women; add in the word *quality* and the number becomes even less.

9. Marriage is a toll road. You pay as you go; even short trips have expensive tolls.

10. You can put a size-12 foot into a size-10 shoe, but there will be blood.

Chapter 12
Eat, Drink, and [Should I] Remarry?

Having read *Divorce Stress Syndrome*, you become more tolerant and no longer summarily reject new prospects; you look into the mirror and do not see Brad Pitt or Angelina Jolie. You agree to take a chance and meet someone who is obviously interested in you. Still, you remain selective and proceed with caution:

- Audience with children

- Audience with a neutral therapist

- Audience with a sex therapist (if necessary)

- Audience with friends, family, and relatives

- Audience with any and all previous spouses

- Audience with court staff to review his/her divorce, criminal, civil files (public information).

Even if you elect to remain single, you realize that you have to interact with others to maintain your social and emotional well-being. You accept that divorce is a common occurrence in today's world and that divorce is experienced by the majority of those who marry and re-marry. This includes the altruistic, benevolent, and charitable, as well as the infamous, successful, and the talented. A mere 15 percent of those in first marriages are said to be emotionally fulfilled and romantically happy.

You acknowledge that you were in the populated company of 85 percent of others who were also not happy with their current relationship stations, yet you progress with a positive attitude and optimistic goals discovered through your recovery of DSS. In reading this book and observing others living through divorce recovery, you gain valuable insights. You discover that those who did not take the required time to work through the mandatory stages of divorce recovery continue to have poor results. You witness that their subsequent unions become replays of their prior marriages, as past problems and confrontations resurface with a new spouse they carefully select and thoroughly screen themselves. Most of these divorce recovery dropouts divorce yet again. Remarrying without resolving former issues places many back in divorce court fighting a new opponent: their newest spouse. Divorce recovery graduation requires successful passage through the steps mentioned here.

You realized that love, marriage, and especially remarriage are all a process, and not an event. You discovered that you had to take time and allow your newfound partner to reveal her/himself, as you also had to be revealed to your new partner. Selection is also a process that requires time, patience, and open-mindedness.

New endings make for new beginnings. U.S. census statistics document an increase in divorce with sequential remarriages (67 percent divorce rate for second marriages and the 74 percent divorce rate for third marriages). Still, most divorced men, and many divorced women, eventually remarry. The risks are higher yet among those who remarry fewer than two years after divorce.

Given the significant number of incomplete marriages, remarriage echoed the words of "The Donald:"

> "I would never marry without a bulletproof Prenuptial Agreement," said Donald Trump, before his first marriage.

> "I would never remarry without two solid bulletproof Prenuptial Agreements," Donald Trump repeated after his first divorce.

"I would never remarry, without three bulletproof, solid, and ironclad Prenuptial Agreements," Donald Trump concluded after his second divorce.

WHAT YOU NOW RECOGNIZED, UNDERSTOOD, AND ACCEPTED

1. Again, there just are more single women than single men.

2. It's truly a matter of numbers; activate and circulate yourself.

3. Unless you're Brad Pitt or Angelina, don't be too picky.

4. Make up your list of required, desired and acceptable attributes.

5. Ask people who know you well to review your list for accuracy.

6. Date with modest expectations; do not expect Mr./Mrs. Right every time.

7. Review all six pre-engagement protocols. Give in where necessary.

8. Do not let resentment contaminate your next marriage or relationship.

9. No one sells happiness insurance—yet.

10. Don't have sex in the mall parking lot; that's what hotels are for.

Your cumulative experiences and the personal growth pathways found in this book brought you self-improvements. You became a better person as you mended and improved yourself and successfully dealt with *Divorce Stress Syndrome*. Congratulations!

Four last things to remember and more:

1. Never refer to your incomplete marriage as a failed marriage. No one failed. It just was incomplete.

2. Love can be lovelier the third, fifth, and even seventh time around. Certainly both Larry King (7) and Zsa Zsa Gabor (9) eventually found happiness and lasting love.

3. Your life is not over; a better life awaits you. Praise yourself for having had the wonderful life experience, to perhaps have loved, been married to and shared your life with more than just one person.

4. Stop, then think of the five most important things in your life and what each one means to you. Think about these five things frequently throughout your day.

5. I sincerely hope that I've lightened your load, brought you a laugh or two, and helped you recover your pre-divorce emotional good health.

   Buona notte Aida, dolci sogni a te (Good night Aida, sweet dreams to you).

   Buona notte Apollina, dolci sogni a te (Good night Apollina, sweet dreams to you).

   Buona notte Monique, dolci sogni a te (Good night Monique, sweet dreams to you).

About the Author

My father was Italian-American, my mother was Mexican-American; they were lifelong marriage partners. We lived in Los Angeles and I attended Catholic grammar school, followed by four years of public high school and then college. My last degree (1972) was received from the University of California, Berkeley, Boalt Hall School of Law.

Drawing upon my 36 years of university teaching and research experience, I am skilled and effective in reporting on pertinent facts, complex issues, and lessons learned from contemporary divorce case-study discussions. My decades of divorce work practice strengthened the writing of Divorce Stress Syndrome. My hope is that this unique, engaging combination of academic aptitude, teaching experience, and specialized legal skills will keep you focused, informed and amused.

Finally, a response to: "How can you give psychology advice when you're not a licensed psychologist?" I'll be the first to acknowledge that I am not a licensed psychologist (though I did minor in psychology as an undergrad). In addition to my undergraduate studies, I have researched psychology-divorce issues and have spiced both my undergraduate and graduate university lectures with this information for over 30 years. I have practiced law for over three decades; I have been given detailed information by hundreds of divorce clients about their personal proclivities and their intimacy issues, and have exchanged extensive commentary with their spouses's lawyers about our respective clients's "marital issues." I have completed several seminars on cross-examining expert witnesses (especially psychologists) and have retained numerous psychologists to aid my clients on their divorce issues. I also have worked with many psychologists on an academic and professional level, have cross-examined others, and have consulted with several on this book.

Interestingly, many of the "Dr" [Phd] psychologists seen on television, who proffer their advice to millions daily, are also not currently licensed psychologists. Other PhD "Drs" offer their advice to many even though they have completed their dissertation work in less demanding disciplines than psychology (i.e., education or counseling). Marriage, Family Therapists (MFTs), have completed a Master's degree in Psychology; most are extremely effective in their counseling work.

Universal university protocols entitle full tenured professors who hold terminal degrees in their respective disciplines (Juris Doctor) to be addressed as "Doctor" by students, staff, and colleagues. I must also mention that many of our students often refer to us by *other names*.

The unlicensed practice of medicine, law, and psychology remains a current problem in many states today; needless to state, television, the Internet, and close relatives have only exacerbated the problem.

Association of State and Provincial Psychology Boards

The Commission concluded that current training of doctoral psychologists provides sufficient experience to be competent for entry-level practice upon completion of the internship and doctoral degree (when they have completed two years of organized, sequential, supervised professional training experience predoctorally). The Commission explicitly affirms the value of organized, sequential, supervised post-doctoral experiences for those who wish to receive further training. Psychologists who do not receive two years of such training predoctorally should have the option of receiving it postdoctorally. The Commission recognized postdoctoral training programs, post-doctoral consultation, and postdoctoral supervision as an important mechanism for the development of advanced competency and expertise for professional practice.

Author's Note

THIS BOOK is about divorce recovery. It is written for the general reader and especially for the person facing divorce or who has been divorced. It is a detailed commentary, popular textbook, and full exploration of *DIVORCE STRESS SYNDROME*, with its confusing causes, encompassing effects, and listed self-condemning consequences. Because of the cumulative nature of the subject matter, the first few chapters provide necessary introductory background information. Much like the openings of many good books, operas, and effective commentary, the valuable principles and enlightening encouragements follow in later chapters.

For the price of this book ($0.076/page) you can buy 8.22 gallons of gas (at $3.12/gal. Nov. 30, 2010), assuming your car averages 26 MPG that would take you 214 miles. Reading this book will get you; your former, present or future spouse; and other loved ones much farther.

Marriage, we are told, fulfills our primal need for emotional intimacy and lasting companionship. Marriage binds individuals into a dynamic relationship with well-defined rights and responsibilities. This unique union also brings emotional and financial challenges, accompanied with societal and individual expectations, all of which can make relationships successful or stressful. No other human relationship can match the scope of individuality, depth of mutuality, and the interrelated complexities of their respective unique and particular challenges. Many of these trials can become insurmountable and lead to divorce. Still, after divorcing, and knowing the uncertainty and instability of marriage, most of us remarry.

As noted, many of our past marriages were interrupted because of poor choices (someone who was exciting to be with and perhaps great in bed). Not always really knowing the person we married (short dating durations and rushed engagements) and apparent failures to grow and remain emotionally connected in later years (divided interest and solo activities). It can be difficult to get beyond those with stellar appearances (impressive features, figures, and dress) or to maintain composure while facing *notable* attributes (someone who is super smooth on diverse dance floors, steep slopes, or on challenging greens).

Being mesmerized by those with substantive material accumulations (expensive houses, cars, and boats) can be difficult. Many of the above mentioned attraction factors might have influenced our past selections. Some spouses, however, sometimes come with unsuited characteristics: entitlement attitudes, excess baggage, and other incompatible traits that are later found to be antagonistic to your particular personality, lifestyle, or expectations.

Mistakenly, many of us may have been previously caught up in speed unions promoted by a culture that clings to the specious notion that spontaneous romantic love—fueled by immediate passion, is essential for a lasting marriage. Others erroneously marry partners who are extremely good to them; however, these benevolent individuals sometimes lack necessary and required intellectual, spiritual, or other desired attributes.

Age brings wisdom, understanding, and an appreciation of what is really important in later life. Stimulating lasting human companionship requires intellectual and emotional compatibility, mutual lasting trust, respect, and total honesty. Age can also bring accompanying declines in rigorous activities like dancing, traveling, and entertaining. These foregoing interest are often replaced by more sedentary involvements and "just-the-two-of-you" activities.

Remarriage requires a closer look at one's finite qualities, values, and common interests be they discussions about politics, the economy, or other shared subjects. Our new focus should be looking for long-lasting companionship potential rather than spontaneous great excitement or expected passion. Don't expect thunderbolts! Look for someone you are genuinely attracted to and who is involved in mutual activities and shares your values. Strangely, you may experience instant comfort along with a feeling that you could fall in love with such a person. Next, you may even be overcome by a strong sense that this is the person you've been looking to find.

But don't be super-selective, because, remarriage is also never perfect. Rather, remarriage is a continuing balancing process that requires constant awareness and a continued realization that the two of you must function as one. Plan for your future and plan carefully.

APPENDIX

Would You Get Married Again if I Died?

GAYLE: "Definitely not!"

GARY: "Why not? Don't you like being married?"

GAYLE: "Yes, of course I do. . ."

GARY: "Then why wouldn't you remarry?"

GAYLE: "Okay, I'd get married again."

GARY: "Would you live in our house?"

GAYLE: "Sure, it's a wonderful, warm house."

GARY: "Would you sleep with him in our bed?"

GAYLE: "Where else would we sleep?"

GARY: "Would you replace my pictures with his?"

GAYLE: "That would be the proper thing to do."

GARY: "Would you take him golfing with you?"

GAYLE: "Yes, those are always good times."

GARY: "Would he use my clubs?"

GAYLE: "Oh, no, he's left-handed."

MEDIAN AGE AT MARITAL EVENT FOR
PEOPLE 15 YEARS AND OVER BY SEX
U.S. CENSUS BUREAU 2007

MEN 42.3 of the married population

First Marriage	White	Black	Asian	Hispanic	Other
Age when married	23.9	25.7	27.8	24.1	23.4
Age when separated	30.4	32.1	32.6	30.3	30.4
Age when divorced	31.6	34.2	34.8	31.6	31.6
Age when widowed	61.8	52.7	U	60.9	62.0

Second Marriage					
Age when married	35.0	37.3	38.1	34.8	35.0
Age when separated	38.3	41.0	U	37.8	38.3
Age when divorced	40.8	43.4	U	41.8	40.8
Age when widowed	61.8	U	U	U	U

WOMEN 44.7 of the married population

First Marriage					
Age when married	21.8	22.8	24.9	21.8	21.8
Age when separated	28.2	28.8	30.8	28.1	28.2
Age when divorced	29.3	30.4	32.3	29.6	29.3
Age when widowed	61.4	53.8	59.2	54.1	62.1

Second Marriage					
Age when married	32.3	34.8	32.8	33.2	32.3
Age when separated	35.5	39.4	U	37.1	35.4
Age when divorced	38.2	41.2	U	38.3	37.8
Age when widowed	57.9	55.3	U	52.8	58.7

Marital History for People 20 Years and Over, by Age and Sex

U.S. Census Bureau 2004

Characteristic Yrs.	25-29	30-34	35-39	40-49	50-59	60-69	70- +
MEN: 109,380,000							
Never married	53.6	30.3	20.2	14.1	8.7	4.8	3.2
Ever married	46.4	69.7	79.8	85.9	91.3	95.2	96.8
Married once	44.3	62.4	68.1	66.8	63.4	66.8	74.9
Still Married	39.7	54.4	56.6	52.8	50.3	54.7	55.1
Married twice	2.0	6.7	10.3	15.7	21.3	20.6	17.0
Still married	1.9	6.0	8.5	12.5	16.1	16.1	12.6
Married three- +	0.1	0.6	1.4	3.3	6.6	7.7	4.9
Still married	-	0.4	1.2	2.7	5.1	5.6	3.1
Ever divorced	5.1	13.1	20.7	30.3	37.5	34.1	20.6
Currently divorced	3.2	6.6	10.9	14.7	16.2	13.0	6.2
Ever widowed	0.1	0.1	0.6	1.1	2.8	7.1	23.8
Currently widowed	-	0.1	0.4	0.6	1.4	4.2	18.9
WOMEN: 117,677,000							
Never married	41.3	22.3	16.2	11.9	7.6	4.3	4.9
Ever married	58.7	77.7	83.8	88.1	92.4	95.7	95.1
Married once	55.5	68.4	67.5	65.3	62.8	71.7	77.4
Still Married	48.6	57.6	54.6	49.7	44.4	46.2	29.0
Married twice	3.1	8.2	14.1	18.9	22.6	18.7	14.9
Still married	2.8	6.6	11.3	14.0	15.5	11.3	5.3
Married three- +	0.1	1.2	2.2	3.9	7.0	5.9	2.8
Still married	0.1	0.8	1.6	2.8	4.4	3.6	1.0
Ever divorced	7.0	17.1	25.6	33.9	40.7	32.3	17.8
Currently divorced	4.1	9.1	11.7	16.4	19.4	15.0	7.2
Ever widowed	0.3	0.7	1.1	2.5	7.8	21.2	54.5
Currently widowed	0.2	0.5	0.9	1.6	5.7	18.0	51.6

Divorce in Other Countries

Divorce is alive and present in most societies of the world; divorce is [still] not allowed in Malta (an archipelago of seven islands off the southern coast of Sicily), the Vatican, or the Philippine Islands. Divorce has now become common throughout the rest of the world. In Portugal, when spouses agree to divorce and to the terms of the divorce, it can be certified by a non-judiciary administrative entity and can then be served electronically. *You've got mail!*

Current statistics show alarming trends in increasing divorce rates all over the world. Many Asian countries are now catching up. Japan retains a markedly lower divorce rate, albeit with increasing rates in recent years. The divorce rate in South Korea is increasing even faster. According to national statistics, the divorce rate in South Korea is growing at an average rate of 56 percent per year. If this rate continues, all of South Korea will be divorced by 2143!

All over the world today, women are initiating divorces and separations more than ever before. Among the chief reasons cited for divorce, 46.4 percent reported that it was due to the husband's/wives' having an affair. Divorce rates in Germany have remained high; perhaps it's because of too many BMWs (bitching, moaning, and whining) on both sides. Statistics show that more than 201,000 German couples divorced in 2008. Most of the couples that divorced had already lived apart for the last six years of the marriage, and at the seventh year began divorce proceedings (I'm sorry, what was your first name again?). The German media have blamed this on rising unemployment rates, rain, sunny days, and other factors. In Belgium and Germany (more BMWs?), divorce rates are approaching the high rates in America, while divorce rates in the Netherlands are roughly the same as in the U.S.

Italy's 12 percent divorce rate is said to be the lowest in Europe. No-fault divorce has been legal in Italy since the 1970s (abortion is also legal), despite loud, local Catholic Church protests. Under current Italian divorce law, dissolution of marriage is divided into two sequential steps: the separation and the divorce. To be allowed to divorce, one or both spouses must first file and request a Separation Decree, then wait three full years before obtaining the final divorce.

The court will grant a final divorce decree only after three (3) uninterrupted years of legal separation. Quanto basta! No more going back home for *a quickie* or *a nooner*. As burdensome as Italian divorces may be, there are still others that are more taxing.

Though wedding rings are said to be the world's smallest handcuffs, they do not always work. Extramarital activity is higher in Europe than in America, but European divorce rates are still lower than in America. Recent newspaper articles in USA Today and other publications report that 45 percent of married men and 36 percent of married women in America have had extramarital affairs, which may help explain why well over half of U.S. marriages fail. This statistic does not speak well for the sanctimonious institution of marriage on either side of the Atlantic.

Politicians and others in Europe seem to have greater extramarital activity than their American counterparts, yet have fewer divorces. Still, Americans are catching up. Wives of American politicians are also becoming more tolerant. Ask Hilary Clinton or Silda Spitzer, but not Elizabeth Edwards or Jenny Sanford. Divorces were seldom granted in China. By 1973, divorces became easier to obtain. This trend continued until the mid 1980s, when the divorce rate soared after Deng Xiaoping *opened the country doors*. Thereafter, millions of Chinese returned to their hometowns and cities from the countryside farms, where Chairman Mao Tse-tung had sent everyone after the Cultural Revolution in 1966. These people had married for political reasons or to ease their daily toil, and many of these marriages ended in divorce.

Unlike the United States, China has a national law governing both marriage and divorce practices throughout their entire country. All of its twenty-two provinces have the same uniform national marriage and divorce laws, as opposed to an individual province-by-province approach as practiced in the U.S. via its individual state-by-state laws. It's noteworthy that China has countrywide marriage eligibility ages of 25 years for women and 26 years for men; thus, in China, Europe and the United States, as well as worldwide, divorce has become accepted and no longer carries its negative stigma.

Notwithstanding China's difficult divorce laws, things are still more complicated in nearby densely populated India. The present divorce rate in India is twice as high as ten years ago. Owing to India's large rural population and incomplete records, there are no formal statistics concerning divorce rates, but it is widely acknowledged that divorce rates have greatly increased.

Divorce in India is still far more complicated than anywhere else. While all major countries have their own laws governing divorce within their respective jurisdictions, India has separate and sometimes overlapping religious regulations regarding divorces in interfaith marriages. In China, India, and other countries, men tend to remain relatively unaffected by divorce, while women, above all those with children, have great difficulty in providing necessities for themselves and their children as well as in finding their way back into society. The phenomenon of family group marriages is notable. In rural India, marriages between families are common: for example, brothers of one family marry the sisters of another family at the same time. But wait; as in group marriage rates, family divorce plans may soon be available.

The divorce rate in Brazil has doubled since 1985, as it has almost everywhere. This increase may have been because of the 1988 abolition of a law that men could only have two divorces in their lifetime. Mercy! Thirty years ago, husbands were allowed to plead *Loss of Honor* (a form of justifiable homicide) if dinner was not ready when they came home from work, and they subsequently killed their wives. Now they can marry and divorce as many times as they want. This change in the law may have lessened the impact of the former limitation of only two divorces in one lifetime and provided a much needed justification for repeal of the former justifiable homicide defense.

Infidelity is one of the main reasons for marriage breakups in Brazil, where the familiar phenomenon of attractive single women seeking out married men is common. In order to help maintain social stability, Brazilian law requires that married couples wait two years after their marriage to get a divorce; furthermore, they must live apart for two additional years, and divorced people must wait two more years after the divorce is final to remarry. That's six years; back to Nevada, where it's only six-weeks.

Divorce in the U.S. Islamic Population

While most organized religions seem to be losing members, Islam is the fastest growing religion in the U.S. (an increase of 110 percent from 1990-2001) and in the world (some estimates claim 25 percent of the world population is now Islamic). The best-adjusted 2009 estimates project the U.S. Islamic population at 6,738,828 approximately, 2.02 percent of the total U.S. population of 308,615,540.

Divorce is also on the increase among the U.S. Islamic population. The U.S. Islamic divorce rate in 1990 was at 32 percent (38 percent in California), which was three times higher than in Egypt and Turkey where the divorce rates remain at 10 percent. Still, the divorce rate among all Islamic countries continues to increase. Based on available data, the chief reasons for American-Islamic divorces are in-laws, infidelity, and incompatibility (so what's new?). Even though Islamic followers consider divorce to be the last resort, it is allowed to end an unsatisfactory, troubled marriage. This must be preceded by extensive negotiation and prolonged discussions between the spouses, along with elders and spiritual advisors.

Chapter 7 Information

We should not be surprised to discover that divorce rates among our public safety servants are at the top of all occupational divorce statistics. Firefighters and our military personnel have high divorce-rates. Police officers experience the greatest number of uncompleted marriages of all occupations. In addition to the listed DSS stresses provided in this book, our public safety servants are compelled to deal with daily life and death-threatening confrontations, deaths of colleagues on the job, flash-back experiences, frequent relocations (promotions and advancement included), and other pressures not experienced by the rest of us.

These heavy loads take their tolls on these over-stressed and often underpaid individuals. While many government agencies are expanding their much needed support services, most neglect the obvious needs of those who bravely serve us. Our public safety servants and their spouses are subjected to far greater levels of marital stress than others.

Some sociologists state that police officers experience a first-marriage divorce rate of 72 percent; others suggest that it's lower (67 percent). The national average for first-marriage divorces is 55 percent.

Most subject commentators isolate police officers's stress to "controlled anger" which is maintained by "continual restraint." This controlled anger and other incipient stresses contaminate healthy marriages and turn them into cesspools of added stress. Police officers also face higher suicide rates than the general population; in fact, twice as many officers are lost by suicide than by death in the line of duty. Given the advancement of modern-day psychology, medicine, and even the limited compelling statistics listed above, it seems as if government has a clear and absolute obligation to increase support services available to our public safety servants and their spouses.

Chapter 9 Information

There are nine important things to do before you file or after you are served. Here is a good list to follow:

1. If you're the one who has or is about to file and you are covered on his/her medical insurance, be sure you have alternative coverage available. While you may be able to be carried on his/her policy until the final judgment is entered, eventually loss of medical insurance coverage may be a problem. You must plan for this contingency because your spouse may be allowed to have you removed once the final judgment has been entered; thus get your teeth capped, cleaned and bleached now.

   Consult with your attorney to be sure that you're properly covered. If you are not the employed spouse, insurance coverage could be a major problem; you can negotiate with your spouse over this for extended coverage and other issues. Some even take this as a part of their spousal support.

2. Before filing or after being served, prepare a revised budget, based on realistic income and necessary expenses.

Sudden new divorce expenses can be ruinous if you're not prepared. You may need a family loan or other financial advance to help bridge this cash shortage to ensure that you can make your essential living expenses.

You'll also need to establish an *emergency cash fund*. Again, consult with your lawyer if you need extra funds to make required ends meet. Perhaps an Order to Show Cause re Support (which will provide an immediate source of cash) may be in order to help you bridge the gap. Both you and your estranged spouse may be required to make significant compromises.

3. When filing for divorce, protect your credit report whether you're the party filing or have been just served. To avoid having late payments on your credit report, close all joint accounts and immediately open new ones in your name only. Open a new checking account in your name only; keep your cash "under the mattress" for a while until the "dust settles."

    DO NOT advance money to your spouse to pay bills in both your names; pay them yourself to ensure that they are paid and that your funds are not diverted.

4. Update insurance and retirement savings. You'll need to reevaluate all your insurance and retirement plans. You may want to change the beneficiary on all of your policies. Make out a new Will and mention that you're going through a divorce and distribute your half of any community property as you may wish. Spend the time necessary in adjusting your financial accounts as required.

    Also, pay for "fun stuff" with cash and charge all necessaries; you want a record of the latter and nothing of the former.

5. Make copies of all financial records before your divorce begins. Make clear copies of all tax returns, loan applications, wills, trusts, financial statements, banking information, all brokerage statements, loan documents, credit card statements, deeds to real property, car registration, insurance inventories, and insurance policies.

6. Copy records that you can use to trace your separate property, like an inheritance or gift from your family. These assets will remain yours as long as you can document them. Copies of each spouse's business records can be a treasure map showing you where hidden assets may be buried.

7. Don't overlook any assets—half of everything is yours! Even if you don't want an asset, it can be used to trade for something you do want. Inventory safe deposit boxes; track down bank and brokerage accounts; and review pay stubs, retirement plans and insurance policies. If your spouse's business generates a lot of cash, you may wish to engage a forensic accountant to look for telltale signs of additional income. Don't overlook hobbies or side businesses that might have expensive equipment or generate income.

8. Both sides must keep a "low financial profile" until the dust, dirt, and dollars settle.

9. Videotape your home and his/her office to make an inventory of what is there, before these items begin to disappear.

One last item of marital property that may need to be divided is the marital bed. Most such beds are used exclusively by the spouses. Some beds (sofas and even dinning room tables), however, become the hosting altars for adulterous frugal husbands or wives, who bring their new lovers to the homeland premises (a.k.a known as, "in house adultery"). Other spouses adhere to, keeping-it-in-the-family, and use the marital bed for sex with the nanny, maid, or butler.

But wait! How do you find out about such recklessness? Actually, several cheating spouses actuality admit this breach of trust; while others are caught in the act by an unexpected returning spouse. For many (especially women), this is the ultimate matrimonial violation. Then there is always DNA testing of residual evidence left behind. Hence the possible origin for the popular encomium phrase: "Get a room!"

FOR SAMPLE PURPOSES ONLY

JOINT PREMARITAL AGREEMENT

Parties

1. HUSBAND residing here, WIFE residing there, collectively herein referred to as "the Parties," in contemplation of their future marriage on July 1, now freely and voluntary enter into this Premarital Agreement (AGREEMENT), as follows:

Purpose

2. The Parties freely enter into this AGREEMENT for the purpose of defining their respective property rights following their contemplated marriage. The Parties mutually intend and expect that property owned, being purchased or acquired by either of them during their marriage, shall forever thereafter remain, the sole and separate property of the party who owns, purchased or acquired said property, unless modified by written agreement between them.

3. The Parties further intend and expect that their respective separate property will include: the property owned by a party before the marriage. All property acquired by a party after the marriage by gift, bequest, devise, or descent; and, the rents, issues and profits of the respective separate property of that party, including any and all appreciation, gains, splits, separate business profits and other normal and expected reasonable returns on said separate property and business, capital and asset interest of each spouse herein.

Property acquired with separate property proceeds of a party shall vest solely in the name of such acquiring party, unless such party agrees to transfer that property to the community or to the separate property of the other party.

4. All of the earnings of the Parties from their work, efforts, and skills during the marriage ("Community Earnings"), and any property purchased or acquired by the Parties with Community Earnings shall be the Parties' community property.

Property purchased or acquired with community property proceeds of the Parties shall be vested in their joint names as community property, unless agreed by the Parties to be transferred to the separate property of one of the Parties. Transfers to a trust shall not change the character of the property.

Disclosure of property

5. Each party has made a full, fair and comprehensive disclosure to the other party of all assets that he or she owns, is in the process of acquiring, all debts, liabilities, contingencies or other obligations, owed by him or her. A comprehensive and complete list of all of the assets owned, financed and obligations owed by HUSBAND is set forth herein in EXHIBIT A, which is attached hereto, and made a part of this AGREEMENT. A comprehensive and complete list of all of the assets owned, financed and obligations owed by WIFE is set forth herein in EXHIBIT B, which is attached hereto, and made a part of this AGREEMENT.

6. The Parties hereto acknowledge and understand that the cumulative totals set forth in EXHIBITS A and B are approximately correct and not exact, and that they reflect the values of the listed property on or about the date of this AGREEMENT.

7. The Parties herein further acknowledge and declare that they have each read EXHIBITS A and B, and that they are each entering into this AGREEMENT freely and voluntarily, and that each has reviewed this AGREEMENT with competent legal counsel of their own choosing.

8. As part of this AGREEMENT each of the Parties hereby fully acknowledge having voluntarily and expressly waived their right to the full and complete disclosure of their listed property, and financial obligations, on the attached EXHIBITS A and B, and that said waivers are a necessary and required part of this AGREEMENT.

9. Children of the Parties: HUSBAND is the father of the listed children by prior marriage:

Anatosicia _____, DOB: _____

Bodacious _____, DOB: _____

WIFE is the mother of the listed children by a prior marriage:

Cladicious _____, DOB: _____

Diogenes _____, DOB: _____

10. The Parties acknowledge and agree that the earnings and income resulting from the work, efforts, and skills of WIFE during the marriage are Community Property of the Parties, in which each will have an undivided one-half interest therein. Any property purchased or acquired by the Parties with the Community Earnings of WIFE or other community property shall be community property of the Parties.

11. HUSBAND hereby further agrees and acknowledges that property coming to WIFE during the marriage, by gift, inheritance, dividend, interest, appreciation and other proceeds from her separate property, other than income or earnings mentioned herein below, shall be the sole and separate property of WIFE and shall be subject to her sole disposition and control as her sole and separate property.

12. The Parties acknowledge and agree that the earnings and income resulting from the work, efforts, and skills of HUSBAND during the marriage are Community Property of the Parties, in which each will have an undivided one-half interest therein. Any property purchased or acquired by the

Parties with the Community Earnings of HUSBAND or other community property shall be community property of the Parties.

13. WIFE, hereby further agrees and acknowledges that property coming to HUSBAND during the marriage, by gift, inheritance, dividend, interest, appreciation and other proceeds from his separate property, other than income or earnings hereinabove, shall be the sole and separate property of HUSBAND and shall be subject to his sole disposition and control as his sole and separate property.

Release of Marital Rights to Separate Property

14. Both of the Parties herein agree to forever waive and release any and all equitable, legal or inchoate claims and rights, actual, inchoate or contingent that he or she may acquire in the separate property, excluding the separate consideration listed in paragraphs 15 and 16 herein below, of the other spouse by reason of their marriage, including but not limited to:

   a. The right to a family allowance;

   b. The right to a Probate Homestead;

   c. The right to claim dower, courtesy, or any statutory Substitutes provided by the laws of the state in which the Parties or either of them reside, die or in which they own property of any kind;

   d. The right of election to take against the will of the other;

   e. The right to a distributive share in the estate of the other should he or she die intestate;

   f. The right to declare a homestead in the separate property of the other; and,

   g. The right to act as estate administrator or trustee of the other.

15. Nothing in this AGREEMENT shall be deemed to constitute a waiver by either party of any bequest or devise that the other party may elect to make to him or her, including the additional consideration listed in paragraphs 15 and 16 herein below.

Additional Consideration

16. In addition to the mutual promises, covenants and other consideration listed herein, HUSBAND has purchased and provided a FIVE HUNDRED THOUSAND DOLLAR ($500,000.00) Term Life Insurance Policy, with Hartford Life Insurance Co., Policy No. FB6879670822 payable to WIFE, to assist and facilitate her relocation transition after his death. Said Term Insurance Life Insurance Policy shall be paid for exclusively by HUSBAND, and shall remain in effect until its stated termination date of October 29, 2023. In the event of their joint-death, or if WIFE dies SIXTY (60) days after HUSBAND the Policy shall then be payable to HUSBAND'S estate as directed.

17. As and for additional consideration, in the event of HUSBAND'S death while the Parties reside in a residence which is either the separate property of HUSBAND or the community property of the Parties, the WIFE may elect to continue to reside in such residence for a period of one (1) year from the date of HUSBAND'S death, free of any and all costs, which shall be borne by the separate property estate of HUSBAND without charge, contribution or indemnification by WIFE.

18. As and for yet an additional and independent element of separate consideration, within thirty (30) days after his death, HUSBAND'S Estate shall payoff any and all remaining balance(s), if any, on the primary vehicle used and driven by WIFE. Title and registration to said vehicle shall also be transferred to WIFE at the time of payoff, or thirty (30) days after his death if no payoff is necessary or required. Payment

of routine household expenses and extraordinary cost shall be paid by WIFE.

19. In the event the Parties reside in a residence owned by either of them, as his or her separate property, the usual and ordinary expenses of the separate property residence shall be borne by the Community Earnings of the Parties to the extent such Community Earnings are sufficient to cover such expenses. Community Earnings used to pay for such items shall not be entitled to reimbursement, contribution, repayment, set-off, deduction, credit, or indemnification. To the extent the Community Earnings of the Parties are insufficient to cover the usual and ordinary expenses of the residence, the separate property of the party owning the residence shall be used to pay said usual and ordinary expenses.

20. The usual and ordinary expense of the residence shall include payments on any note(s) secured by deed(s) of trust, property taxes, property insurance, maintenance, utilities, minor repairs, and replacement of minor items such as doors, windows, window-screens and all other such routine costs and expenses.

21. Capital improvements and major repairs to a residence owned by either of the Parties, in which the Parties reside, shall be borne by the separate property of the owner Party. Such capital improvement and major repairs shall include, but not be limited to: new carpeting, roof replacement, slab repairs, major pool repairs and replacements, and other improvements and replacements exceeding FIVE THOUSAND DOLLARS (5,000.00).

Execution of Instruments

22. Each party agrees, after careful review and explanation by his and her own independent legal counsel, to execute and deliver, and properly acknowledge any and all necessary and required documents to carry out the full intentions and expectations of this AGREEMENT, and to further execute and deliver, properly acknowledged deeds and other necessary or required

instruments, in order that free and marketable title to any and all separate property can be conveyed by either party, free from claim, right or demand, from the other party herein by reason of their marriage.

Representation by Separate Counsel and Joint Preparation of Agreement

23. Each party hereby acknowledges and attests that each has been represented by separate and independent legal counsel in the negotiations, modifications and explanations of this AGREEMENT; however, that the drafting, editing, revisions and finalization of this AGREEMENT was a joint product and effort of their two independent counsels.

Presentation of Agreement

24. Each party further acknowledges that counsel representing each party is of their own selection and that each party had read the entire AGREEMENT and understands it. Each of the Parties further state and declare that not less than fourteen (14) days have elapsed between the time this AGREEMENT was presented to them, and that each was advised to seek and obtain their independent legal counsel before the signing of this AGREEMENT.

Binding Effect on other Parties

25. This AGREEMENT shall bind and inure to the benefit of the parties and their respective heirs, personal representatives, successors and assigns.

Integration Clause

26. This AGREEMENT constitutes the entire understanding, expectations and agreement between the Parties concerning the subject matters covered. Any and all oral representations, modifications or alterations made or claimed, whether made

before or after the execution of this AGREEMENT, contrary, challenging or inconsistent with the expressed subjects addressed therein, shall be void, unenforceable and have absolutely no force or effect on this AGREEMENT, but for subsequent written modifications made by the Parties and independent and separate legal counsel of their own selection.

Effect of Partial Invalidity

27. If any term, provision, paragraph, promise or condition of this AGREEMENT is determined to be invalid, void or unenforceable, by a court of competent jurisdiction, in whole or in part, then the remainder of this AGREEMENT shall remain in full force and effect and shall in no way affect, impair, invalidate or compromise thereafter.

Signed in Counterparts

28. This AGREEMENT may be executed in counterparts. Each is hereby declared and recognized to be an original; all however, shall be deemed to be one and the same AGREEMENT. Both photographic and photostatic copies of this AGREEMENT may be introduced into evidence without further foundation or production of both originals, in any necessary or required action(s) or proceeding(s).

Governing Law

29. This AGREEMENT shall be strictly governed by the laws of the State of Chaos, notwithstanding the possible relocation or residence of the Parties.

EXECUTION AND ACKNOWLEDGEMENT

IN WITNESS WHEREOF, the Parties have executed and signed this AGREEMENT on the day and year set forth herein below.

_____   _____

HUSBAND   Date

_____   _____

WIFE   Date

Legal Counsel for HUSBAND   _____

                                       Dewey Cheatum

Legal Counsel for WIFE   _____

                                       Ann Howe

FOR SAMPLE PURPOSES ONLY

JOINT POSTNUPTIAL AGREEMENT

AGREEMENT, made this_____ day of _____ 2010 by _____ (Husband) and between _____ (Wife) hereinafter jointly referred to as the Parties, and their respective attorneys _____ and _____

PURPOSE

The Parties married each other on _____. Each has separate property, the nature and extent of which is fully disclosed in the attached Financial Disclosure Statement (statements of assets and liabilities as Exhibits 1). The Parties are also setting forth their respective rights in and to all listed property, either owned at the date of their marriage, and in and to all property acquired, and to the property that may have been acquired individually or jointly during the marriage.

The Parties, and their respective counsel, hereby mutually stipulate and agree that this Agreement is equitable, fair and reasonable as to either party, or that said Agreement was negotiated, drafted and authored by joint counsel.

EFFECT OF AGREEMENT

The Parties shall separately retain all rights in the property he or she now owns as set forth in greater detail in their respective attached Exhibits, including all appreciation, as well as property and income acquired separately in the future ("Separate Property").

1. Each of the Parties shall have the unrestricted right to dispose of such Separate Property, free and clear of any claim that may be made by the other by reason of their marriage and with the

same effect as if no marriage had been consummated between them.

2 Separate Property shall include substitutions and exchanges for such property now in existence, and income and property acquired separately hereafter, and any proceeds therefrom, and from any income derived from such property, and any property purchased from the proceeds or income from such property. Separate property shall also include gifts or inheritances one party receives from a third party pursuant to local statutes.

3. PROPERTY DISTRIBUTION. The Parties agree that all furniture, furnishings, and property accrued jointly in both names during the marriage as outlined in detail in Form A11 shall be divided equally between them with the exception that: In the event either of the Parties should desire to sell, encumber, convey or otherwise dispose of or realize upon his or her Separate Property or any part or parts thereof, the other will, upon request, join in such deeds, bills of sale, mortgages, renunciations of survivorship or other rights created by law or otherwise, or other instruments, as the party desiring to sell, encumber, convey or otherwise dispose or realize upon may request and as may be necessary and appropriate.

4. DEBT DISTRIBUTION. The Parties mutually agree that all liabilities presently existing, as detailed on their respective Financial Disclosure Exhibits attached hereto, and or which may be incurred by either party during the marriage, and which were incurred in their name alone shall remain as an individual liability as to the party so incurring said liability; and, at no time hereafter shall the other party have any obligation or responsibility to pay liabilities so incurred by said other party.

5. All debt accrued jointly in both names shall be paid equally between the Parties. The Parties hereby further stipulate and agree that in the event of any audits of all past filed tax returns; each party shall be responsible to pay one-half of any assessments, penalties and interests charges for said past filed

tax returns which pre-date this Agreement. The Parties hereby further stipulate and agree that in the event of any audits of all future filed tax returns, each party shall be individually responsible to pay the full amount(s) of any assessments, penalties and interest charges which are attributable to his or her failure to declare income or due to his or her taking improper deductions which may arise for that period.

6. JOINT PROPERTY. This Agreement does not restrict, prohibit or condition any conveyance, devise, bequest or transfer by the Parties, or either of them alone, of the Separate Property of either party into tenancy in common, joint tenancy, tenancy by the entireties or any other form of concurrent and or undivided estate or ownership between the Parties. This Agreement does not restrict, prohibit or condition the acquisition of any property in any such form of ownership by any one of the Parties.

7. The incidents and attributes of ownership and other rights of the Parties with respect to any property so conveyed, transferred or acquired shall be determined under the state laws of the Partie's domicile, or the state laws of the subject property's location, and shall be, to the extent possible, necessary or required by law, or otherwise determined with reference to this Agreement.

8. SEPARATE PROPERTY. The Parties agree that the rights and obligations created by this Agreement have monetary value to each of the Parties and each of the Parties agrees to make no claim to the Separate Property of the other party, either during the joint lives of the Parties hereto or thereafter, and, if a party is not a prevailing party (as may be legally finally determined) with respect to any such claim, to indemnify the other party against all costs, attorney and court fees and expenses arising from any such claim.

9. WAIVER OF RIGHTS. Except as otherwise provided in this Agreement, each party hereby waives, releases and relinquishes any and all right, title or interest whatsoever, whether arising by common law or present or future statute of any jurisdiction

or otherwise, in the Separate Property and probate estate of the other, including but not limited to distribution in intestacy, the right of election to take against the will of the other, any rights accruing by reason of events occurring prior to their marriage, and any right to dower, courtesy, statutory allowances, and spousal support.

Such waiver, release and relinquishment shall not apply and is not effective with respect to any rights or entitlements a party may have as a surviving spouse under the Social Security laws or with respect to any other governmental benefit or governmental program of assistance. This Agreement shall not limit the right of either party to make such transfers of property to the other as he or she may wish during their respective lifetimes, or by will, or to acquire property jointly or in any other form of ownership referenced in sections 4, and other applicable and relevant sections.

10. DIVORCE/SEPARATION/ANNULMENT. Except as otherwise provided in this Agreement, each party specifically agrees that neither shall make any claim for or be entitled to receive any money or property from the other as alimony, spousal support, or maintenance in the event of separation, annulment, divorce or any other domestic relations proceeding of any kind or nature.

11. Each of the Parties further forever waives and relinquishes any and all claims for alimony, spousal support or maintenance, including, but not limited to, any claims for services rendered, work performed, and labor expended by either of the Parties during any period of cohabitation prior to the marriage and during the entire length of the marriage. The waiver of spousal support shall apply to any and all claims, including both pre- and post-judgment.

12. ERISA RIGHTS. Each party hereby specifically waives any right, whether created by statute or otherwise, to pension, profit-sharing, or other retirement benefits earned by or credited to the other, including, but not limited to, any joint or

survivorship rights and any right which might arise in the event of the Parties' separation or the dissolution of the marriage. Each party shall execute all such necessary and required waivers or other documents as the other may reasonably request to evidence such waiver(s).

13. FINANCIAL DISCLOSURE. Each party has attached a statement of assets and liabilities as Exhibits to this Agreement, 1 and 2 respectively. Each party accepts and acknowledges that they have been given ample opportunity to inquire further as to the financial information provided by the other, and each party specifically waives any right to any further disclosure of the property and financial obligations.

14. RIGHT TO CONTEST. Nothing contained herein shall be deeded or implied to limit the right of either party to contest any domestic relations suit between the Parties or to file a countersuit against the other party; however, in any hearing on such suit, this Agreement shall be considered a full, final and comprehensive settlement of any and all property rights between the Parties under local laws and the laws of states where other property of the Parties may be located. In such case, neither party shall maintain any claim or demand whatsoever against the other for property, money, attorney fees and costs, which is inconsistent, repugnant or otherwise in conflict with or not provided for in this Agreement.

15. INTEGRATION. This Agreement sets forth the entire agreement between the Parties with regard to the subject matter hereof. All prior agreements, covenants, representations, and warranties, expressed or implied, oral or written, with respect to the subject matter hereof, are contained herein.

Any and all prior or contemporaneous conversations, negotiations, possible and alleged agreements, representations, covenants, and warranties, with respect to the subject matter hereof, are hereby forever waived, merged, and superseded hereby and herein in this integrated agreement.

16. BINDING ON SUCCESSORS. Each and every provision contained in this Agreement shall inure to the benefit of and shall be binding upon the heirs, assigns, personal representatives, and all successors in the interest of the Parties.

17. SEVERABILITY. In the event any provision of this total Agreement is deemed to be void, invalid, or unenforceable, that provision shall be severed from the remainder of this Agreement so as not to cause the invalidity or unenforceability of the remainder of this Agreement. All remaining terms and provisions of this Agreement shall then, therefore, continue in full force and effect. If any provision shall be deemed to be invalid or unenforceable due to its scope, breadth or lack of consideration, such provision shall be deemed valid, to the extent possible, as permitted by law.

18. PARAGRAPH HEADINGS. All headings of particular paragraphs and subparagraphs are inserted only for convenience and are not part of this Agreement and are not to act as a limitation as to the scope or purpose of the particular paragraph to which the heading refers.

19. MODIFICATION. This Agreement may be modified, superseded, or voided only upon the written agreement of the Parties, and their individual legal counsel. Furthermore, the physical destruction or loss of this Agreement shall not be construed as a modification.

20. ACKNOWLEDGEMENTS. Each party acknowledges that he or she has had an adequate opportunity to read and study this Agreement, to consider it, and to consult with his or her Attorneys, Certified Public Accounts and other individually selected necessary or required experts, by each party, without any form of coercion, duress or pressure. Each party further acknowledges that he or she has examined the Agreement before signing it, and has been advised by independent legal counsel concerning the rights, liabilities, waivers and implications of this document.

21. STATE LAW. It is intended that this Agreement be valid and enforceable within the provisions of the Parties' State Law, and that the Parties' case law that governs its interpretation.

22. CERTIFICATION OF RECEIPT OF AGREEMENT. By signing below, both certify that each individually received a true and correct copy of this Agreement. No representations of any kind have been made to him or her as an inducement to enter into this Agreement, other than the representations set forth herein.

23. IN WITNESS WHEREOF, the Parties hereto have set their hands and seals.

EXECUTION AND ACKNOWLEDGEMENT

IN WITNESS WHEREOF, the parties have executed and signed this AGREEMENT on the day and year set forth herein below.

_____   _____

HUSBAND   Date

_____   _____

WIFE   Date

Legal Counsel for HUSBAND   _____

                           Dewey Cheatum

Legal Counsel for WIFE   _____

                           Ann Howe

APPENDIX 2

A speeding car passed a female state trooper
driving along an interstate highway. The trooper
activated her siren and red lights, however; the
driver failed to stop.

After a three-mile slow-speed chase, the
driver finally pulled over. The state trooper
cautiously approached the woman driver.

The female state trooper then asked,
"Do you know why I stopped you?"

The woman-driver, in a state of obvious
apprehension, replied, "Two years ago my former
husband ran-off with a woman state trooper;
I thought you were bringing him back!"

For years past, the U.S. Department of Health and Human Services (HHS) sought to shine the spotlight on the problem of child support enforcement. In 1995, HHS released a joint report with the Department of Commerce. The report showed that in 1991, of the 54% of custodial parents who had support obligations in place, only 67% of outstanding child support obligations were met. This report showed that a smaller percentage of mothers who receive support from out-of-state fathers actually receive the support that is due than mothers who receive support from in-state fathers.

This focus on the problems of interstate support enforcement led to the Full Faith and Credit for Child Support Orders Act (FFCCSOA). The following pages contain excerpts from said act.

The journal entry suggestions provided here are examples to assist you in starting your individualized entries. Open your heart and record your darkest feelings and deepest pains.

U.S. Department of Health Human Services

ACTION TRANSMITTAL

OCSE-AT-02-03

TO: STATE AGENCIES ADMINISTERING CHILD SUPPORT ENFORCEMENT PLANS UNDER TITLE IV-D OF THE SOCIAL SECURITY ACT, TRIBES AND TRIBAL ORGANIZATIONS, AND OTHER INTERESTED INDIVIDUALS

SUBJECT:

Clarifying the Applicability of the Full Faith and Credit for Child Support Orders Act (FFCCSOA) to States and Tribes.

PURPOSE:

The purpose of this action transmittal is to inform states and tribes of provisions of the Full Faith and Credit for Child Support Orders Act (FFCCSOA) and their application to both jurisdictions.

Congress enacted FFCCSOA (28 U.S.C. 1738B) in 1994 because of concerns about the growing number of child support cases involving disputes between parents who live in different states and the ease with which noncustodial parents could reduce the amount of the obligation or evade enforcement by moving across state lines. FFCCSOA requires courts of all United States territories, states and tribes to accord full faith and credit to a child support order issued by another state or tribe that properly exercised jurisdiction over the parties and the subject matter.

Congress amended FFCCSOA in the Personal Responsibility and Work Opportunity Reconciliation Act of 1996 to be consistent with the requirements of the Uniform Interstate Family Support Act (UIFSA) regarding which of several existing orders prospectively controls the current support obligation, as well as UIFSA's choice of law provisions. Most of the provisions regarding modification of orders in FFCCSOA and UIFSA are consistent as well. While tribes are not obliged to enact UIFSA as a condition of receipt of Federal funding of their child support enforcement programs operated under title IV-D of the Social Security Act, states are obligated to do so.

FFCCSOA addresses the need to determine, in cases with more than one child support order issued for the same obligor and child, which order to recognize for purposes of continuing, exclusive jurisdiction and enforcement.

Definitions applicable to FFCCSOA appear in section 1738B(b). FFCCSOA defines "state" to include "Indian country" as this term is defined in 18 U.S.C. section 1151. This means that wherever the term state is used in the Act, it includes tribe as well. "Court" is defined as "a court or administrative agency of a state [or tribe] that is authorized by state [or tribal] law to establish the amount of child support payable by a contestant or make a modification of a child support order."

Provisions of the Full Faith and Credit for Child Support Orders Act

General Rule:

FFCCSOA section 1738B(a) provides that the appropriate authority in each state and tribe shall enforce a child support order made consistent with the provisions of FFCCSOA in another state or tribe according to its terms and that a state or tribal court may not modify an order of another state or tribal court except in accordance with subsections (e), (f) and (i) of FFCCSOA. Where a state or tribal court or administrative agency issues an order that is consistent with FFCCSOA the order must be recognized and enforced by other states and tribes.

Requirements of Child Support Orders:

Section 1738B(c) of FFCCSOA contains the requirements of child support orders. In order for a child support order to be consistent with FFCCSOA, a court with subject matter jurisdiction and personal jurisdiction over the contestants must have issued it. Additionally, the contestants must have been given reasonable notice and opportunity to be heard.

Continuing Jurisdiction:

Section 1738B(d) of FFCCSOA contains the provisions on continuing jurisdiction. A state or tribe has continuing, exclusive jurisdiction over an order issued by a court of that state or tribe if the state or tribe is the child's residence or the residence of any individual contestant unless the court of another state or tribe, acting in accordance with subsections (e) and (f) has modified the order.

Recognition of Child Support Orders:

Section 1738B(f) contains the provisions for determining the order recognized for continuing, exclusive jurisdiction. Both FFCCSOA and UIFSA have consistent rules for determining which order is the single effective order entitled to prospective enforcement when multiple orders exist. The rules are:

"If one or more child support orders have been issued with regard to an obligor and a child, a court shall apply the following rules in determining which order to recognize for purposes of continuing, exclusive jurisdiction and enforcement:

(1) If only one court has issued a child support order, the order of that court must be recognized.

(2) If two or more courts have issued child support orders for the same obligor and child, and only one of the courts would have continuing, exclusive jurisdiction under this section, the order of that court must be recognized.

(3) If two or more courts have issued child support orders for the same obligor and child, and more than one of the courts would have continuing, exclusive jurisdiction under this

section, an order issued by a court in the current home state of the child must be recognized, but if an order has not been issued in the current home state of the child, the order most recently issued must be recognized.

(4) If two or more courts have issued child support orders for the same obligor and child, and none of the courts would have continuing, exclusive jurisdiction under this section, a court having jurisdiction over the parties shall issue a child support order, which must be recognized.

(5) The court that has issued an order recognized under this subsection is the court having continuing, exclusive jurisdiction under subsection (d)."

<u>Authority to Modify Orders:</u>

A state or tribe may modify its own order as long as it has continuing, exclusive jurisdiction. The authority to modify the child support order of another state or tribe under FFCCSOA is found at section 1738B(e). Under this section, a state or tribal court may modify the order of another state or tribe if it has jurisdiction and the issuing state or tribe no longer has continuing, exclusive jurisdiction or if each individual contestant files written consent with the state or tribe of continuing, exclusive jurisdiction. FFCCSOA prohibits a state or tribe from modifying an existing order issued by another state or tribal court, unless these criteria are met.

<u>Enforcement of Modified Orders:</u>

Section 1738B(g) of FFCCSOA contains the enforcement provision. If a state or tribe no longer has continuing, exclusive jurisdiction it may enforce the nonmodifiable aspects of the order and collect on arrearages that accrued before the date on which the order was modified under subsections (e) and (f).

<u>Choice of Law:</u>

Section 1738B(h) contains FFCCSOA's choice of law provision. In a proceeding to establish, modify, or enforce a child support order, the law of the forum state or tribe applies. As an exception to this rule, courts must apply the law of the state or tribe that issued the order when interpreting the order's obligations, such as the amount and duration of support payments. In a proceeding for arrearages, the statute of limitations under the laws of the forum state or tribe or the issuing state or tribe, whichever is longer, applies.

Registration for Modification:

Section 1738B(i) contains FFCCSOA's registration for modification provision. If all of the individual contestants have left the issuing state or Indian country, the contestant seeking to modify an order issued in another state or tribe must register that order in a state or tribe with jurisdiction over the nonmoving contestant for purposes of modification. Either a state IV-D agency or a tribal CSE agency may be a party who is seeking to modify and enforce an order under this subsection.

Related References:

For further information on determining which order is entitled to prospective enforcement in cases with more than one order, consult OCSE-IM-01-02 which issued a TEMPO on determining controlling orders and DCL-00-64 which provided material and resources to help states and tribes make determinations of controlling order. Both are available at OCSE's website at www.acf.hhs.gov/programs/cse/poldoc. htm.

INQUIRIES TO: ACF Regional Administrators
ATTACHMENT: 28 U.S.C. 1738B

Sherri Z. Heller, Ed.D.
Commissioner
Office of Child Support Enforcement
(http://www.acf.hhs.gov)

Child Support Enforcement Interstate

Full Faith and Credit for Credit for Child Support Orders Act (FFCCSOA)

GENERAL INFORMATION

1. This topic contains information on the following:

    1. An overview of the Full Faith and Credit for Child Support Orders Act (FFCCSOA);

    2. Enforcing another state's order under FFCCSOA;

    3. Collecting interest under FFCCSOA.

FFCCSOA - OVERVIEW

1. Effective October 20, 1994, the Full Faith and Credit for Child Support Orders Act (28 U.S.C. Section 1738B) required states to enforce the terms of any permanent or temporary order (including paternity orders) issued by a court or administrative authority of the issuing state, and it prohibits modification of other states' child support orders unless certain jurisdictional requirements are met.

    Any payments or installments of support due under a support order are considered final judgments by operation of law and are entitled to full faith and credit. The state where the obligor resides (or is employed) is referred to as the "forum state". The Full Faith and Credit for Child Support Orders Act (FFCCOA) applies to all states, territories, possessions, and Indian tribes of the United States.

    The purpose of FFCCSOA is to facilitate the enforcement of child support orders among the states. By adhering to the guidelines of FFCCSOA, jurisdictions are ensured that cases are handled uniformly and consistently. The main premise remains that the child support order of the issuing state, as registered in the responding state, shall be enforced based on the terms as found therein. Under the FFCCSOA, a child support order issued by a court in another state must be enforced if:

1. The issuing state had subject-matter jurisdiction to hear the matter and enter an order;

2. The issuing state had personal jurisdiction; and

3. The parties were given reasonable notice and opportunity to be heard.

FFCCSOA – ENFORCING ANOTHER STATE'S ORDER

1. When North Carolina is the forum for enforcement of another state's support order, the same procedures and remedies available to N.C. orders are applied to the enforcement of the out-of-state order. The law of the issuing state governs the interpretation of the order, but in procedures to collect arrearages, the longer statute of limitations applies.

2. Example: North Carolina is asked to enforce an order entered in New York that requires current support for the child up to age twenty-one (21). FFCCSOA requires N.C. to continue enforcement of support until the child is twenty-one (21), rather than age eighteen (18) or through high school up to age twenty (20), as required by N.C. law.

FFCCSOA – COLLECTION OF INTEREST

1. The collection of interest on arrearages is another example of FFCCSOA. N.C. law does not address collection of interest on child support arrearages, but N.C. can collect the interest if another state's law allows it.

2. Example: An order from California has a sum certain amount for child support and three percent (3%) interest on the arrearages. North Carolina pursues collection of the interest on the arrearages. (The initiating state should determine the amount of interest to be collected.)

For questions or clarification on any of the policy contained in these manuals, please contact your local county office.

North Carolina Department of Health and Human Services
http://www.ncdhhs.gov/

Personal Journal Starting Suggestions

If I'm being honest with myself, I first noticed my relationship was in trouble when:

_____

_____

_____

I came to see that I contributed to the demise of my fallen marriage by:

_____

_____

_____

Learning about the three phases of DSS assisted me in directing my attention to personal concerns by:

_____

_____

_____

Accepting grief as a necessary and required phase of recovery helped me prepare for passage by:

_____

_____

_____

I long ago realized that most marriages have their problems; still, I now realize that it's an ongoing process and that both spouses must work extra hard by:

_____

_____

_____

Divorce from my spouse, who was my lover, partner and best friend, left me brokenhearted. It's as if:

_____

_____

_____

Separations frequently ignite into full-divorce mode because of offensive responses or objectionable behaviors that surface during this hurtful period. I recall that I felt as if:

_____

_____

_____

My self-confidence, self-respect and desire to live all seemed suddenly gone. I felt as if:

_____

_____

_____

Letting go of the past allows me to enjoy the present today and the future tomorrow. A great burden will be lifted because:

_____

_____

_____

Once I forgive, I will start to heal. Eventually my inner demons and emotional toxicants will dissipate. I will start by:

_____

_____

_____

Moving on means I must stop thinking about him/her and to acknowledge and accept that they are forever gone and will not return. This I will do by:

_____

_____

_____

My recovery can be impacted by attitude and expectations. I will not regard my loss as an unalterable tragedy; I will learn from my mistakes and grow by:

_____

_____

_____

My desire to find fulfilling companionship and lasting happiness can become a self-fulfilling prophecy by:

_____

_____

_____

Now that I'm alone, I can stand back and look at myself from an outsider's perspective and make necessary adjustments to achieve new goals and desired objectives by:

_____

_____

_____

PUBLISHER'S NOTE

Publishing and selling this book created an increase demand among cruise ship passages, Queen Mary visitors, and many others to visit the homes and former homes of many of the celebrities mentioned in this book. To fill this demand, we associated with SunseekerS TOURS, www. SunseekertourS.us and 562.331.1230.

See in person the familiar sights you so well know from movies, books, and the many celebrity divorces mentioned here!

"We start by traveling north to the splendid world famous hilltop Hollywood Sign where you can take pictures of yourself and others."

We Visit these Hollywood Landmarks:

Grauman's Chinese Theater	Muscle Beach
Hollywood Boulevard	Ports of LA/Long Beach
Hollywood Roosevelt Hotel	Rodeo Drive
Hollywood Walk of Fames	Santa Monica Pier
Kodak Theater	Sunset Strip
Mel's Diner	Venice Beach

GLOSSARY STARTER
OF
MODERN DIVORCE DEFINITIONS

This glossary starter is provided as a checklist for unfamiliar legal and quasi-legal terms. Because these terms often have individualized different state definitions, they are provided here as a starting place for you to check definitions for your particular state. Some have satirical definitions to keep your interest.

BE SURE YOU CHECK your particular state's definition.

Abandonment: What happens when you introduce your spouse to a younger, thinner more attractive man or woman.

Abuse: Endless weekend and holiday viewing of sports.

Adultery: Wishful thinking.

Affidavit: Guys you date after divorcing David.

Alienation of Affection: See Abandonment above.

Alimony: Court-ordered spousal support, sometimes payable till death due you part.

Alimony a Pendente: Support paid by an Italian ex-husband.

Annulment: The court's judgment that a so-called marriage was never legally valid or became invalid after the marriage.

Appeal: What you feel when you see an attractive person you would like to meet.

Arbitration: Talking things over with your in-laws, a neutral third party, or a private judge.

Bifurcation: Marriage dissolution and property rights/support obligations are handled separately.

Canons of (Legal) Ethics: State rules, usually established by lawyers that regulate the behavior of lawyers. Violations can lead to warnings, fines, suspensions, and even license revocation.

Child Support: Court-ordered, monthly payments from the non-custodial parent to the custodial parent that are tax deductible by the non-custodial parent.

Child Support Guidelines: State guidelines requiring the noncustodial parent to pay child support based on a percentage of income.

COBRA: Covers ex-spouses even after one party remarries.

Code of Professional Responsibility: There is no such thing.

Cohabitation: Unmarried persons living together (in sin) as if married (in sin). A.K.A: sharing expenses and having great sex.

Common Law Marriage: A judicially-recognized marriage in some states, generally based on cohabitation, despite the parties's failure to comply with marriage statutes.

Community Property: A system of property division which divides all property acquired during the term of the marriage equally—excluding inheritances, gifts, and proceeds from other separate property.

Confidential Relationship: See Privilege.

Conflict of Interest (Rules): Lawyers are prohibited from entering certain relationships in which a lawyer received confidential information about the opposing party.

Conjugal Rights: What you used to have when you were dating.

Consolidation: When your in laws move in with you.

Constipated marriage: One where both spouses are full of s_ _ _ .

Contempt of Court: Legal action by plaintiff/petitioner that alleges a willful failure to obey a court order or judgment.

Contested Divorce: When your ex shows up at the courthouse after all.

Contingency Fee: An unethical type of divorce fee agreement that provides the lawyer with a percentage of your settlement.

Co-respondent: A third-party in a divorce action who was sexually involved with your ex.

Counterclaim. See Answer and Counterclaim.

Court Arbitrator: His/her mother-in-law.

Court Investigator: Your mother-in-law.

Courtroom Etiquette: Always wear something sexy; make him (and others) realize what his not getting anymore.

Coverture: The sad days when you were married.

Cruel and Abusive Treatment: Why you are filing for divorce.

Custodial Parent: The one stuck with the kids.

Custody: Possession of the TV remote.

Decreeo Absoluto: Italian folksong.

Decreeo Dissolutioni: Another Italian folksong.

Decree Nisi: Divorce from a second-generation Japanese spouse.

Deposition: See Discovery; Pretrial Discovery.

Desertion: See abandonment above.

Disciplinary Rules: See Canons of (illegal) Ethics above.

Discovery: Post divorce dating.

Discovery Problems: Finding a date for Saturday night.

Disinherit: To deprive a rightful heir from his or her inheritance.

Divorce Decree or Judgment of Divorce: Free at Last; Free at Last!

Docket: See Court Docket.

Domicile: A person's legal home, i.e., where the person spends most of his time or intends to return if living elsewhere.

Equitable Distribution: Distribution of property based on rotating choices, subject to equal values.

Ethics: There is no such thing as Legal Ethics; it's an oxymoron!

Evidence: Text messages, someone else's undergarments, or other such demonstrative material.

Evidentiary Hearing: Checking out text messages and sizes.

Ex Parte: Having a party without notice to the host.

Expert Witness: In divorce cases, everyone is an expert.

Fair and Reasonable: No such thing; everything about divorce is unfair and unreasonable.

Final Judgment: After a court enters a final judgment, you may remarry. Why?

Financial Statement: Credit card bills.

Find: A great date.

Forensic: Of, or pertaining to, courts of law.

Fraud: All of those undelivered things promised before marriage.

Full Faith and Credit: Shopping without limits.

Garnishment: Wages automatically deducted from a paycheck and assigned (paid) to another party (usually to an ex-wife).

Ground(s) for Divorce: Anything and everything!

Guardian ad Litem: Your ex-'s new dating title.

Hearing on the Merits: Going to confession.

Hold Harmless Agreement: You take the hit; other side gets off free.

Impeachment: What Congress did to Bill Clinton after the Monica incident.

Infant: How your ex reacted when you said you wanted a divorce.

Inheritance Rights: What you thought you were going to get.

Injunction Relief: A court order prohibiting certain activity.

Innocent Spouse: No such person; it [always] take two!

Investigator: A person appointed by the court, usually to investigate child-related matters and file a report with the court.

Irretrievable Breakdown: What happens to most marriages.

Joint Custody: See Custody, Legal and Custody, Physical.

Judicial Separation: Separate bedrooms, checking, and email accounts.

Legal Ethics: See Ethics; Legal Ethics.

Legal Separation: Changing the locks.

Lien on Marital Property: See Attachment.

Maintenance: See Alimony.

Malpractice (Legal): The improper or incompetent behavior of your attorney.

Marital Tort: Usually served with guacamole.

Marriage Certificate: The official certification (with raised seal) of your marriage issued by a public entity.

Master: See Special Master.

Mediation: An informal, voluntary process allowing parties to work with a neutral third party to develop a separation agreement.

Memorandum of Law: Expensive legal research in support.

Motion for Attachment: She gets your paycheck before you do.

Motion to Vacate the Marital Home: Get Out Notice!

Negotiated Settlement: She takes all the assets; he takes the liabilities.

No-Fault Divorce: No such thing; it's always someone's fault!

Notice: Legal Notice: Coming home and finding all of your clothes in the driveway.

Nullity of Marriage: See Annulment.

Nuptial: Of, or pertaining to, marriage.

Palimony: Shack-up payments similar to alimony made to a former co-habitator.

Prejudice: What you feel towards your ex.

Preliminary Hearing: Any court proceeding that occurs prior to trial.

Premarital Assets: Assets acquired before marriage that are excluded from you ex.

Prenuptial Agreement (a.k.a. *Trump Armor*): A written, premarital contract dealing with divorce which sets forth the rights and responsibilities of the parties upon such occurrence.

Pretrial Conference: A meeting of all parties and counsel with the trial judge, sometimes held in the judge's chambers.

Pretrial Discovery: See Discovery; Pretrial Discovery.

Pretrial Memorandum: See Trial, Pretrial Memorandum.

Pretrial Motion: Last minute reconciliation based on new promises.

Primary Physical Custody: See Custody Physical.

Privileged: Shopping or vacationing by yourself.

Production of Documents: See Discovery; Pretrial Discovery.

Process. (noun): See Service; Service of Process.

Protective Order: Practicing safe sex.

Restraining Order: A temporary court order prohibiting a party from certain activities.

Retainer Agreement: Giving your credit card to your attorney.

Secretion of Assets: The hiding of assets.

Self-Incrimination: The right of the accused to remain silent.

Separate Maintenance: Doing your own laundry.

Separate Property: Includes property brought into the marriage and inheritance or gifts received during the marriage.

Separation: Separate bedrooms.

Service of Process: The legal process of informing,

Shared Custody: See Custody.

Sole Custody: Your own fish dinner.

Special Master: The one who used to sleep next to you.

Spousal Lien on Marital Property: See Attachment.

Spousal Support: See Alimony.

Subpoena Duces Tecum: A court order to attend a legal proceeding such as a trial or deposition, with requested documents. Latin for, "darn it, I should have burnt them!"

Summons: The court's official notice to the defendant that he/she must respond to the attached complaint or petition.

Supervision Visitation: See Visitation.

Survival Agreement: Estranged spouses living together.

Temporary Restraining Order (TRO): A pretrial order compelling a party to do something or prohibiting the party from certain activities.

Temporary Support: Dream on; it's usually not temporary.

Testimony: Any statement made under oath (from to hold one's testicles while responding. Hey, that's where the word comes from).

Vacate the Marital Home: A request to the court made telling the husband to get out NOW.

Venue: The location of the court, in contrast to jurisdiction, which determines whether a court has legal authority to hear a case.

Visitation, Grandparent: Babysitters.

Wage Assignment: Wage Attachment. See Garnishment.

White Marriage: A marriage without sex; so what's new?

Writ of Attachment. See Attachment: Motion for Attachment.

Writ Ne Exeat (Arrest): You have the right to remain silent …

Index

Author's Note

All public figures, public officeholders, and other celebrities are identified by their true names. All others are presented anonymously. Total anonymity ensures absolute privacy for those who may be recognized by others or innocently associated with me; hence, pseudonyms and altered occupations are used for all non-public and non-celebrity persons, as well as for fictitious persons used herein.

Acknowledgments

My PhD academic colleagues from subject-related disciplines, as well as professional colleagues and competent clinicians, have contributed creative comments and personal perspectives; their judicious advice and sagacious suggestions have been ardently accepted. Helpful individuals who must also be acknowledged include the scores of courtroom judges, bailiffs, and clerks, as well as certified stenographic reporters, and, of course, my lawyer colleagues who I opposed in trial but shared many of their case-stories regardless.

Readers can also share experiences, follow discussions, and communicate with one another on my blog at my website: www.divorcestresssyndrome.com

Lawyers refer to divorce cases as a "disso" (short for Dissolution of Marriage, as used in most state statutes); hence the namesake for my email addresses: contact@mydisso.com and buybook@mydisso.com

"There's no denying that divorce has become a pervasive component of contemporary society, both in America and abroad. The results can often be indeed traumatic. Yet Dr. Pastrana skillfully explores the subject with a compassion and even humor that surprisingly puts it all into full perspective."

Gene Dinielli, Emeritus Professor of English, CSULB

"As a twice-divorced person, like you, I can't say enough good things about your book's content: its message of being prepared for marriage/ divorce before, during, and after; its comprehensiveness; the interesting, up-to-date, and well-researched celeb stories; its humor; cerebral breaks; and best of all, its reminders to being kind and forgiving through the process are all paced with great writing."

B. R. Milbourn, Nashville, TN

"The book delves into the interdisciplinary messy facets of divorce such as the financial, emotional and legal entanglements that inevitably crop up no matter how 'amicable' the split may be. Pastrana offers real world advice and guidance for people who are struggling to cope. He even manages to bring a smile to the reader's face as he mixes wit with empathy in a truly one-of-a-kind resource that even those who have never been divorced could benefit from reading."

Lynnette Baum, President SCWA

"A valuable resource on a topic of wide relevance and great importance, Divorce Stress Syndrome is reasoned and impartial in its perspective. It cogently combines academic knowledge with professional experience. Commentary contributed by the author's two ex-wives adds a delicate seasoning of irony and wit."

Ron Kenner, former Metro staff writer, *The Los Angeles Times*

"I want to thank you for sharing your time and your book with me yesterday. I found it interesting and insightful; I liked the manner in which you mixed reality with humor (which many of us going through divorce need).

"The short celebrity snippets make it easy and enjoyable to read; the way it is sectioned-off allows a person to skip from one chapter to another if they desire.

"You had an excellent mix of divorced people, including Madonna and Mel Gibson, as well as a great selection of those with troubled marriages like Tiger Woods and Charlie Sheen. I also liked the broad selection of referenced greats like Fitzgerald, Puccini, Tolstoy, and so many others.

"Well done; much success."

RMJ, Professor of Comparative Literature, Boston, MA

"…You have a great sense of humor that comes out in your writing and it is fun.

"…It sort of takes the focus off our own problems for a while and most of us aren't too comfortable with self-examination, which, in my opinion, is where all the problems reside anyway—within ourselves.

"…many of your readers will identify this book as a how-to-avoid divorce tutorial…I conclude you are writing this to help people, not just entertain them.

"Truly a great read."

Dr. John Holcomb, Chicago, IL

"There's no denying that divorce has become a pervasive component of contemporary society, both in America and abroad. The results can often be indeed traumatic. Yet Dr. Pastrana skillfully explores the subject with a compassion and even humor that surprisingly puts it all into full perspective.

"While never sweeping the many negative aspects of divorce under the rug, the author instead confronts the practical reality of the situation head on. Statistics don't lie. Lots of people are getting divorced. Does it hurt? Sure it does; but it doesn't have to be the end of the world. And it isn't.

"The book delves into the interdisciplinary messy facets of divorce such as the financial, emotional and legal entanglements that inevitably crop up no matter how 'amicable' the split may be. Dr. Pastrana offers real world advice and guidance for people who are struggling to cope. He even manages to bring a smile to the reader's face as he mixes wit with empathy in a truly one-of-a-kind resource that even those who have never been divorced could benefit from reading.

"Thanks."

Dave Tribino, Hoboken, NJ

"Your encouraging book is wonderful and will be a big hit! This book will help countless people caught in the syndrome you so eloquently and analytically describe. I love your teaching methods; my son was one of your past students and he recommended your book to me; I shall graciously recommend it to others."

Roberta Stephano, San Diego, CA

Divorce Stress Syndrome

Dr. David E. Pastrana, Abruzzi Press (2011) Reviewed: Olivera
Baumgartner-Jackson for Reader Views (2/11)

First and foremost, the factor which made me not only pick up this book,
but actually finish it, was that reading it was a real delight. Let me start
with the author's unique perspective—both as a trained professional
(lawyer– and professor), he obviously speaks with insightful authority.
For somebody so well versed in this subject, it would have been all too
easy for him to slip into "know-it-all" or preachy mode, or to make it
sound so convoluted that few people could—or would want to—read it,
but he deftly managed to keep the content approachable, easy to relate
to and decidedly fresh. His oftentimes tongue-in-cheek style of humor
was a welcome break in the otherwise rather somber topic, as were the
references to many actors, celebrities, CEOs, politicians and other famous
individuals who either ended divorced or came really close to a divorce.

"Divorce Stress Syndrome" is a comprehensive resource for all issues
surrounding the complexity of a divorce, from those which happened
before it and likely contributed to it, to the technicalities of the process
itself and on to the scary "new" world a divorced individual faces as a
newly single-again person. It makes it clear that divorce can sometimes
be halted and reversed, but only if both parties truly desire to resolve the
underlying issues; and that sometimes things are irretrievably broken and
cannot be repaired. It also stresses that one should not rush into a new
relationship too fast, since time to reflect and heal is a necessity. Most
importantly, in my opinion, it teaches how to keep one's dignity and
maintain sanity during a truly difficult and challenging time in one's life.

In spite of its title, I would recommend "Divorce Stress Syndrome"
to a wide range of people, not just the freshly divorced ones. If you are
in a relationship and thinking about taking the next step, this book just
might point out some areas to consider before doing so. If you are married
and facing tough times, it could well put things in perspective for you. If
you are in the process of divorcing, it will remind you to dot the i's and
cross the t's. And most importantly, its abundance of information, humor
and slight irony are plain good reading.